THE THEORY OF FINANCIAL MARKETS AND INFORMATION

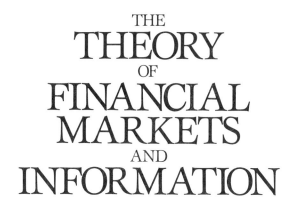

THE THEORY OF FINANCIAL MARKETS AND INFORMATION

JAMES A. OHLSON
Graduate School of Business
Columbia University

1987

NORTH-HOLLAND
New York • Amsterdam • London

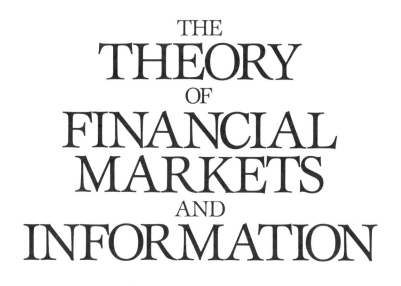

Elsevier Science Publishing Co., Inc.
52 Vanderbilt Avenue, New York, NY 10017

Distributors outside the United States and Canada:

Elsevier Science Publishers B.V.
P.O. Box 211, 1000 AE Amsterdam, The Netherlands

Library of Congress Cataloging in Publication Data

Ohlson, James A.
The theory of financial markets and information.

Bibliography: p.
Includes index.
1. Finance. 2. Capital market. 3. Money market.
I. Title.
HG173.034 1987 332.6 87-9100
ISBN 0-444-01161-7

Current printing (last digit):
10 9 8 7 6 5 4 3 2 1

Manufactured in the United States of America

CONTENTS

LIST OF DEFINITIONS

PREFACE

Basic results in the theory of financial markets are dispersed throughout a large number of academic articles and books. This causes considerable difficulties for anyone who wishes to improve his or her knowledge, particularly so because many articles need only partial reading. In order to provide for a more productive learning environment, this book attempts to synthesize the theory in terms of its central concepts and results with minimum detail. I hope that not only graduate (Ph.D.) students in economics, finance, and accounting should benefit but also scholars in the field who want to acquire a (perhaps different) perspective on how the theory's various parts fit together.

To read the book, the only mathematics required is elementary Lagrangean optimization theory and elementary linear algebra. The probability theory used does not go beyond what is taught in an introductory course during the first couple of weeks. However, although the reader needs only relatively modest technical knowledge, the material covered is frequently quite subtle in content and purpose. This suggests that some experience in formal economic analysis is essential. More specifically, knowledge of classical equilibrium analysis and second year MBA-level finance greatly facilitates a reading of the book.

The book consists of five chapters that combine into three parts. The first part, Chapter 1, provides an overview of ends and means, and it outlines the topics covered within each chapter. The second part comprises Chapters 2 and 3. Starting from basics, this part develops a simple two-date one budget constraint model within partial equilibrium (Chapter 2) that extends to general equilibrium (Chapter 3). Most of this material is relatively straightforward and known to graduating Ph.D. students in finance. Chapters 4 and

5 make up the final part. It deals with more complex models that involve multiple budget constraints due to information and the passage of time. The results presented are also generally well known, but much less than those in the second part. The chapter on partial equilibrium (Chapter 4) relies somewhat on Chapter 2 but not at all on 3; the one on general equilibrium (Chapter 5) refers extensively to both Chapters 3 and 4. The following summarizes the logical organization:

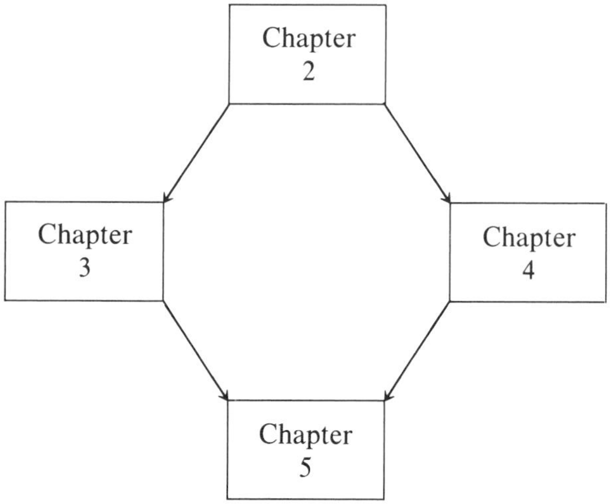

The material develops around formal propositions. These propositions state the more important economic results or facts that are exceedingly useful to keep firmly in mind. The propositions generally have little to do with clever or complex mathematical manipulations (the few exceptions will be noted!). Accordingly, many propositions come without formal proofs because, (1) the steps required are obvious in view of prior results, and/or (2) the necessary ingredients for a formal proof should be fully apparent from the discussion immediately following or preceding the proposition. (The latter may, in fact, differ little from a formal proof.) An asterisk at the end of a proposition marks the absence of a formal proof. Appendixes after each chapter supply proofs for all other cases. These proofs may often appear redundant to at least some readers; this simply reflects my policy to opt for a proof even when in doubt about its need. The overall organization expresses my belief that, in order to facilitate a comprehension of the material, neither the learner nor the expositor should focus on mathematical steps and techniques.

This book's composition does not reconcile with the chronological and intellectual evolution of the field. Any attempt to do so would have run counter to my aims of providing a synthesis and theoretical unity. I have therefore not tried to trace and attribute more or less well-known results to specific individuals. In any event, to perform such a task involves considerable difficulties since the number of individuals who can lay claim to partial or concurrent contributions is exceedingly large. Out of the many references that are possible I have mostly chosen those that I, personally, have found helpful in learning the subject matter. For the many omissions I apologize to any slighted authors.

Finally, I wish to acknowledge my gratitude to friends and colleagues who commented on various parts and versions of the manuscript. Greg Buckman, Joel Demski, John Fellingham, Jerry Feltham, Robert Freeman, Nils Hakansson, Paul Newman, Steve Penman, Stefan Reichelstein, Mark Rubinstein, and Don Vickrey have all been most helpful.

THE THEORY OF FINANCIAL MARKETS AND INFORMATION

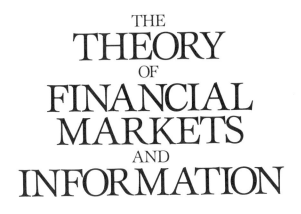

CHAPTER ONE

INTRODUCTION AND OVERVIEW

This book provides a comprehensive analysis of the economics of financial markets, the role of information within such markets, and the factors that determine the values of securities. Topics of interest include the efficiency characteristics of financial markets and the ways that individuals' welfare relate to alternative specifications of the markets and the information available. Markets and information derive their economic relevance from the simple fact that they have an effect on individuals' exchange opportunities. This concern with exchange and welfare is of interest not only in its own right, but also for its insights into what determines the structure of values and security prices. Conversely, assumptions about values and security prices frequently have important welfare implications. Thus one can turn the relatively abstract welfare analysis into a powerful tool for gaining insights about the more concrete issue of how security prices interrelate at a given date and how they change over time. Perhaps one of the most overlooked aspects of financial markets theory is the close relationship between welfare and valuation analysis. The interconnection between the two issues runs as a theme throughout this book.

Quite aside from the problem of recognizing interesting questions and conclusions that make good economic sense, there is—at least from a student's viewpoint—a more important issue: What concepts are useful generally, and what are the more commonly exploited "strategically simplifying assumptions" in financial markets theory? This book deals with these questions by emphasizing the theory's *structure,* rather than the theory's empirical content and its implications for corporate and social policy. Consistent with this perspective, the empirical validity of assumptions is much less important than their potential use in developing constructive results. In financial markets theory one encounters "theorems" and "propositions" involving principal concepts such as Pareto efficiency, state contingent prices, Arrow-Debreu securities, dynamically complete markets, risk aversion, logarithmic utility, state independent utilities, linear risk tolerance preferences, and homogeneous beliefs. Even a cursory examination of the literature suggests that these concepts are significant and useful in a variety of contexts, and understanding them becomes absolutely critical.

The treatment of the subject is best characterized as basic, for at least three reasons. First, the approach here assumes that the state space, which defines the economy's uncertainty, is finite. Second, the analysis excludes endogenous production possibilities and thus falls solely within the domain of pure exchange. Third, asymmetric (or "private") information does not enter into the analysis. The first of these restrictions eliminates many, if not all, potential mathematical complications; the second and third restrictions allow a model with the simplest possible concept of equilibrium. These are important methodological advantages. While the theory appears relatively unsophisticated when compared to the state-of-the-art, it should be noted that more advanced theoretical topics outside the book's scope—continuous time dynamic equilibria, the theory of stockholder production and financing unanimity, equilibrium in asymmetric information economies, and so forth—refer to results and concepts developed from more primitive models. The insights that underpin modern financial markets economics serve a broad purpose.

The material in this book is organized as follows.[1] Chapter 2 specifies the general assumptions about preferences and opportunities in financial markets. The resulting model provides a simple prototype of an individual's consumption/portfolio choice problem in a two-date uncertainty economy. Much of the discussion concerns different specialized preferences that play important roles in later propositions. The analysis also details the structure of investment opportunities, that is, security prices and related uncertain payoffs. The key attribute of the investment opportunities is its exclusion of arbitrage, which has two major implications: the existence of an implicit (state-contingent) price system, and a solution to the individual's choice problem. A close examination of the model shows that securities are best regarded as a means to future (uncertain) consumption. With great advantage, this perspective leads to a restatement of the individual's choice problem in real terms rather than in financial terms. Patterns of consumption become the objects of choice, and the implicit prices simply assign values to patterns that are available through existing markets. This mode of analysis highlights the idea that markets, no less than wealth and prices, also determine an individual's opportunities. Thus the analysis of investment opportu-

[1] This content outline necessarily refers to concepts that may be unfamiliar to some readers. The readers who so wish can skim, or even omit, this outline in a first reading. Chapter 2 develops the model from basics.

nities leads naturally to a distinction between incomplete and complete markets, and Arrow-Debreu markets evolve as a special case of the latter.

An alternative and more traditional approach to the analysis of the individual's portfolio choice problem applies Lagrangean theory. The inspection and manipulation of the Lagrangean optimality conditions are such an integral part of the theory that the literature states them without derivations. Of particular interest, therefore, is the demonstration of how the optimality conditions vary with alternative specifications of markets and preferences. Another obviously useful application of the optimality conditions considers preferences with linear risk tolerance (the "LRT" class of preferences). Combined with Arrow-Debreu markets, these preferences have optimality conditions leading to closed form solutions for the security holdings. These derivations are not only of pedagogical interest, for they also lead to the two major implications of such preferences: portfolio separation applies, and the optimal security holdings are linear in the total amount invested in securities. Generalizations to incomplete markets follow. Given the importance of LRT preferences in financial markets theory, subsequent chapters frequently refer back to these results.

Chapter 3 develops the competitive equilibrium model that follows from the prototype choice problem. The initial discussion presents the general ingredients in pure exchange and then defines an equilibrium from two different perspectives: in financial terms and in real terms. This dual perspective on an equilibrium greatly facilitates an understanding of most key results. Further groundwork introduces the efficiency properties that characterize competitive equilibria. Of interest is constrained Pareto efficiency, and, as a special case thereof, (full) Pareto efficiency. The analysis then extensively treats Pareto efficient allocations, with an emphasis on the conditions under which incomplete markets reach such allocations. The latter results are central to financial markets theory. Every Pareto efficient incomplete markets economy "disguises" an essentially equivalent Arrow-Debreu economy. Moreover, although Arrow-Debreu economies are supposedly contrived—in contrast to incomplete market economies—they are also rich in implications. The search for Pareto efficient incomplete market economies thus becomes an important matter.

A different aspect of market analysis traces the redistributive welfare effects resulting from changes in individuals' endowments or changes in the set of available securities. Because the subject highlights endowments, a clear distinction emerges between efficiency evaluation and changes in each individual's welfare. The analysis specifically notes that redistributive welfare effects do not relate narrowly to the (re-)distribution of endowments.

A special section considers the potential use of put and call options to improve on an economy's performance through more efficient risk sharing. The analysis evaluates the strengths and limitations of put and call options, thereby highlighting many previous results.

The final part of the chapter addresses a basic question: How do security values interrelate? The subject is subdivided into two parts. The first part concerns arbitrage pricing and relative security valuation. The resulting valuation theory explicates popular applications, such as the pricing of options and forward contracts. More important, the theory prepares the ground for a comprehensive analysis of the different versions of the famous Modigliani-Miller Theorem. Because these theorems focus on the relationship between welfare and valuation invariance, the insights reveal the core of financial markets theory. The second part of the valuation analysis discusses how the individuals' preferences and beliefs influence security prices. The general idea of a security's risk develops, with few complications, from an individual's optimality conditions. The derivations illuminate the specialized nature of the Capital Asset Pricing Model, as well as some other less well known valuation models.

Chapter 4 introduces information and evaluates the effects of information on an individual's consumption/portfolio selection problem. The modeling of information follows the standardized framework developed by Marschak and Radner (1972); the discussion reviews basic implications of their scheme, such as the meaning of "more information" and conditional probability revision. A key point further notes that the absence of information differs little from the absence of markets in the consumption/portfolio selection problem. The absence of either markets or information puts linear constraints on attainable mixes of consumption plans. Hence, the previous analysis of markets usefully directs the information analysis.

Information introduces other important features in the analysis. It permits the modeling of dynamic decision environments—in this case the individual trades securities both before and after observing an uncertain signal. More generally, information may be interpreted as the passage of time, and therefore adds descriptive richness to the consumption/portfolio selection problem. The prototype dynamic decision model, however, represents only one possible choice setting; the chapter also specifies two alternative portfolio/consumption models in which information affects the choice. These two alternative models are of theoretical interest because an analysis of them highlights the structure of the dynamic setting. At one extreme, the dynamic problem converts into a simple static problem that allows plans to be fully coordinated across the (uncertain) signals. This desirable outcome occurs when markets are dynamically complete. Thus, notions of market completeness become more intricate in a dynamic context. At the other extreme, the dynamic problem converts into a problem that entirely rules out coordination of plans across signals. In the general case the dynamic problem falls between these two extremes.

The chapter also identifies conditions under which incremental information improves an individual's welfare. The issue is relevant in each of the three decision environments. Furthermore, the analysis evaluates the extent to which "more information" is equivalent to "more markets." A few key insights and results bring out the considerable similarities between the two concepts, thereby providing a useful foundation for the subsequent equilibrium chapter.

By incorporating information and the passage of time, Chapter 5 extends the simple two-date equilibrium analysis. Of particular interest are the attributes of sequential equilibria—that is, those equilibria that build on individuals solving their dynamic consumption/portfolio optimization problems. The efficiency/welfare issues involve more subtleties than previously. Many of the renowned conclusions that one associates with classical models lose their validity or require significant modifications. The analysis departs from generalized definitions of constrained and full Pareto efficiency and then considers in detail the conditions under which the constraints are nonbinding, that is, circumstances such that additional markets and information cannot improve on efficiency. This analysis provides benchmark allocations, and these are essential for evaluating the relative efficiency of sequential equilibrium economies. Conditions under which the sequential equilibria achieve full Pareto efficiency are established. As one should expect, the conditions restrict either markets or preferences/beliefs. But it is also shown that sequential equilibria can be truly inefficient, amounting to a breakdown in the celebrated effectiveness of the "invisible hand." Two particularly important and closely related results are demonstrated: enriched markets may make all individuals worse off—a seminal result due to Hart (1975)—and a similar conclusion holds for incremental information.

Although sequential equilibria occupy center stage in the welfare analysis, the chapter evaluates the two alternative equilibrium settings as well. By juxtaposing the welfare characteristics of the three equilibrium models one gains insights into why and how information and the passage of time affect equilibria. The final part of the chapter considers valuation and information. The major results establish conditions under which implicit prices do not depend on information, and express the relationship between two sets of signal-dependent security prices based on identical implicit prices. These two problems relate closely to the Modigliani-Miller Theorem. A more specialized result originating from these concepts is the so-called Martingale Hypothesis. Finally, the discussion deals with the behavior of security prices and how it reflects and relates to the economy's welfare attributes.

CHAPTER TWO

MICROANALYSIS UNDER FIXED INFORMATION

2.1. Introduction

This book analyzes financial markets within a standard neoclassical framework. The model's development naturally begins with the central figure, the prototype individual who trades securities and consumes goods. To derive the individual's economic behavior consists of identifying the optimal consumption and portfolio choice. This mundane observation emphasizes that the initial assumptions concern the individual and his choice environment; no matter how sophisticated or elaborate the final model, these basic assumptions always affect conclusions even when these apparently have little to do with an individual's choice per se. One must therefore carefully consider the assumptions about the individual and his choice environment.

A model's generality rests directly on its assumptions. This suggests that one should work with assumptions that are as general as possible. On the other hand, general assumptions by their nature cannot lead to sharp insights and results, which implies that a rich theory must build, at least partially, on specialized assumptions as well. Identifying such assumptions successfully often provides the more dramatic and celebrated results; in this regard, financial markets theory does not differ from other branches of economics. Nevertheless, the task of "identifying assumptions successfully" poses considerable difficulties since the implications of various assumptions do not reveal themselves automatically. Research seeks strategically simplifying assumptions through an iterative process of trial and error. Given any particular result, one can thereafter try to find more general assumptions. To facilitate this search, an essential first step will be to consider alternative assumptions. In broad terms, the analysis that follows places restrictions on (i) the individual's preferences or on (ii) his opportunities.

Results in this chapter show how alternative combinations of restrictions on preferences and opportunities yield conclusions about the individual's behavior or about his relative well-being (expected utility). Although this chapter considers microanalytic issues only—that is, an individual's behavior given a fixed price system—the reader should keep in mind that similar manipulations of assumptions will prove no less rich in implications as the model evolves in complexity. A striking aspect of the theory of financial markets is that the same few variations in assumptions yield constructive results for the full range of questions about welfare and valuation.

2.2. The Model

2.2.1. Outcomes and Preferences

Economic activity in the model occurs at only two dates: date-zero ("today") and date-one ("tomorrow"). At date-zero an individual makes a decision, and this results in consumption at date-zero and uncertain wealth at date-one. The wealth realized at date-one is available for consumption at that date; to keep matters simple, the analysis in this chapter does not explicitly include date-one investment opportunities. The discussion therefore simply refers to consumption at the two dates as the consequence of an individual's choice. It is useful to think of the consumption levels as measured in dollars, and this means that the model disregards how dollars may be spent on different consumption goods at the two dates.

Let the scalar c denote the certain consumption at date-zero. The uncertainty of consumption at date-one, however, implies a dependence on the *state* that prevails. The model has a finite number of states, $s = 1, \ldots, S$; by definition, the S states are mutually exclusive and exhaustive. It is often convenient to let S also denote *the set of all possible states,* in which case the appropriate notation is $s \in S$. (This dual use of the symbol S will not be a source of confusion; the context in which S appears will make its meaning clear.) Let w_s denote the date-one consumption realized given state s, and let $w = (w_1, \ldots, w_S)$ denote the S-dimensional row vector of consumption levels across the conceivable states.[1] The $(S + 1)$-dimensional row vector

$$\alpha \equiv (c,w) \equiv (c, w_1, \ldots, w_S),$$

is referred to as the individual's *consumption pattern across dates and states*. The consumption pattern at date-one is *certain* or *risk free* if $w_1 = w_2 = \cdots = w_S$. This pattern is of course rather extreme, and the outcome w_s generally depends on the state.

[1] In the interest of simplicity, the notation does not indicate whether a vector is a row or column vector. The reader should memorize such facts. Some less experienced readers may also find it helpful to initially rework subsequent matrix algebra expressions using summation operations.

An individual has preferences with respect to the available consumption patterns. The function $V(\alpha)$ represents these preferences. Specifically, $V(\alpha'') > V(\alpha')$ if and only if the individual strictly prefers α'' to α'; $V(\alpha'') = V(\alpha')$ implies, and is implied by, indifference between α'' and α'.

Under relatively mild rationality axioms one may assume that an individual has probability-beliefs over state occurrences, and that the form of $V(\cdot)$ satisfies additivity in states. To be more precise, the analysis presumes that for each consumption pattern α the preference function $V(\cdot)$ admits an *expected utility* representation:[2]

$$V(\alpha) = \sum_{s \in S} \pi_s U_s(c, w_s) \tag{2.1}$$

where $\pi \equiv (\pi_1, \ldots, \pi_S)$ defines the vector of probability-beliefs, $\pi_s > 0$, and $\sum_s \pi_s = 1$. The function $U_s(\cdot,\cdot)$ denotes the utility of consumption in state s. The subscript s as it appears in $U_s(\cdot,\cdot)$ simply indicates that the enjoyment of a specific consumption level might depend on the state in which it is experienced.

Since the elements in α represent consumption, a basic assumption maintains that more is strictly preferred to less: $\alpha'' \geq \alpha'$ implies that $V(\alpha'') > V(\alpha')$.[3] Note further that V satisfies this property for all positive π if, and only if, the U_s increase in their arguments:

$$U_s(c'', w''_s) > U_s(c', w'_s) \quad \text{if} \quad (c'', w''_s) \geq (c', w'_s), \qquad \text{all } s \in S.$$

A rich and powerful theory about individuals' behavior imposes additional structure on $V(\cdot)$. Of particular significance is *strict concavity*. Formally, $V(\cdot)$ satisfies strict concavity if

$$V(k\alpha'' + (1 - k)\alpha') > kV(\alpha'') + (1 - k)V(\alpha'),$$

where $0 < k < 1$, and α'', α' are distinct but otherwise arbitrary. Given further that $V(\cdot)$ satisfies the expected utility representation Eq. (2.1), strict concavity follows from

$$U_s(k(c'', w''_s) + (1 - k)(c', w'_s)) > kU_s(c'', w''_s) + (1 - k)U_s(c', w'_s).$$

With no restrictions on π (except that it be positive), this inequality is also clearly necessary for the strict concavity of $V(\cdot)$.

Although not generally critical, assuming that $V(\cdot)$ is differentiable in its arguments frequently simplifies the analysis. This condition and the two

---

[2] Most basic graduate textbooks on consumer choice analyze how a function $V(\alpha)$ derives from primitive preference axioms and when, under uncertainty, the preferences permit an expected utility representation.

[3] When two *vectors*, x'' and x', are compared the following notation is used: $x'' \geqq x'$ means that $x''_j \geq x'_j$ for each element j; $x'' \geq x'$ means that $x'' \geqq x'$ and $x''_j > x'_j$ for at least one j.

previous assumptions about preferences—that $V(\cdot)$ is increasing and strictly concave—will be maintained throughout.

DEFINITION 2.1. MISC EXPECTED UTILITIES. *The expected utility of a consumption pattern* α,

$$V(\alpha) = \sum_s \pi_s U_s(c, w_s),$$

*is monotonically increasing and strictly concave—MISC—*for any $\pi > 0$ *if for all* s

$$\partial U_s / \partial c \equiv u_s^1 > 0, \ \partial U_s / \partial w_s \equiv u_s^2 > 0,$$

and

$$U_s(k(c'', w_s'') + (1 - k)(c', w_s')) > kU_s(c'', w_s'') + (1 - k)U_s(c', w_s'),$$

where $0 < k < 1$ *and* $(c'', w_s'') \neq (c', w_s')$.

Many results obtain for less restrictive preferences, and a few require only the existence of a preference ordering. Beyond these few cases the most critical assumption relates to the letter I—increasing—in MISC: an individual prefers more to less. As one should suspect, no meaningful theory can be developed without it. Concavity either is necessary for particular kinds of results or permits more transparent and direct proofs. No results depend in any critical sense on the differentiability of V, but this condition aids any elementary exposition of the theory. Similar comments apply to the expected utility hypothesis itself. For many results an examination of proofs will indeed reveal that Eq. (2.1) serves no purpose, but in other cases it is necessary. The reader will experience little difficulty making such discriminations. Accordingly, maintaining the Definition 2.1 preferences throughout is convenient. Choosing as a minimal assumption MISC expected utilities reflects a trade-off between the conflicting objectives of using the weakest possible assumptions for specific results and a development of the theory unencumbered by excessive detail. One can further argue that Definition 2.1 serves as a natural (and popular) starting point because it does not exclude cases of obvious theoretical interest.

The MISC assumption does not always suffice, however, and a number of interesting theoretical insights necessitate additional restrictions. One such assumption, *state independence,* applies when the U_s remain identical over states. Thus, given state independence, express $V(\cdot)$ as

$$V(\alpha) = \sum_s \pi_s U(c, w_s).$$

The literature often represents the last expression by using the random variable notation ~ and the expectation-operator E:

$$V(\alpha) = EU(c, \tilde{w}).$$

State independence combined with the concavity of $V(\cdot)$ leads to particularly interesting preferences. The individual exhibits *risk aversion*. To develop this idea, compare the expected utility of an uncertain consumption pattern α' to that of a certain pattern α'' where $c'' = c' \equiv c$ and $w_1'' = \cdots = w_S'' = E\tilde{w}'$. State independence and concavity permit an application of *Jensen's Inequality* such that

$$V(\alpha') \equiv EU(c,\tilde{w}') < U(c,E\tilde{w}') = \sum_{s} \pi_s U(c,E\tilde{w}')$$
$$= EU(c,\tilde{w}'') \equiv V(\alpha'')$$

for every probability vector π. In other words, having the uncertain consumption pattern is always inferior to having the expected level of consumption with certainty. To prove that the inequality holds in the case $S = 2$, put $k = \pi_1$, $(1 - k) = \pi_2$ in the definition of concavity, and use the state independence of utilities. (For $S > 3$, one shows without difficulty that concavity implies that $V\left(\sum_j k_j\alpha^j\right) > \sum_j k_j V(\alpha^j)$ where $k_j > 0$, $\sum_j k_j = 1$, and at least two patterns satisfy $\alpha^j \neq \alpha^k$.) Risk aversion has no meaning without state independence; one can construct examples such that $V(\alpha'') > V(\alpha')$ holds even though $V(\cdot)$ satisfies MISC, and $c' = c''$, $w_1' = \cdots = w_S' = E\tilde{w}''$.

Another frequently useful, but essentially arbitrary, restriction relates to *time-additive* preferences. The condition implies that $U_s(c,w_s) \equiv U^1(c) + U_s^2(w_s)$, and

$$V(\alpha) = U^1(c) + \sum_s \pi_s U_s^2(w_s). \tag{2.2}$$

This expected utility function satisfies MISC if and only if, in addition to $u^1, u_s^2 > 0$, the second derivatives of U^1 and U_s^2 (that is, $\partial u^1/\partial c$ and $\partial u_s^2/\partial w_s$) are negative.

Also of interest is *time-additivity combined with state independence:*

$$V(\alpha) = U^1(c) + \sum_s \pi_s U^2(w_s) = U^1(c) + EU^2(\tilde{w}).$$

The above structure may be augmented with the assumption that U^1 *has the same form as* U^2: $U^2(x) = U^1(x)/\rho \equiv U(x)$, where ρ is a positive constant. The expected utility of a pattern α is expressed as

$$V(\alpha) = \rho U(c) + \sum_s \pi_s U(w_s) = \rho U(c) + EU(\tilde{w}). \tag{2.3}$$

The parameter ρ reflects a *patience factor* where a smaller ρ indicates a more patient individual.

The most confined modes of analyses combine time additivity and state independence with a specific analytical form of U^2 (and possibly U^1). The better-known examples are the *logarithmic utility,* $U^2(w_s) = \log w_s$; the *quadratic utility,* $U^2(w_s) = -(\varphi - w_s)^2$, $\varphi > 0$; and the *negative exponential utility*, $U^2(w_s) = -\exp\{-\varphi w_s\}$, $\varphi > 0$. All three cases satisfy MISC, except that for quadratic U^2 w_s must be less than φ. These preferences, as well as some others that section 2.4 introduces, lead to important theoretical insights. The analysis considers their implications throughout.

Common sense suggests that negative consumption ought to be impossible. That $V(\alpha)$ applies only for $\alpha \geqq 0$ therefore seems a reasonable and innocuous restriction. Nevertheless, its explicit incorporation into formal analysis often proves burdensome. A more convenient approach disregards this constraint, and the procedure works without complications if the constraint does not bind the individual's behavior. No recognition will therefore generally be given to the constraint $\alpha \geqq 0$. The only exceptions occur in some basic existence results—Lemma 2.2, Proposition 2.2, and Proposition 3.3—in which cases the constraint $\alpha \geqq 0$ is too critical not to be listed as a condition for the result. In all other propositions the preferences are understood to be MISC, and $\alpha \geqq 0$ is nonbinding. Suffice it to mention that few, if any, theoretical insights need substantial modification or qualification if the analysis explicitly includes the possibility of a binding constraint.

2.2.2. Market opportunities and the individual's resources

In addition to a market in the current consumption good, a market in *securities* offers the individual trading opportunities. There are $j = 1, \ldots, J$ securities (stocks, bonds, convertible bonds, options, etc.), and a_{js} denotes the gross dollar payoff of security j in state s. The $J \times S$ matrix

$$A \equiv \begin{bmatrix} a_{11} & \cdots & a_{1S} \\ \vdots & & \vdots \\ a_{J1} & \cdots & a_{JS} \end{bmatrix} \equiv \begin{bmatrix} a_1 \\ \vdots \\ a_J \end{bmatrix}$$

summarizes the gross payoffs across securities and states.

The matrix A is referred to as the *securities-states tableau* or, more colloquially, as the *payoff matrix*, the *market structure*, or simply the *markets*. The row vector a_j enumerates the payoffs of security j in the S states. Although the theory maintains no particular restrictions on the payoff matrix, some settings usefully impose the *limited liability* condition $a_j \geq 0$.

The direct objects of choice are current consumption, c, and *portfolios of securities*, where the row vector $z \equiv (z_1, \ldots, z_J)$ summarizes the portfolio of security holdings. A portfolio z yields a payoff $w_s = \sum_j z_j a_{js}$ in state s; that is, the linear combination $w = \sum_j z_j a_j$ determines the vector of date-one consumption payoffs. In matrix algebra notation

$$w = zA, \quad \text{and} \quad \alpha = (c, zA),$$

where w, z, and α are all row vectors. The algebra shows that the collection of payoff vectors $\{a_1, \ldots, a_J\}$ generates a vector space in which the date-one consumption pattern w is an element. In more compact jargon, w must be *attainable* or in the *span* of the matrix A. This concept of spanning plays an extremely important role in subsequent developments.

The individual acquires securities and portfolios at a cost. One unit of security j is priced at P_j; the total cost of a portfolio z therefore adds up to $z \cdot P\left(= \sum_j z_j P_j\right)$, where $P \equiv (P_1, \ldots, P_J)$ defines a column vector. By convention, but at no loss of generality, the unit cost of the current consumption good equals one. Hence, a *plan* (c, z) costs $c + z \cdot P$.

The individual's resources are his *endowed wealth,* denoted by $\bar{\bar{w}}$. Its value depends on the individual's endowments in the current consumption-good, $\bar{c}$, and the securities, $\bar{z}$, such that $\bar{\bar{w}} \equiv \bar{c} + \bar{z} \cdot P$. Both market opportunities and endowments limit the individual's opportunities. The choice of a plan (c, z) must satisfy the *budget constraint:*

$$c + z \cdot P \leq \bar{\bar{w}} \equiv \bar{c} + \bar{z} \cdot P.$$

The budget constraint may also be expressed as

$$(c - \bar{c}) + (z - \bar{z}) \cdot P \leq 0,$$

where $c - \bar{c}$ and $z - \bar{z}$ represent the individual's *trades*.

To achieve analytical tractability the model includes two subtle and important assumptions about opportunities. First, the portfolio choice takes place within *competitive* markets in the sense that the price vector is beyond the individual's control. In analytical terms, the individual treats P as independent of z. Second, markets are *perfect*. The model rules out frictions such as taxes and transactions costs. Trades and security holdings are infinitely divisible. The individual may sell securities short ($z_j < 0$) without limitations, such as "margin requirements," on how the proceeds may be used. (Note that the restriction $\alpha \geqq 0$ by no means implies that z must be nonnegative even if $a_{js} \geq 0$.) The analysis maintains competitive and perfect markets throughout. Although limiting, these assumptions are standard in the theory because to eliminate them generally introduces significant complications.

2.2.3. The standard problem

Combining the preferences of an individual with his endowments and the market opportunities leads to Definition 2.2, the statement of the individual's optimization problem.

Definition 2.2. standard problem. *The individual solves*

$$\max_{\alpha} V(\alpha) = \max_{(c,z)} V(c, zA) = \max_{(c,z)} \sum_s \pi_s U_s(c, \sum_j z_j a_{js})$$

subject to

$$c + \sum_j z_j P_j \leq \bar{c} + \sum_j \bar{z}_j P_j .$$

The optimization problem may be viewed either in terms of finding an optimal consumption pattern α or in terms of finding an optimal holding (c, z) of securities. Each plan (c, z) maps into a pattern α. Accordingly, given a preference ordering $V(\alpha)$ and a market structure A, an induced preference ordering for the plans (c, z) can be inferred from $V(c, zA)$; that is, (c'', z'') is strictly preferred to (c', z') if and only if $V(c'', z''A) > V(c', z'A)$.

Having posed the standard problem, one obviously wants to identify conditions that ensure the existence and uniqueness of an optimal solution. Preferences are MISC, and the analysis maintains this assumption precisely because such preferences are "well-behaved." However, "well-behaved" regular preferences do not suffice: the existence of an optimum also requires the absence of *arbitrage opportunities.* Arbitrage opportunities within competitive and perfect markets means that an individual can "get something for nothing," regardless of his preferences/beliefs and wealth. Intuition suggests that under the circumstances every portfolio can be improved upon, and thus the standard problem (SP) does not have an optimal solution. To restore meaning to SP one needs a no-arbitrage condition that introduces restrictions on the market characteristics (A, P).

Before providing a formal definition of no-arbitrage opportunities, consider an example in which arbitrage opportunities *are* present. Suppose that two limited liability securities, j and k, satisfy $a_j = a_k \geq 0$ but $P_j > P_k$. Because identical payoff patterns ought to be priced equally, this price difference surely implies that one can get something for nothing. Any purchase-sales plan with $-z_j = z_k > 0$, z_k large, yields the large positive proceeds $z_k(P_j - P_k) > 0$ at date-zero. These proceeds can then be used for current consumption or for the purchase of other securities. The outcome has obvious attraction since $z_j a_j + z_k a_k = 0$; that is, one can rest assured that the portfolio *never* results in any future obligations. As an alternative strategy for arbitrage, one can choose portfolios costing zero that nevertheless have nonnegative payoffs in all states *and* a strictly positive payoff in at least one state. Appropriate scaling makes these positive payoffs as large as desired. Let z_k be any large positive number, and put $z_j = -z_k P_k / P_j$ (which implies that $z_j P_j + z_k P_k = 0$); the portfolio costs nothing, but the date-one payoff vector satisfies $z_j a_j + z_k a_k = (z_j + z_k) a_k \geq 0$ since $a_j = a_k \geq 0$ and $z_j + z_k > 0$.

Less transparent cases of arbitrage opportunities can be concocted. For example, let $a_1 = (5,4)$, $a_2 = (6,2)$, $P_1 = 23$, and $P_2 = 29$. The second security is too expensive relative to the first, although this may seem unclear since $a_{21} > a_{11}$. To construct an arbitrage portfolio, choose any $z_1 > 0$ and $z_2 < 0$ such that $z_1 P_1 + z_2 P_2 = 0$; a direct calculation then shows that $z_1 a_1 + z_2 a_2 > (0,0)$. Alternatively, choose z_1, z_2 such that $z_1 a_1 + z_2 a_2 = (0, k)$

where $k > 0$, and calculations reveal that $z_1P_1 + z_2P_2 < 0$ for all k (each k yields a solution for z). Both strategies result in arbitrage outcomes since consumption opportunities become unbounded by scaling the quantities purchased and sold. Given that an individual prefers more consumption to less, arbitrage thus prevents the existence of a solution to SP.

The analysis needs a formal definition of no-arbitrage opportunities. The two examples indicate how the problem must be approached. The only subtlety involves the recognition of the two dates, and one resolves this aspect by relating the date-zero net current proceeds of a portfolio to its implied date-one payoffs. First, if the proceeds from short sales exceed the cost of long positions $\left(\sum_j z_jP_j < 0\right)$, the absence of arbitrage means that the portfolio yields a negative payoff in at least one state. Second, if a portfolio has nonnegative payoffs in all states and a strictly positive payoff in at least one state, the net cost (value) of the portfolio must be positive. *No*-arbitrage opportunities is therefore defined formally as in Definition 2.3.

DEFINITION 2.3. NO-ARBITRAGE OPPORTUNITIES. *There exists no portfolio z such that $z \cdot P \leq 0$, $zA \geqq 0$, and with at least one strict inequality in the $S + 1$ equations.*

Note that the definition does not depend on the probability beliefs in the sense that it applies for all strictly positive π. Hence, the absence or presence of arbitrage is not a subjective matter given that the model supplies an unambiguous set of *possible* states. (Although far from irreproachable, the assumption is maintained throughout.)

The definition of no-arbitrage opportunities raises the following questions: Does a P exist such that (A,P) exclude arbitrage? If so, how does one construct such a P? More generally, a useful result identifies the set of no arbitrage P given some A. A powerful equivalent statement of no-arbitrage solves this problem.

PROPOSITION 2.1. *There exists a vector $R > 0$ such that $P = AR$ if and only if the market characteristics (A,P) preclude arbitrage.*[4]

The S-dimensional positive column vector R need not be unique; if the rank of A is less than S, then, in fact, there exist at least two vectors R' and R'', such that $P = AR' = AR''$ although $R' \neq R''$, and $R', R'' > 0$. Moreover, the existence of some $R \not> 0$ such that $P = AR$ does *not* imply arbitrage opportunities unless, of course, R is unique. *No-arbitrage opportunities follow from the existence of at least one positive vector R*, and this is also the necessary condition.

[4] Proofs are found in appendices following each chapter. If the proposition ends with an asterisk no proof is supplied. The formal steps should be obvious in view of the discussion that precedes or follows the statement.

To illustrate Proposition 2.1, consider the following example. Let

$$A = \begin{bmatrix} 2 & 2 & 4 & 4 \\ 0 & 2 & 4 & 6 \end{bmatrix}$$

and $P_1 = 3.5$, $P_2 = 3$. The specification admits no-arbitrage because $R = (1/2,\ 1/4,\ 1/4,\ 1/4)$ satisfies $P = AR$. Compare this to the two previous examples with arbitrage opportunities. First, note that $a_j = a_k$ but $P_j \neq P_k$ permits no R, positive or not, such that $P = AR$. In the second example, where A is 2×2, the only R that solves $AR = P$ equals $(5, -1/2)$.

Proposition 2.1 thus shows that one easily constructs no-arbitrage P by calculating AR for positive R. On the other hand, given some (A,P), the identification of a positive R, or a demonstration that it does not exist, may pose considerable difficulties when A has a large number of rows and columns. However, the explicit numeric derivation of a specific R from an (A,P) combination typically is of no interest. The significance of Proposition 2.1 stems from its guaranteeing that the expression $P = AR$, $R > 0$, has analytical validity in all no-arbitrage settings, and, conversely, the expression imposes no undesirable hidden restrictions on (A,P). The nonuniqueness of R does not prevent the representation from being theoretically significant and exceedingly useful.

The last point may be explained as follows. Securities serve as a means to an end: to permit choices of future consumption patterns. This suggests that the analysis can benefit from a direct focus on w rather than on z. Accordingly, a useful scheme values every w within the span of A; other ws are irrelevant since they are unattainable. No-arbitrage makes such valuation possible. If the portfolio z results in the pattern w, then the value of w (the cost of acquiring w) is determined by

$$z \cdot P = z \cdot AR = zA \cdot R = w \cdot R.$$

In words, R_s values one unit of consumption in state s. The nonuniqueness of R causes no concern because $w \cdot R$ remains constant for all R satisfying $P = AR$, (A,P) fixed, provided that A spans w. That is, the operation $w \cdot R$ is without validity unless some z exists such that $zA = w$. (Hence, if $w = (0, \ldots, 0,1,0, \ldots 0)$ is attainable for some z, then and only then is R_s unique.)

That R_s can be interpreted as the price of a unit of consumption in state s is an exceedingly useful insight. The literature accordingly graces the vector R with a specific label.

DEFINITION 2.4. IMPLICIT PRICE SYSTEM. *Any vector R satisfying $P = AR, R > 0$, is said to be the implicit price system of market characteristics* (A,P).

The concept of implicit prices (or *state contingent* prices) greatly facilitates the development of the theory. The identification of such prices makes good economic sense simply because it stresses what a portfolio z accomplishes and why z has a value in the first place. If z results in $w(= zA)$, the value of z is $w \cdot R$, and the implicit price system serves as the linear valuation operator that assigns a value to every attainable payoff pattern. The linearity property follows immediately because $(w' + w'') \cdot R = w' \cdot R + w'' \cdot R$, thereby shadowing the relationship $(z' + z'') \cdot P = z' \cdot P + z'' \cdot P$.

Because the implicit prices assign values to all portfolios, there are no compelling analytical reasons to accord the corner portfolios $z = (0, \ldots, 0,1,0, \ldots, 0)$ elevated status, except that one needs observable and "explicit" security prices to make the R-vector "implicit." This suggests that viewing the implicit price system as being derived from (A,P) is somewhat arbitrary. An equally valid perspective departs from (A,R), $R > 0$, and considers the relationship $P = AR$ *definitional*. The only justification for not adhering to such a flow of logic rests on the observability of security prices. But this should not obscure that the development of theory takes a neutral stance on which set of prices is more "basic." Taste and analytical convenience generally determine the appropriate emphasis.

To further illustrate the versatility of implicit prices, consider the return on a risk-free security or portfolio. In an economy with only one good—cash—at the two dates, the value of a unit of consumption today relative to the value of a unit of certain consumption tomorrow defines the risk-free return (one plus the rate-of-return). Given that the value of one consumption unit today is \$1, the risk-free return equals the inverse of the cost of a portfolio yielding one unit of consumption in every state. Hence, let R_F denote the risk-free return, and $R_F = (w \cdot R)^{-1}$ with $w = 1$, so that $R_F = \left(\sum_s R_s\right)^{-1}$. The question "What is the return on a risk-free security?" therefore permits an answer that does not specifically refer to the A-matrix or to the price vector P. Besides no-arbitrage opportunities, the solution $R_F = \left(\sum_s R_s\right)^{-1}$ requires only that the securities span the unit vector (i.e., that at least one z exists such that $1 = zA$). Other assumptions about A are superfluous. In particular, a security j with a pattern a_j proportional to the unit vector may or may not exist. Further, note again that nonuniqueness in implicit prices causes no problems. Given $1 = zA$ and $AR' = AR''$, it follows immediately that $\sum_s R'_s = \sum_s R''_s = z \cdot P$ even though $R'' \neq R'$.

The discussion next considers the SP, and the relevance of no arbitrage and implicit prices. The first result shows that the critical condition for SP to have a solution is no-arbitrage.

LEMMA 2.2. *Consider the standard problem with a continuous preferences/beliefs function $V(\cdot)$ defined for $\alpha \geqq 0$. Then no-arbitrage opportunities are necessary and sufficient for an optimal solution to exist.*

The conditions on preferences in the lemma do not suffice for a unique optimal α. One deals usefully with this uniqueness problem by invoking the MISC preferences. However, a unique α does not imply a unique z; elementary linear algebra implies that $z'A = z''A$, $z' \neq z''$, holds if, and only if, A has linearly dependent rows. The following basic proposition therefore applies.

PROPOSITION 2.2. *Let $V(\cdot)$ be MISC for $\alpha \geqq 0$, and suppose that there are no-arbitrage opportunities. Then SP has a unique optimal pattern α; the optimal plan (c,z) is unique if and only if in addition $\{a_1, \ldots, a_J\}$ are linearly independent.*

One way of acquiring insights into SP is to analyze a superficially different yet fundamentally equivalent problem. The development of this problem, the constrained contingent claims problem (CCCP), builds on the recurring idea that securities serve as a means to acquire a future consumption pattern. This view suggests that α should be considered *the* choice vector and that a direct reference to the J specific securities is unnecessary. Maintaining a consistent perspective, consumption patterns and their implicit prices express the budget constraint. Finally, the optimization problem must incorporate constraints such that no w can be chosen outside the span of A.

DEFINITION 2.5. THE CONSTRAINED CONTINGENT CLAIMS PROBLEM. *The individual solves*

$$\max_{(c,w)} \sum_s \pi_s U_s(c, w_s)$$

subject to

$$c + w \cdot R \leq \bar{c} + \bar{w} \cdot R, \qquad \text{(i)}$$

and

$$w \cdot b_k = 0 \qquad \text{(ii)}$$

where $k = 1, \ldots, K$ and the K equations are linearly independent. The convention $K \equiv 0$ indicates the absence of the second set of constraints.

The terminology CCCP emphasizes that (i) the individual trades in patterns of (c,w)—claims where w is a direct choice of how much to consume in each date-one contingency (i.e., state) and (ii) K equations in addition to the budget constraint constrain the choice of w. The K constraints go beyond the budget constraint and do not relate to the individual's endowed wealth. Accordingly, the subsequent discussion refers to these constraints as *extrabudget* constraints.

The K extrabudget constraints can be summarized by $wB = 0$, where $B \equiv [b_1, \ldots, b_K]$; B has S rows and K columns, and 0 is a K-dimensional row vector. To make SP and CCCP equivalent requires identifying B such that $wB = 0$ holds if and only if A spans w. As the next proposition asserts, such a B matrix always exists.[5]

PROPOSITION 2.3. *Consider SP and CCCP with identical endowments in consumption plans, $\bar{z}A = \bar{w}$. Suppose further that (A,P) in SP relates to R in CCCP by $P = AR$. Then a matrix B exists such that SP and CCCP are equivalent, and B depends only on the space spanned by A.*

Economic intuition suggests that the number of constraints in CCCP should be inversely related to the dimension spanned by A. The intuition is valid. The proof shows that the vector space generated by the column vectors in B has dimension $K = S - \dim\{a_j\}_j$; in addition, this vector space is orthogonal to the one generated by the row vectors in A. Formally, $\{w \mid w = zA\} = \{w \mid wB = 0\}$ if and only if $a_j \cdot b_k = 0$ and $\dim\{a_j\}_j + \dim\{b_k\}_k = S$. The K extrabudget constraints are independent of the implicit prices and the prices of securities. The observation confirms that an individual is constrained not only by his budget and prices but also by the richness of the market opportunities. A straightforward but critical implication is that an individual's welfare (expected utility) may be no less dependent on the market opportunities than on his endowed wealth.

The following example illustrates Proposition 2.3. For SP, let

$$A = \begin{bmatrix} 1 & 1 & 1 \\ 1 & 3 & 5 \end{bmatrix} \quad P_1 = 11/12,\ P_2 = 35/12,$$

and $(\bar{c},\bar{z}) = (5,6,6)$. The related budget constraint thus equals

$$c + z_1 \times 11/12 + z_2 \times 35/12 \leq 5 + 6 \times 11/12 + 6 \times 35/12 = 28 \equiv \bar{\bar{w}}.$$

To express an equivalent CCCP[6] put

$$B^t = [1\ -2\ 1],\ R^t = (1/4,\ 1/3,\ 1/3),$$

and $(\bar{c},\bar{w}) = (5,12,24,36)$. This implies a budget constraint determined by

$$c + w_1 \times 1/4 + w_2 \times 1/3 + w_3 \times 1/3 \leq 5 + 12 \times 1/4 + 24 \times 1/3 + 36 \times 1/3 = 28$$

and a single extrabudget constraint determined by

$$w_1 - 2 \times w_2 + w_3 = 0.$$

To verify equivalence between SP and CCCP, note that $P = AR$, $\bar{w} = \bar{z}A$, $AB = 0$, and $\dim(A) + \dim(B) = 2 + 1 = 3 = S$.

[5] In what appears to be a little-known article, Fischer (1972) develops the CCCP and its equivalence to SP.

[6] The notation x^t, where x is a vector (or matrix), denotes transposition.

To identify an extrabudget constraint B matrix in the equivalent CCCP requires only linearly independent securities in A. Stated somewhat differently, a security j' is a *redundant* security if the remaining securities, $\{a_j\}_{j,\ j \neq j'}$ span the vector $a_{j'}$. The word "redundant" describes the case, since one can put $z_{j'}$ equal to zero without affecting the set of attainable w patterns.[7] And, on the cost side, redundant securities do not facilitate any search for the least costly plan z that attains a given w. Proposition 2.1 implies that all portfolios resulting in w cost the same ($w \cdot R$). (More directly, $z''A = z'A$ implies $z'' \cdot P = z' \cdot P$ since $z''AR = z'AR$.) Further note that Proposition 2.2 reflects the redundancy of linearly dependent securities: an optimal plan (c, z) is unique if and only if $\{a_j\}_j$ are linearly independent.

Extreme cases of the CCCP deserve a closer examination. First, the matrix B vanishes in the CCCP ($K = 0$) if and only if A is of full rank (i.e., $\dim\{a_j\}_j = S$). This optimization problem reduces to:

$$\max_{(c,w)} \sum_s \pi_s U_s(c, w_s)$$

subject to

$$c + w \cdot R \leq \bar{\bar{w}}.$$

This simple problem includes only a budget constraint and, in contrast to the general case when $K \geq 1$, the individual can choose any consumption *mix* he desires. The implicit price vector turns into a unique price vector since $\text{rank}(A) = S$ implies that $P = AR$ has a unique solution R. (The conclusion follows from elementary linear algebra.)

The case $K = 0$ is of great theoretical importance because, notation and preferences aside, the optimization problem is equivalent to the classical model of consumer choice. This setting makes it unnecessary to refer to financial markets at all; the richness of the markets permits a conversion of the financial markets problem SP into a regular consumption choice problem. The designation of the underlying financial markets as *complete* is most telling.

DEFINITION 2.6. COMPLETE MARKETS. *Markets are said to be complete if the securities-states tableau A has full rank, that is, if* $\dim\{a_j\}_j = S$.

Naturally, markets are said to be incomplete if A is of less than full rank (i.e., if $\dim\{a_j\}_j < S$).

According to Proposition 2.3, the space generated by A suffices to determine the space that B needs to span, and conversely. Without changing SP, it follows that one can replace any (A', P') with (A'', P''), provided that (i) A'' spans the same space as A' and (ii) the pricing P'' remains consistent

[7] Proof: Let $a_J = k_1 a_1 + \cdots + k_{J-1} a_{J-1}$, and consider any portfolio z'. Put $z'' = (z'_1 + z'_J k_1, \ldots, z'_{J-1} + z'_J k_{J-1}, 0)$. It follows that $z''A = (z'_1 + z'_J k_1) a_1 + \cdots + (z'_{J-1} + z'_J k_{J-1}) a_{J-1} = z'_1 a_1 + \cdots + z'_{J-1} a_{J-1} + z'_J (k_1 a_1 + \cdots + k_{J-1} a_{J-1}) = z'_1 a_1 + \cdots + z'_J a_J = z'A$.

with P'. Pricing consistency means, of course, that the two settings have a common implicit price vector, that is, some $R > 0$ exists satisfying both $P' = A'R$ and $P'' = A''R$. Thus, specifically, *all* complete markets SP settings with fixed R reduce to identical CCCP problems with $K = 0$. *Given complete markets one might as well assume that A equals the identity matrix: $A = I$. In that case the equivalence between SP and CCCP becomes a trivial matter*: $P = R$ and $z = w$. These securities have a unique and curious property. Security j pays one dollar if state $s = j$ occurs, and zero otherwise ($s \neq j$). The security price $P_j (j = s)$, or R_s, is the price of one date-one consumption unit in state s alone. The securities' empirical implausibility and contrived nature do not prevent them from being important in theoretical analyses. The literature refers to such securities as *Arrow-Debreu securities* or *primitive securities*.

Although an Arrow-Debreu securities market defines a special case of complete markets, the restrictiveness is thus more apparent than real. On a more concrete level, if w represents the solution in the Arrow-Debreu setting, then the related optimal z satisfies $w = zA$, A complete. Hence, assuming (with no substantive loss of generality) that A has no redundant securities, matrix inversion applies and $z = wA^{-1}$. This analysis highlights the means-to-an-end perspective on securities: in the extreme one bypasses the markets entirely by letting the individual select an unconstrained consumption mix as described by CCCP with $K = 0$.

As a second extreme case, let $J = 1$, or, equivalently, $K = S - 1$. This setting makes every attainable w proportional to $a_1 (= A)$. Quite aside from the wealth endowment, the individual therefore encounters extensive extra-budget constraints that severely limit opportunities. He could be made better off—or at least no worse off—if there were additional opportunities to buy and sell securities *and* if R and $\bar{\bar{w}}$ do not change. To generalize this idea, note that (i) fixing the implicit price system and the endowments fixes the budget constraint in the CCCP, and that (ii) the row vectors in A' span a subspace of A'' if and only if in the equivalent CCCPs the column vectors of B'' span a subspace of B'. Leaving the first constraint (i) unchanged while relaxing the second set of constraints (ii), $\{w \mid wB' = 0\} \subseteq \{w \mid wB'' = 0\}$, implies that all patterns available in the single-primed CCCP setting remain available in the double-primed CCCP setting. Hence, given Proposition 2.3, the following applies.

PROPOSITION 2.4. *Consider two sets of no-arbitrage market characteristics (A', P') and (A'', P''). Let (c', z') and (c'', z'') denote the two respective solutions of the related SP with endowments $(\bar{c}', \bar{w}') = (\bar{c}'', \bar{w}'')$. Suppose further that A' spans a subspace of A'' and that some $R > 0$ exists such that $P' = A'R$ and $P'' = A''R$. Then (c'', z'') is no worse than (c', z'):*

$$V(\alpha'') \equiv V(c'', z''A'') \geq V(c', z'A') \equiv V(\alpha').*$$

A corollary to the last proposition demonstrates the meaning of economically equivalent (A'',P'') and (A',P') pairs, and their effect on optimal portfolio choices.

COROLLARY 2.4.1. *If the assumptions of Proposition 2.4 apply and A' and A'' span identical spaces, then $V(\alpha') = V(\alpha'')$. Furthermore, there exists a $J' \times J''$ matrix T such that $A' = TA''$, and $z'' = z'T$ connects optimal z', z''.*

In general, the two spaces generated by A' and A'' may of course not be subspaces of each other. Nevertheless, Proposition 2.4 requires such a subspace condition since the set of available consumption patterns in the single-primed setting would otherwise not be a subset of those available in the double-primed setting. But this subset relationship drives the result, and thus it also becomes clear why the result requires the two settings to have at least one common vector of implicit prices as well.[8] This raises the following, more complex, question: Can (A'',P'') dominate (A',P') relative to expected utility for a class of preferences/beliefs even though the related sets of available consumption patterns do not have a subset relationship or the settings do not have a common implicit price vector? An answer to the question relies on the idea that the conclusion of Proposition 2.4 may still obtain if one loosens some of the restrictions on the market characteristics in exchange for a tightening of those on preferences/beliefs. Section 2.4 in this chapter considers the issue.

2.3. Analysis of the Standard Problem's Optimality Conditions

This section develops the optimality conditions associated with the solution of the standard problem. To delineate the conditions greatly facilitates an understanding of subsequent chapters. The analysis disregards the constraint $\alpha \geqq 0$; as section 2.2.1 notes, this approach presumes that the constraint does not bind SP's solution. Given this simplification, the optimality conditions for the optimal plan (c, z) derive from a solution to the Lagrangean problem

$$\max_{(c,z,\omega)} L(c,z,\omega) \equiv \max_{(c,z,\omega)} V(c,zA) - \omega[(c + z \cdot P) - \bar{\bar{w}}], \tag{2.4}$$

where ω denotes the Lagrangean multiplier, and, as usual, $\bar{\bar{w}} \equiv \bar{c} + \bar{z} \cdot P$. Differentiating L with respect to its arguments and setting the derivatives

[8] Note that not *all* implicit price vectors may be common simply because one common vector exists. That is, in the expression for "at least one,"

$$\{R''|A''R'' = P'',R'' > 0\} \cap \{R'|A'R' = P',R' > 0\} \neq \phi,$$

one cannot replace "$\cap$" with "=". Using basic linear algebra one shows that the only exception occurs when A' and A'' span identical spaces.

equal to zero yields the following equations:

$$\partial L/\partial c = v^1(c,w) - \omega = 0, \tag{2.5a}$$

$$\partial L/\partial z_j = \sum_{s \in S} v_s^2(c,w_s)a_{js} - \omega P_j = 0, j = 1, \ldots, J, \text{ and} \tag{2.5b}$$

$$\partial L/\partial \omega = c + z \cdot P - \bar{\bar{w}} = 0, \tag{2.5c}$$

where

$$\partial V/\partial c \equiv v^1 = v^1(c,w) = \sum_s \pi_s u_s^1(c,w_s), \tag{2.6}$$

and

$$\partial V/\partial w_s \equiv v_s^2 = v_s^2(c,w_s) = \pi_s u_s^2(c,w_s). \tag{2.7}$$

The function v^1 is the marginal expected utility of current consumption, and v_s^2 is the marginal expected utility of date-one consumption in state s. The system of Eq. (2.5a), (2.5b), and (2.5c) has $J + 2$ equations and the same number of variables. Given the MISC regularity conditions, Lagrangean optimization theory implies that a solution to the systems of Eqs. (2.5a), (2.5b), and (2.5c) is both necessary and sufficient for (c,z) to be optimal.[9]

Elimination of the multiplier, ω, makes additional simplification possible. Solving for ω in Eq. (2.5a) and substituting into Eq. (2.5b) leads to J equations:

$$\sum_s [v_s^2(c,w_s)/v^1(c,w)]a_{js} = P_j. \tag{2.8a}$$

Substituting Eq. (2.6) and Eq. (2.7) into Eq. (2.8a) yields

$$\sum_{s \in S} [\pi_s u_s^2(c, \sum_j a_{js} z_j)/ \sum_s \pi_s u_s^1(c, \sum_j a_{js} z_j)]a_{js} = P_j. \tag{2.8b}$$

Letting $\lambda \equiv (\lambda_1, \ldots, \lambda_S) \equiv (v_1^2/v^1, \ldots, v_s^2/v^1, \ldots, v_S^2/v^1)$ permits a more compact expression for the optimality conditions Eq. (2.8a):

$$A\lambda = P. \tag{2.9}$$

It is understood that λ depends directly on the decision variables, which in turn relate back to all parameters affecting the optimal decision (i.e., $\bar{\bar{w}}$, A, P, and preferences/beliefs $V(\cdot)$). The vector λ will be referred to

---

[9] Provided that $V(\alpha)$ is strictly concave in α, one easily proves that $V(c,zA)$ is concave in (c,z). The concavity is strict if there are no redundant securities. Hence, the well-behavedness of $V(\alpha)$ carries over to the indirect preference ordering $V(c,zA)$ of (c,z).

From the optimality conditions, one infers that the conditions $v^1(0,w) = \infty$ any $w \geqq 0$, and $v_s^2(c,0) = \infty$, any $c \geq 0$, imply that $\alpha > 0$ at an optimum. The constraint $\alpha \geqq 0$ is safely neglected under the circumstances. The following example fulfills the conditions: let utilities be state independent and time-additive with $U^1(x)/\rho = U^2(x) = \log x$.

as the vector of *marginal rates of substitution* (*MRS*) *of consumption across states*. This terminology derives from the classical consumer choice model, and it makes sense since

$$\lambda_s \equiv [\partial V/\partial w_s]/[\partial V/\partial c]. \tag{2.10}$$

As a practical matter, in most instances the optimality conditions do not lend themselves to a clearly identifiable solution structure beyond the system of equations (2.9). Explicit "closed form" solutions for the optimal plan (c,z), or for the pattern α, rarely exist. Nevertheless, the absence of explicit solutions does not prevent the development of theory. For most theoretical questions the key analyses center on the marginal rates of substitution vector λ rather than (c,z) directly, and detailed examination of Eq. (2.8b) serves a useful purpose only for models with considerable structure.

Before looking at such specific models some further general observations about λ are of interest. First, given any specification of $V(\cdot)$, α suffices for an evaluation of λ_s, and, in general, this evaluation must consider all components in α. The market structure A and security holdings z affect λ only indirectly via their effect on $\alpha = (c, zA)$. Nor do P and $\bar{\bar{w}}$ have any direct effect on λ, except that the optimal α depends on P and $\bar{\bar{w}}$. There is again no real surprise, since all critical perspectives rely on the concept that securities are a means to acquire (uncertain) future consumption. Second, every SP with MISC preferences results in a unique λ; this follows since SP has a unique optimal α (Proposition 2.2). The possibility of a nonunique optimal plan (c,z) does not impinge on the conclusion. Third, the vector λ can serve as a valid implicit price system. Its validity follows immediately from (i) the definition of an implicit price system and Eq. (2.9), and (ii) in Eq. (2.9) $\lambda_s > 0$ since $v^1, v_s^2 > 0$. Given any solution α and the related λ, one may therefore always put $R = \lambda$. The value of a pattern w is then equivalent to $w \cdot \lambda$, that is, to the consumption summed across states weighted by the marginal rates of substitution evaluated at an optimum. Similar to the classical analysis, $c' + w' \cdot \lambda' \leq c + w \cdot \lambda'$ when (c', w') defines the optimal consumption pattern and $V(\alpha) \geq V(\alpha')$. However, the financial markets setting additionally restricts w' and w to be in the span of A.

The vector R differs conceptually from λ because R is generally nonunique and derives from (A,P) alone. In contrast, λ is unique and ultimately depends on the characteristics of the individual, $(V, \bar{\bar{w}})$, as well. The need for distinguishing between λ and R is apparent in Proposition 2.4: the common implicit prices condition, $P'' = A''R$ and $P' = A'R$, some $R > 0$, does *not* imply $\lambda'' = \lambda'$ since the optimal pattern α'' may differ from α'. Knowing the set of admissible R yields only partial knowledge about λ, except for complete markets, in which case $R = \lambda$ perforce. Complete markets, as usual, lead to sharp and important implications.

One should expect the optimality conditions Eq. (2.8a) and (2.8b) and the expression for λ to become less cumbersome given additional structure on preferences or on markets. As illustrations, the literature frequently relies on the following two models as starting points. First, time-additive V simplifies Eq. (2.5a) to

$$\omega = u^1(c), \tag{2.11a}$$

and

$$\lambda_s = \pi_s u_s^2(w_s)/u^1(c). \tag{2.11b}$$

Time-additivity facilitates the analysis because λ_s depends directly only on the characteristics that relate to state s; w_t has no direct effect. Second, combining time-additivity with Arrow-Debreu securities reduces Eq. (2.8b) to

$$\pi_s u_s^2(w_s)/u^1(c) = P_s = R_s = \lambda_s. \tag{2.12}$$

The last expression thus shows the equivalence of security prices, implicit prices, and the marginal rates of substitution of consumption.

Because of their simplicity Eqs. (2.11a), (2.11b), and (2.12) have certain virtues, but they also sharply narrow the general optimality equations, Eqs. (2.8a) and (2.8b). By letting U_s^2 be state independent and of specific functional form, the simplification of Eqs. (2.8a) and (2.8b) becomes even more extreme. The next section introduces a class of models with explicit analytic functions as preferences, and, of lesser significance, Arrow-Debreu markets.

2.4. An Analysis of a Class of Utility Functions: Linear Risk Tolerance Utilities

Working with highly stylized models having straightforward and clearly discernible implications often has considerable value. Only with "strategically simplifying" assumptions does the analysis provide unambiguous conclusions about the demand for securities as a function of the individual's characteristics and the security prices. Hence, one useful byproduct of such models is that they illustrate how one manipulates optimality conditions to derive a "closed form" solution. Moreover, the models that will be analyzed are of theoretical interest in their own right. One should expect simple settings to have interesting implications, even though these may occasionally border on the pathological. In other words, the model implications tend to be extraordinary, and a general relaxation of assumptions typically eliminates their occurrence. However, a thorough understanding of a paradigm flows from a careful analysis of the peculiar insights acquired only in highly restrictive settings. Results thus derived provide useful guidance when one seeks out substantive theoretical questions. The process of identifying relatively weak assumptions for a particular result is aided by a benchmark setting for which the conclusion holds.

The class of utility functions analyzed here is commonly referred to as *linear risk tolerance* (*LRT*) *utilities,* or *HARA utilities* (HARA stands for "hyperbolic absolute risk-aversion"). These utility functions satisfy state independence and time-additivity. In addition, the literature generally identifies LRT $U^2(\cdot)$ as a solution to a particular differential equation.

DEFINITION 2.7. LINEAR RISK TOLERANCE. *The time-additive and state independent utility function $U_s(c, w_s) = U^1(c) + U^2(w_s)$ satisfies linear risk tolerance if $U^2(w_s)$ solves the differential equation*

$$-[\partial U^2(w_s)/\partial w_s]/[\partial^2 U^2(w_s)/\partial w_s^2] = \varphi + \beta w_s,$$

where φ and β are independent of w_s.

From the definition it is seen that every LRT U^2 is identified by two parameters: the intercept, φ, and the slope, β.

The differential equation in Definition 2.7 has three sets of solutions, depending on the value of β. Let $b \equiv 1/\beta$ when $\beta \neq 0$; the solutions are as follows:

$$\beta \neq 0,1\text{: } U^2(w_s) \sim [b/(1 - b)](\varphi + \beta w_s)^{1-b}, \tag{2.13a}$$

$$\beta = 1\text{: } U^2(w_s) \sim \log(\varphi + w_s), \tag{2.13b}$$

$$\beta = 0\text{: } U^2(w_s) \sim -\varphi \exp\{-w_s/\varphi\}. \tag{2.13c}$$

In the above context the symbol "~" means that the solutions are unique up to a positive linear transform. One inserts the constants $[b/(1 - b)]$ and $-\varphi$ in Eq. (2.13a) and (2.13c), respectively, out of convention and convenience (see below).

The three classes of utility functions are, respectively, *generalized power utility, generalized logarithmic utility,* and *negative exponential utility*. The word "generalized" applies in the first two cases whenever $\varphi \neq 0$. For $\varphi = 0$, utilities are of the *power* (2.13a) or *logarithmic* (2.13b) type. These cases are also said to be *iso-elastic,* and the utilities display *constant proportional* (relative) *risk aversion* (CPRA). The latter terminology derives from the relationship $-w_s[\partial^2 U^2/\partial w_s^2]/[\partial U^2/\partial w_s] = \beta^{-1}$, which defines a measure of the individual's relative disposition toward risk. *Quadratic utility* follows by letting $\beta = -1$, and other, less important, polynomial utilities follow by letting $1/\beta = -2, -3, \cdots$. Finally, note that negative exponential utility ($\beta = 0$) satisfies *constant absolute risk aversion:* $-[\partial^2 U^2/\partial w_s^2]/[\partial U^2/\partial w_s] = \varphi^{-1}$ independent of w_s. Subsequent analysis will not refer to the two risk-aversion concepts ("relative" and "absolute"). Nevertheless, the reader should be aware that the literature frequently relies on these two characterizations of utility functions.

MISC requires $u^2 > 0$, $\partial u^2/\partial w_s < 0$, and the two inequalities therefore constrain the LRT parameters φ and β. The parameterization Eq. (2.13a), (2.13b), and (2.13c) is exceedingly useful for this purpose. One easily verifies that $U^2(\cdot)$ is MISC at a point w_s if and only if φ, β, and w_s satisfy $\varphi + \beta w_s > 0$. The notion of a "relevant range" for w_s is therefore generally applicable, the only exception occurring when $\beta = 0$. Equation (2.13c) is MISC for all w_s if and only if $\varphi > 0$. If $\beta > 0$ the relevant range of w_s is $w_s > -\varphi/\beta$ (a lower bound), and for $\beta < 0$ the restriction is $w_s < -\varphi/\beta$ (an upper bound). MISC quadratic utility therefore holds if and only if $w_s < \varphi$. To allow for positive w_s in the upper-bound cases requires in addition that $\varphi > 0$. The analysis assumes throughout that w_s is within its relevant range.

Consider next the derivation of optimal policies in settings with Arrow-Debreu securities and LRT utilities. As a useful first step, restate the optimality condition Eq. (2.12) of the previous section as

$$u^2(w_s) = \omega(P_s/\pi_s) \equiv \omega\hat{R}_s, \quad (s = 1, \ldots, S), \tag{2.14}$$

where $\hat{R} \equiv (\hat{R}_1, \ldots, \hat{R}_S)$ are the *probability-normalized* implicit prices and $\omega = u^1(c)$. Next, restate the budget constraint as

$$\sum_s P_s w_s = \bar{\bar{w}} - c \equiv \bar{I}, \tag{2.15}$$

where $\bar{I}$ defines the total amount invested in securities. The emphasis will be on the derivation of w as a function of $\bar{I}$, β, φ, $\hat{R}$, and P; the explicit determination of $\bar{I}$ (and thus of c) is unimportant for the time being. Special assumptions about U^1 are unnecessary since $\bar{I}$ is fixed in this analysis. (The explicit derivation of $\bar{I}$ and c is straightforward if one assumes that $\rho U^2 = U^1$; see below.)

To solve for the vector w, consider first the cases in which $\beta \neq 0, 1$, that is, where the utility function is of the generalized power type, Eq. (2.13a). Upon differentiating Eq. (2.13a) with respect to w_s, the optimality condition (2.14) equals to

$$(\varphi + \beta w_s)^{-b} = \omega\hat{R}_s \quad (\text{all } s \in S) \tag{2.16}$$

Solving for w_s and using $b = \beta^{-1}$ implies that

$$w_s = b\omega^{-\beta}\hat{R}_s^{-\beta} - \varphi/\beta \equiv b\omega^{-\beta}\hat{R}_s^{-\beta} - \theta, \tag{2.17}$$

where $\theta \equiv \varphi/\beta$. Multiplying both sides of Eq. (2.17) by P_s and summing over states yields

$$\sum_s w_s P_s \equiv \bar{I} = b\omega^{-\beta} \sum_s P_s\hat{R}_s^{-\beta} - \theta/R_F, \tag{2.18}$$

where $R_F \equiv \left(\sum P_s\right)^{-1}$ is the return on a risk-free portfolio. Solving for $b\omega^{-\beta}$ in Eq. (2.18) and substituting into Eq. (2.17), one obtains the demand for w_s as a function of $\bar{I}$, β, φ, $\hat{R}$, and P (partially via θ and R_F):

$$w_s = -\theta + \hat{R}_s^{-\beta}[\bar{I} + \theta/R_F]/\left[\sum_s P_s\hat{R}_s^{-\beta}\right]. \tag{2.19}$$

The above analysis applies equally to generalized logarithmic utility; put $\beta = 1$ in Eq. (2.16) through (2.19). Because $\sum P_s\hat{R}_s^{-1} = 1$, Eq. (2.19) reduces to

$$w_s = -\varphi + \hat{R}_s^{-1}[\bar{I} + \varphi/R_F]. \tag{2.20}$$

With iso-elastic utilities $\varphi = \theta = 0$, and Eq. (2.19) is even simpler:

$$w_s = \hat{R}_s^{-\beta}\bar{I}/\left[\sum_s P_s \hat{R}_s^{-\beta}\right]. \tag{2.21}$$

Nor does the case of negative exponential utility ($\beta = 0$, $\varphi > 0$) pose any problems. The optimality condition Eq. (2.14) equals

$$\exp\{-w_s/\varphi\} = \omega\hat{R}_s. \tag{2.22}$$

Solving for w_s, one gets

$$w_s = -\varphi \log \omega - \varphi \log \hat{R}_s. \tag{2.23}$$

Next, multiply both sides of Eq. (2.23) by P_s and sum over s to get

$$\sum_s P_s w_s \equiv \bar{I} = -\varphi[R_F^{-1} \log \omega + \sum_s P_s \log \hat{R}_s]. \tag{2.24}$$

Solving for $\log \omega$ in Eq. (2.24) and substituting into Eq. (2.23) yields

$$w_s = -\varphi[\log \hat{R}_s - R_F \sum_s P_s \log \hat{R}_s] + R_F\bar{I}. \tag{2.25}$$

Equations (2.19), (2.20), and (2.25) thus identify respectively the demand functions for w_s when utility is generalized power (Eq. (2.13a)), generalized logarithmic (Eq. (2.13b)), and negative exponential (Eq. (2.13c)). A couple of interesting observations may be deduced directly from the "closed form" solutions.

First, in all three models one can express w_s as a function linear in $\bar{I}$: $w_s = q_{1s} + q_{2s}\bar{I}$ where (2.19), (2.20), and (2.25) supply the details for the $\bar{I}$-independent but generally s- and (φ,β)-dependent q_{1s} and q_{2s} quantities. These demand functions are exceptional; if one restricts the utilities to be state independent, it can be shown that LRT utilities are not only sufficient but also necessary for w_s to be linear in $\bar{I}$ (Milne, 1979). Accordingly, a basic equivalence exists between LRT and linear demand functions. This equivalence is one reason why theoretical and empirical analyses frequently postulate LRT utilities. A related, seemingly innocuous, property of the linear demand functions may be pointed out, although the reader has to await the next chapter before its significance becomes transparent. The slope coefficient $\partial w_s/\partial\bar{I} = q_{2s}$ is independent of φ, a fact that powerfully enhances the analytical usefulness of LRT utilities.[10] For both generalized

[10] The w_s solutions may be condensed to highlight their dependence on $(\varphi,\bar{I})$:

$$w_s = \begin{cases} \varphi K_1(\beta,\hat{R},P,\hat{R}_s) + K_2(\beta,\hat{R},P,\hat{R}_s)\bar{I}, & \beta \neq 0 \\ \varphi K_3(\beta = 0,\hat{R},P,\hat{R}_s) + R_F\bar{I}, & \beta = 0. \end{cases}$$

The K functions may be retrieved from Eqs. (2.19) and (2.25).

power (Eq. (2.19)) and generalized logarithmic (Eq. (2.20)) utilities, $\partial w_s/\partial \bar{I} = \hat{R}_s^{-\beta}/\left(\sum_s P_s\hat{R}_s^{-\beta}\right)$. In the case of the negative exponential utility Eq. (2.25), $\partial w_s/\partial \bar{I} = R_F$. (The latter result has a curious implication: as additional wealth becomes available for investment in securities, the individual puts it all incrementally into a risk-free portfolio. The conclusion follows immediately since $[\partial w_s/\partial \bar{I}]/[\partial w_t/\partial \bar{I}] = 1$.)

Second, careful examination of the solutions (Eq. (2.19), (2.20), and (2.25)) reveals that the optimal solution varies little in response to certain individual specific parametric variations. Thus, the optimal solution of a particular decision problem in some sense is closely related to the optimal solutions of other decision problems because the decision problems have sufficiently similar solution structures. The idea can be made precise. If one fixes β and examines the vector w as a function of φ and $\bar{I}$, a linear combination of the unit vector and one additional row vector, $h \equiv (h_1, \ldots, h_S)$, expresses the optimal pattern w:

$$w(\varphi,\bar{I}) = k_1(\varphi,\bar{I})1 + k_2(\varphi,\bar{I})h, \tag{2.26}$$

where $k_1(\cdot,\cdot)$ and $k_2(\cdot,\cdot)$ are scalar functions of φ and $\bar{I}$. The two functions k_1 and k_2 thus furnish the coefficients for the vectors 1 and h. Even though k_1 and k_2 may indeed depend on φ, $\bar{I}$, the point is that *the vector h does not*. (Because β is treated as fixed, the notation disregards that k_1, k_2, h, and w are all potentially functions of β.)

From a direct inspection of the solutions (Eq. (2.19), (2.20), and (2.25)) one can identify h up to an arbitrary scale factor:

$$\beta \neq 0 \text{ implies that } h_s = \hat{R}_s^{-\beta}, \tag{2.27a}$$

and

$$\beta = 0 \text{ implies that } h_s = \log \hat{R}_s. \tag{2.27b}$$

The related functions k_1 and k_2 are also readily identified from Eq. (2.19), (2.20), and (2.25):

$$\beta \neq 0 \text{ implies that } k_1 = -\varphi/\beta \text{ and } k_2 = [\bar{I} + \varphi/(\beta R_F)]/\left[\sum_s P_s\hat{R}_s^{-\beta}\right], \tag{2.28a}$$

and

$$\beta = 0 \text{ implies that } k_1 = \varphi R_F \sum_s P_s \log \hat{R}_s + R_F\bar{I} \text{ and } k_2 = -\varphi. \tag{2.28b}$$

Equations (2.26) through (2.28a) and (2.28b) amount to the following: the unit vector and h define two portfolios, and the set of all optimal portfolios as $(\varphi,\bar{I})$ vary are linear combinations of these two portfolios. For this reason one refers to the unit vector and h as the two *basis portfolios*. The two basis portfolios are obviously not unique, but the ones chosen have the virtue of deriving readily from the optimal solutions (Eq. (2.19), (2.20), and (2.25)). More generally, if one picks any two pairs $(\varphi',\bar{I}')$ and $(\varphi'',\bar{I}'')$ not resulting in proportional $w' \equiv w(\varphi',\bar{I}')$ and $w'' \equiv w(\varphi'',\bar{I}'')$ vectors, then $\{w'',w'\}$ span $w(\varphi,\bar{I})$ for any $(\varphi,\bar{I})$; in addition, $\{w'',w'\}$ span the unit vector.

The existence of two basis portfolios spanning the set of all optimal portfolios—where the class of optimization problems implied by "all" must be specified carefully—is generally referred to as *two-fund portfolio separation*. Thus, in the examples discussed, the idea is that 1 and h define the two funds. Carrying this perspective one additional step, if $\beta \neq 0$ (but is otherwise fixed) *and* $\varphi = 0$, then *one-fund separation* obtains for all $\bar{I}$. The optimal portfolios equal $w = k_3\bar{I}h$ where the constant k_3 derives from $k_3\bar{I} = k_2(\varphi = 0,\bar{I}) = \bar{I}/\sum_s P_s\hat{R}_s^{-\beta}$. The last relationship follows from Eq. (2.28a), and k_3 is indeed independent of $\bar{I}$. (Eq. (2.27a) still defines the vector h.) In sum, one-fund separation applies for iso-elastic utility functions with fixed β, and the optimal portfolios are proportional to one another as $\bar{I}$ varies.

The preceding analysis combines two different sets of restrictions: that preferences belong to the LRT class and that the markets consist of Arrow-Debreu securities. Of course, complete markets work as well. Equation (2.26) still applies, but $\{1,h\}$ now define *basis consumption patterns* as opposed to basis portfolios. For complete markets without redundant securities one infers the optimal portfolio $z(\varphi,\bar{I})$ by postmultiplying Eq. (2.26) by A^{-1} and by letting $z' = 1A^{-1}$ and $z'' = hA^{-1}$ serve as basis portfolios:

$$z(\varphi,\bar{I}) = k_1(\varphi,\bar{I})z' + k_2(\varphi,\bar{I})z''. \tag{2.29}$$

Less clear, however, is the extent to which one can consider incomplete markets without destroying the portfolio separation conclusions. The need for specialized assumptions on utilities can hardly be challenged. The only other approach leading to as strong a result as portfolio separation requires assumptions about the joint probability distribution of payoffs, that is, assumptions about A and π (3.7 considers this approach). Nevertheless, it turns out that the previous separation conclusion does not depend on complete markets, and, surprisingly, the availability of a risk-free portfolio suffices. The following proposition states this well-known portfolio separation property of LRT utilities formally.

PROPOSITION 2.5. *Suppose that utility is LRT with parameters φ and β, β fixed. Suppose further that some z' satisfies $1 = z'A$. Then a portfolio z'' and scalar functions $m_1(\varphi,\bar{I})$ and $m_2(\varphi,\bar{I})$ exist such that the optimal plan $z(\varphi,\bar{I})$ is given by*

$$z(\varphi,\bar{I}) = m_1(\varphi,\bar{I})z' + m_2(\varphi,\bar{I})z''.$$

The optimal consumption pattern $w(\varphi,\bar{I})$ *is given by*

$$w(\varphi,\bar{I}) = m_1(\varphi,\bar{I})1 + m_2(\varphi,\bar{I})w'',$$

where $z''A = w''$.

COROLLARY 2.2. *If* β *is fixed,* $\beta > 0$, *and* $\varphi = 0$, *then one fund separation obtains:* $z(\bar{I}) = z''\bar{I}$ *where* z'' *is the basis portfolio, and* $w(\bar{I}) = w''\bar{I}$ *where* $w'' = z''A$. *The result holds for arbitrary A.**

Note, again, that portfolio separation requires a fixed β; that is, $w(\varphi,\bar{I},\beta)$ is *not* spanned by two portfolios if β varies.

The proof of Proposition 2.5 shows that the function $m_2(\varphi,\bar{I})$ is proportional to, and thus essentially the same as, the function $k_2(\varphi,\bar{I})$, which derives in the complete markets setting (Eqs. (2.28a) and (2.28b)). The function $m_1(\varphi,\bar{I})$, however, differs from $k_1(\varphi,\bar{I})$, and it does not have a simple closed form expression. Even so, the portfolio holdings $z_j(\varphi,\bar{I})$ remain linear in $\bar{I}$ for all j. This conclusion follows by examining the function $z(\varphi,\bar{I})$ as it appears in the proof of Proposition 2.5.[11]

The discussion next turns to the determination of $\bar{I}$ and c, a problem whose solution U^1 and $\bar{\bar{w}}$ affect. Conversely, the latter function and parameter can be unspecified when one focuses only on the choice of z *given* some $\bar{I}$. This suggests a recursive solution procedure: first, identify an optimal plan z for each $\bar{I}$, and second, solve for the optimal $\bar{I}$. That is, for the second stage, solve

$$\max_{\bar{I}}\{U^1(\bar{\bar{w}} - \bar{I}) + U^{2*}(\bar{I})\},$$

where $U^{2*}(\bar{I})$ denotes the optimal expected utility of date-one consumption given $\bar{I}$:

$$U^{2*}(\bar{I}) \equiv \max_{z} \sum_{s} \pi_s U_s^2\left(\sum_{j} z_j a_{js}\right)$$

subject to

$$z \cdot P = \bar{I}.$$

Although the notation suppresses the dependence, note that U^2, π, A, and P affect U^{2*}.

The recursive solution procedure can, at least in principle, be used for any U^1 and U^2 specification. To illustrate its application, consider LRT U^2,

---

[11] Another property retained in the incomplete markets setting with the negative exponential utility is that $z_j(\varphi,\bar{I})$ is independent of $\bar{I}$ for all risky securities, and $\partial P_J z_J(\varphi,\bar{I})/\partial\bar{I} = 1$ where the Jth security is risk-free. Incremental dollar amounts available for investment are therefore used entirely to buy more of the risk-free security.

Given $a_J = 1 \times$ constant, note from the proof that $z_j' = 0$, $1 \le j < J$, and $z_J'' = 0$. Hence, in this case z_j/z_k, j, $k < J$, does not depend on $(\varphi, \bar{I}, U^1)$.

$\beta > 0$. The proof of Proposition 2.5 supplies the necessary information to express the form of U^{2*}. U^{2*} separates usefully into one part that depends on $\bar{I}$ and one part that does not. Specifically, one finds the optimal $\bar{I}$ by solving

$$\max_{\bar{I}}\{U^1(\bar{\bar{w}} - \bar{I}) + m_2(\varphi,\bar{I})^\gamma K_1\}, \quad (\beta \neq 1), \tag{2.30a}$$

and

$$\max_{\bar{I}}\{U^1(\bar{\bar{w}} - \bar{I}) + \log m_2(\varphi,\bar{I}) + K_2\}, \quad (\beta = 1), \tag{2.30b}$$

where K_1 and K_2 depend only on A, P, and π (and are thus independent of $\bar{\bar{w}}$, U^1, φ, and $\bar{I}$), $m_2 = \varphi/\beta + R_F\bar{I}$, and $\gamma = 1 - 1/\beta$. Differentiating the expressions inside { } in Eq. (2.30a) and (2.30b) with respect to $\bar{I}$ yields the optimality condition:

$$u^1(\bar{\bar{w}} - \bar{I}) = R_F m_2(\varphi,\bar{I})^{-1/\beta}K_3, \tag{2.31}$$

where $K_3 = \gamma K_1$, and $K_3 \equiv 1$ if $\beta = 1$.[12]

The additional assumption that $U^1/\rho = U^2$, introduced in Eq. (2.3), implies that u^1 has "the same form" as $m_2^{-1/\beta}$ and Eq. (2.31) becomes:

$$\rho[\varphi + \beta(\bar{\bar{w}} - \bar{I})]^{-b} = R_F[\varphi/\beta + R_F\bar{I}]^{-b}K_3. \tag{2.32}$$

The optimal solutions for $\bar{I}$ and c now derive easily; as expected, both are linear in $\bar{\bar{w}}$. The result applies in spite of the incomplete markets.

The backward recursion solution procedure illustrates the derivation of optimal choice within a two-date context. Nevertheless, the theoretical usefulness of a recursive procedure must not be overrated, and frequently it becomes outright cumbersome and impractical. The general optimality conditions that section 2.3 develops contain all the information needed about optimal choice, and for this reason subsequent chapters do not rely on recursive optimality. (This is true even when the analysis generalizes SP to a dynamic model which includes multiple decision points.)

One apparent case that bypasses Eq. (2.32) assumes complete markets in addition to LRT U^2 and $U^1/\rho = U^2 \equiv U$. The linear solutions for $\bar{I}$ and c derive directly. Define $\pi_0 \equiv \rho$, $c \equiv w_0$, and let s range from zero (rather than one) to S. Express expected utility Eq. (2.3) as

$$V(\alpha) = \sum_{s=0}^{S} \pi_s U(w_s). \tag{2.33}$$

To solve for α and not just w, the analysis of this section's first part may be utilized—simply replace $\bar{I}$ with $\bar{\bar{w}}$ and let $P_0 \equiv 1$, $\hat{R}_0 \equiv \rho^{-1}$, and $R_F^{-1} \equiv \sum_{s=0}^{S} P_s$.

---

[12] An additional less-important but well-known independence result follows from a direct observation of Eq. (2.30b): given generalized logarithmic utility ($\beta = 1$, but U^1 is arbitrary), the optimal $\bar{I}$ is independent of the probabilistic characteristics of the risky investment opportunities. That is, $\bar{I}$ depends on R_F but not otherwise on A, P, and π.

The solutions (Eqs. (2.19) and (2.25)) extend to w_0 as well, keeping in mind that s runs from $0, \ldots, S$ and, most important, where the optimal solution α depends on $\bar{\bar{w}}$ directly rather than $\bar{I}$. (Of course, in this case R_F should not be interpreted as the usual risk-free rate, and $\sum_{s=0}^{S} \pi_s$ exceeds one. The last observation modifies Eq. (2.20) since $\sum_{s=0}^{S} P_s \hat{R}_s^{-1} \neq 1$.)

The distinction between the two assumptions—(i) U^2 is LRT and U^1 is arbitrary (but MISC), and (ii) U^2 is LRT *and* U^1 has the same form as U^2 (that is, $\rho U^2 = U^1$)—is an important one. In case (i) the portfolio separation relates to w, and w is linear $\bar{I}$. In case (ii) the separation relates to every component of α, including c, and α is linear in $\bar{\bar{w}}$. Consequently, the stronger assumption about current consumption preferences leads to a stronger statement about the solution. The literature generally pays little attention to the significance of the two different assumptions. Looking beyond the current chapter, the following is of interest. For portfolio separation to have analytical power the weaker form, that is, case (i), suffices. On the other hand, linear demand functions have analytical power only when all of α is linear in $\bar{\bar{w}}$, that is, in case (ii).

Proposition 2.5 shows that for LRT utilities variations in $(\varphi, \bar{I})$ have only a limited effect on z and w. Another aspect of this setting focuses on the expected utility ranking of opportunity *sets* rather than the relationship between optimal policies. Roughly speaking, given the similarity of optimal policies across $(\varphi, \bar{I})$, or $(\varphi, \bar{\bar{w}}, U^1)$, one should expect the relative expected utilities associated with different market characteristics to satisfy a similar specification independence. The following proposition expresses this idea.

PROPOSITION 2.6. *Let (A', P') and (A'', P'') be two sets of no-arbitrage market characteristics. Assume the risk-free rate is the same in both cases, that is, $1 \cdot R' = 1 \cdot R''$. Suppose further that U^2 satisfies LRT with parameters φ and β. Let α' and α'' be the solutions to the two respective SP in which $\bar{\bar{w}}' = \bar{\bar{w}}'' \equiv \bar{\bar{w}}$. Then the sign of*

$$V(\alpha'') - V(\alpha')$$

is independent of U^1, φ, and $\bar{\bar{w}}$.[13]

The above result relies on fewer restrictions on the market characteristics than Proposition 2.4. The spaces generated by A'' and A' need not be subsets of each other, and common implicit prices may not exist (although $1 \cdot R'' = 1 \cdot R'$ must hold). The weaker market characteristics assumption suffices because of the stronger preferences (LRT) assumption.

---

[13] To be sure, more precise but cumbersome notation can be used to indicate that both the optimal α and the specification of the preferences V depend on ϕ. For example, express the optimal expected utility as $V_\phi(\alpha(\phi))$.

Propositions 2.4 and 2.6 compare an individual's welfare in two different (single-primed and double-primed) settings. This theme recurs throughout. It is therefore worth noting again that Propositions 2.4 and 2.6 jointly illustrate a frequently applied general principle. Two broad strategies are available for deriving propositions about individuals' relative welfare in different settings: either make relatively strong assumptions about the market structure and the prices, or make relatively strong assumptions about individuals' attributes. As is typical in economics, to support particular conclusions there are trade-offs between different sets of assumptions.

The microanalysis of this chapter relies on exogenous specifications of the price structure. The next chapter considers the more complex task of evaluating individuals' welfare when prices are determined endogenously, that is, in settings of general equilibrium.

Appendix 2.1 Proofs

Proof of Proposition 2.1. To prove the existence of an $R > 0$ such that $P = AR$ given no-arbitrage is not elementary. The result applies Steimke's Theorem, which in turn closely relates to Farkas' Lemma. Mangasarian (1969) provides a comprehensive analysis of these results.

However, the converse—that $P = AR$, $R > 0$, implies no-arbitrage—is straightforward. Suppose $z \cdot P < 0$; then $zA \cdot R < 0$ and zA has at least one negative component since $R > 0$. Similarly, if $z \cdot P = 0$, then $zA \cdot R = 0$ and zA has at least one negative component unless $zA = 0$.

Remark: The above result is robust; it restricts neither P nor A to be nonnegative.

Proof of Lemma 2.1. Suppose first that arbitrage is possible. Then for any α' there exists some other attainable and affordable α'' such that $\alpha'' \geq \alpha'$. This follows by putting $(c'', z'') = (c', z') + (0, \hat{z})$, where $\hat{z}$ is any arbitrage portfolio; $c'' + z'' \cdot P \leq \bar{\bar{w}}$ since $\hat{z} \cdot P \leq 0$. Hence, $V(\alpha'') > (\alpha')$ and no optimum exists.

Suppose next that arbitrage is impossible. Proposition 2.1 then implies that α satisfies

$$c + w \cdot R \leq \bar{\bar{w}}, \quad \text{where } R > 0.$$

It follows that $0 \leqq (c, w) \leqq (1, R_1^{-1}, \ldots, R_S^{-1})\bar{\bar{w}}$ so that feasible α are bounded. The set of feasible α is also readily seen to be a closed set. (If (c^n, z^n), $n = 1, 2, \ldots$ are affordable, then so is $\operatorname{Lim}_n (c^n, z^n)$.) Since $V(\alpha)$ is continuous, it is now well known that a maximizing α exists.

Proof of Proposition 2.2. Suppose that α'' and α' are distinct optimizers. Let $(c''', z''') = k(c'', z'') + (1 - k)(c', z')$ where $0 < k < 1$; then (c''', z''') is affordable and $\alpha''' = k\alpha'' + (1 - k)\alpha'$. Further, since $V(\cdot)$ is strictly concave, $V(\alpha''') > kV(\alpha'') + (1 - k)V(\alpha') = V(\alpha'') = V(\alpha')$. But the last inequality contradicts the presumed optimality of α'' and α'.

The (non)uniqueness of z follows, since for each w there is a unique z satisfying $w = zA$ if and only if $\{a_j\}_j$ are linearly independent.

Remark: The strict concavity can be relaxed to strict quasi-concavity; see Mangasarian (1969). This generalization appears to be of little significance in the theory of financial markets.

Proof of Proposition 2.3. The existence of a B matrix derived from the span of A follows from basic linear algebra. If Q is a linear subspace of a Euclidean space, then there exists a complementary linear subspace $\bar{Q}$ such that the basis vectors of Q and $\bar{Q}$ combined span all of the Euclidean space, and where the inner product $q \cdot \bar{q} = 0$ for all $q \in Q$ and $\bar{q} \in \bar{Q}$. Hence, if the span of A generates Q, then choose any set of basis vectors that generates $\bar{Q}$ to construct the columns in B. (Most standard linear algebra texts supply the result.)

Proof of Corollary 2.4.1. The equivalence of α' and α'' is immediate from Proposition 2.3 and the uniqueness of the optimal patterns (Proposition 2.2). Further, from standard matrix algebra it is known that a matrix T such that $A' = TA''$ exists if the spans of A' and A'' are identical. Since $w' = z'A' = z'TA''$, it follows that $z'' = z'T$ implies $\alpha'' = \alpha'$.

Proof of Proposition 2.5. Consider first the cases of $0 < \beta \neq 1$:

$$V^* \equiv \max_{(c,z)} V(c, zA) = \max_{(c,z)} \left\{ U^1(c) + \mu \sum_s \pi_s \left(\theta + \sum_j z_j a_{js} \right)^{\gamma} \right\},$$

where $\gamma \equiv 1 - 1/\beta$, $\theta \equiv \varphi/\beta$; β has been factored out in Eq. (2.13a), so that $\mu \equiv [b/(1-b)]\beta^{\gamma}$ and where μ is a function of β only. Without loss of generality, assume that the Jth security is risk-free: $a_J = 1$. Further, let $J^- = \{1, \ldots, J-1\}$ and note that $z_J = (\bar{\bar{w}} - c - \sum_{j \in J^-} z_j P_j)/P_J = \bar{I} R_F - \sum_{j \in J^-} z_j R_F P_j$ due to the budget equation, and since $\bar{I} \equiv \bar{\bar{w}} - c$ and $R_F = 1/P_J$. Substituting the expressions $c = \bar{\bar{w}} - \bar{I}$ and the one for z_J into V^*, the optimization problem can be restated as an iterated maximization:

$$V^* = \max_{\bar{I}} \left\{ U^1(\bar{\bar{w}} - \bar{I}) + \max_{(z_1, \ldots, z_{J-1})} \mu \sum_s \pi_s \right.$$
$$\left. \times \left(\theta + R_F \bar{I} + \sum_{j \in J^-} (a_{js} - R_F P_J) z_j \right)^{\gamma} \right\},$$

where $\bar{I}$ and $(z_1, \ldots, z_{J-1})$ are unconstrained optimizers.

Define $\hat{a}_{js} \equiv a_{js} - R_F P_j$, and $m_2(\varphi, \bar{I}) \equiv \theta + R_F \bar{I} = \varphi/\beta + R_F \bar{I}$ where the arguments of the function m_2 are the contextually relevant variables. Also, let $x_j \equiv z_j / m_2(\varphi, \bar{I})$ and maximize over x_j rather than z_j:

$$V^* = \max_{\bar{I}} \left\{ U^1(\bar{\bar{w}} - \bar{I}) + m_2(\varphi, \bar{I})^{\gamma} \max_{(x_1, \ldots, x_{J-1})} \mu \sum_s \pi_s \right.$$
$$\left. \times \left(1 + \sum_{j \in J^-} x_j \hat{a}_{js} \right)^{\gamma} \right\}.$$

The optimal solution x_j^*, $j \in J^-$ does not depend on φ, $\bar{I}$ (or $\bar{\bar{w}}$, U^1); it depends only on π, A, P, and β. It follows that the optimal holdings of *risky* securities, z_j, $j \in J^-$, expressed as a function of $(\varphi,\bar{I})$, are simply proportional to the portfolio x_j^*:

$$z_j(\varphi,\bar{I}) = m_2(\varphi,\bar{I})x_j^* \text{ where } j = 1, \ldots, J-1.$$

The optimal investment in the *risk-free* security, $z_J(\varphi,\bar{I})$, derives directly from the budget equation:

$$\begin{aligned} z_J(\varphi,\bar{I}) &= \left[\bar{I} - \left(\sum_{j\in J^-} z_j(\varphi,\bar{I})P_j\right)\right]/P_J \\ &= \bar{I}R_F - m_2(\varphi,\bar{I}) \sum_{j\in J^-} x_j^* P_j R_F \equiv m_1(\varphi,\bar{I}). \end{aligned}$$

Let $z' = (0,0, \ldots, 0,1)$ and $z'' = (x_i^*, \ldots, x_{J-1}^*,0)$. These two portfolios are basis portfolios since

$$z(\varphi,\bar{I}) = m_1(\varphi,\bar{I})z' + m_2(\varphi,\bar{I})z''.$$

For the case $\beta < 0$, initially factor out $-\beta$ (rather than β), and the remaining steps will follow as above with only trite modifications in the expressions.

The cases $\beta = 0,1$ are analyzed similarly. Consider $\beta = 1$; express V^* as

$$\begin{aligned} V^* = \max_{\bar{I}} \Big\{ & U^1(\bar{\bar{w}} - \bar{I}) + \log m_2(\varphi,\bar{I}) + \max_{(x_1,\ldots,x_{J-1})} \sum_s \pi_s \\ & \times \log\left(1 + \sum_{j\in J^-} x_j \hat{a}_{js}\right)\Big\} \end{aligned}$$

and where $m_2(\varphi,\bar{I})\ (= \varphi + R_F\bar{I})$, x_j are as previously defined. The conclusion is now immediate by following the same steps as in the $\beta \neq 0,1$ derivation.

Finally, consider $\beta = 0$. One easily demonstrates that V^* equals

$$\begin{aligned} V^* = \max_{\bar{I}} \Big[& U_1(\bar{\bar{w}} - \bar{I}) + \exp\{-R_F\bar{I}/\varphi\} \max_{(x_1,\ldots,x_{J-1})} - \sum_s \pi_s \\ & \times \exp\Big\{-\sum_{j\in J^-} \hat{a}_{js} x_j\Big\}\Big] \end{aligned}$$

where $x_j \equiv z_j/\varphi$, $j \in J^-$. (The derivation uses $\exp\{q_1 + q_2\} = \exp\{q_1\}\exp\{q_2\}$, but is otherwise essentially identical to previous cases.) Again, the basis portfolios $(0,0, \ldots, 0,1)$ and $(x_1^*, \ldots, x_{J-1}^*,0)$ span all optimal policies $z(\varphi,\bar{I})$. Specifically, put $m_2(\varphi,\bar{I}) = \varphi$ and $m_1(\varphi,\bar{I}) = z_J = R_F\left(\bar{I} - \left(\sum_{j\in J^-} x_j^* P_j\right) m_2(\varphi,\bar{I})\right)$.

Remarks: The proof, which is due to Hakansson (1969), does not use optimality conditions. The approach here avoids unnecessary complications that may arise, especially when U^1 is arbitrary.

For the necessity of LRT for portfolio separation, see Vickson (1975).

The proof shows that one needs to add a boundary condition to the conditions of the proposition: $\varphi/\beta + R_F\bar{I} > 0$ for optimal $\bar{I}$. This is of no economic significance and is omitted in the formal statement. (See also Vickson [1975].)

In case $\beta = 0$, note that optimal $z_j, j \in J^-$, do not depend on $\bar{I}$ (and $\bar{\bar{w}}$).

The LRT portfolio separation achieves true theoretical significance only in the complete markets case. Contrary to what one might expect, no fundamental results flow from the additional incomplete markets generality. (This will become clear in the next chapter, section 3.2.) The reader can therefore concentrate on the closed form analysis in section 2.4 rather than the above proof.

Proof of Proposition 2.6. The proof uses results developed in the proof of Proposition 2.5. The definitions of $\hat{a}_{js}$, γ, and μ are retained, and $a_J = 1$, $R_F = 1/P_J$.

Consider the optimization problems

$$\max_{(x_1,\ldots,x_{J-1})} \mu \sum_s \pi_s \left(1 + \text{sign}(\beta) \sum_{j \in J^-} x_j \hat{a}_{js}\right)^{\gamma} \equiv f(A,P;\beta) \quad (\beta \neq 0,1)$$

$$\max_{(x_1,\ldots,x_{J-1})} \sum_s \pi_s \log\left(1 + \sum_{j \in J^-} x_j \hat{a}_{js}\right) \equiv f(A,P;\beta = 1)$$

$$\max_{(x_1,\ldots,x_{J-1})} - \sum_s \pi_s \exp\left(- \sum_{j \in J^-} x_j \hat{a}_{js}\right) \equiv f(A,P;\beta = 0)$$

Note that $f(A,P;\beta)$ does not depend on U^1, φ, or $\bar{\bar{w}}$.

It will be shown that if $f(A'',P'';\beta) > f(A',P';\beta)$, then $V(\alpha'') > V(\alpha')$, a conclusion that holds regardless of the particularization of U^1, φ, or $\bar{\bar{w}}$.

The proof of Proposition 2.5 shows that the solutions to $\max_{\alpha} V(\alpha) \equiv V^*$ for different βs equal:

$$V^* = \max_{\bar{I}} [U^1(\bar{\bar{w}} - \bar{I}) + m(\varphi,\bar{I};R_F,\beta) f(A,P;\beta)], \ \beta \neq 1$$

and

$$V^* = \max_{\bar{I}} [U^1(\bar{\bar{w}} - \bar{I}) + m(\varphi,\bar{I};R_F,\beta) + f(A,P;\beta)], \ \beta = 1.$$

The proof of Proposition 2.5 also implicitly defines $m(.,.;.,.)$, and $m(.,.;.,.) > 0$ if $\beta \neq 1$.

Let $\bar{I}^{*\prime}$ and $\bar{I}^{*\prime\prime}$ denote the optimal investment in the securities, and let $V^{*\prime}$ and $V^{*\prime\prime}$ be the optimal expected utilities in the two respective settings.

Assume that $f(A'',P'';\beta) > f(A',P';\beta)$. Then, for $\beta \neq 1$,

$$\begin{aligned} V^{*''} &= U^1(\bar{\bar{w}} - \bar{I}^{*''}) + m(\varphi,\bar{I}^{*''};R_F,\beta)f(A'',P'';\beta) \\ &\geq U^1(\bar{\bar{w}} - \bar{I}^{*'}) + m(\varphi,\bar{I}^{*'};R_F,\beta)f(A'',P'';\beta) \\ &> U^1(\bar{\bar{w}} - \bar{I}^{*'}) + m(\varphi,\bar{I}^{*'};R_F,\beta)f(A',P';\beta) = V^{*'}, \end{aligned}$$

a conclusion that does not depend on the particularization of U^1, φ, and $\bar{\bar{w}}$. In case $f' = f''$ it follows directly that $\bar{I}^{*''} = \bar{I}^{*'}$ and $V^{*'} = V^{*''}$. Finally, if $\beta = 1$, then $\bar{I}^{*''} = \bar{I}^{*'}$ and the required result is again obvious.

CHAPTER THREE

GENERAL EQUILIBRIUM ANALYSIS UNDER FIXED INFORMATION

3.1. The Allocation of Securities and Consumption Patterns in Multiperson Economies

This chapter examines the welfare and value implications for economies in which the standard problem determines individuals' demands for securities and the associated equilibrium. The support for such a financial markets equilibrium will not differ substantively from the concepts one encounters in classical analysis. Aside from the standard market clearing and optimization conditions, the model presumes competitive and perfect markets. These two assumptions have particular appeal when individuals trade financial claims. One can reasonably assert that a large number of individuals participate in financial markets, and that their price taking within the model approximates behavior in reality. Likewise, compared to most other markets, financial markets are relatively free from transactions costs.

The economies modeled deal solely with *pure exchange*: the consumption patterns summed over individuals' holdings cannot exceed the exogenously *fixed social totals*. Pure exchange does not imply an absence of interesting questions about welfare, nor do the questions have to be narrow in scope. A possibly tempting but misleading perspective views pure exchange as a "fixed pie" economy, in which nothing can be done to improve an individual's welfare without damaging someone else's. To conceptualize pure exchange in these terms does not properly reflect the essence of welfare analysis. A "pie" of fixed size can generally be apportioned in a number of different ways, and when the "pie" has numerous ingredients certain divisions might well be preferred by everyone. The choice setting model in the previous chapter expresses an individual's preferences over risky consumption patterns. Hence, in that model efficient apportionment of the "pie" corresponds to *efficient sharing of risks*. This economic function of financial markets must not be underrated, even though the same markets also perform the more obviously important role of allocating capital resources in decentralized production economies. The buying and selling (issuing) of financial instruments in pure exchange—whether stocks, bonds, convertible bonds, options such as puts and calls, forward and future contracts, insurance contracts, etc.—allow individuals to acquire portfolios that have particularly appropriate risk-characteristics given their uniqueness as individuals. Thus, even with fixed social totals, securities markets usefully allocate consumption mixes to individuals in accordance with their beliefs, attitudes toward risk, intertemporal consumption preferences, and any other more or less peculiar tastes or desires.

If one grants that trading serves a useful economic purpose, it follows naturally that some structures of the financial markets may be preferable to others. The analysis will indeed demonstrate that positive welfare effects may occur. Enriched markets lead to greater exchange opportunities, which, in turn, facilitate the "packaging" of risks to meet individuals' diverse preferences/beliefs. Thus, market enrichment *potentially* makes all individuals better off, and from such a perspective it implies improved economic efficiency. Nevertheless, the word "potentially" qualifies this claim significantly. First, certain additional markets may be irrelevant when individuals have sufficiently similar attributes (such as homogeneous beliefs). In that case, market enrichment may not affect the risk sharing, and the analysis therefore needs to discriminate between strict and no (weak) efficiency improvement. The theory pays considerable attention to the possibility of no improvement. Specifically, a central issue in financial markets theory is: What restrictions on endowments/preferences/beliefs/markets cause a financial equilibrium to achieve its maximum (i.e., Pareto) efficiency? Second, the potential for improved welfare may not materialize because *distributive effects* can make a subset of individuals worse off. The hypothetical welfare improvement made possible by enriched markets must be distinguished from the complicated issue of comparing each individual's welfare in two alternative economic settings. The nature of, and reasons for, such distributive effects will also be made precise. As the analysis makes apparent—and this point is indeed important—the issue of distributive welfare effects does not relate in a simple and direct fashion to the endowments of individuals or the value of their endowments.

The analysis of security prices relates closely to an economy's welfare attributes. This observation does not depend on the fact that prices affect wealth calculations, nor is there any element of causation. The point is more subtle. Only confined and stylized settings admit reasonably precise statements about pricing relationships. But the introduction of restrictive assumptions more likely than not has important welfare implications, and this suggests a general "association" between welfare characteristics and the structure of security prices. The claim makes economic sense and can be carried one step further: the welfare analysis of markets usefully precedes the theory of security valuation.

The structure of prices generally depends on *all* securities available in the economy. Hence, one cannot analyze prices effectively without first establishing the effect of the markets on the equilibrium outcome. These considerations about markets fall within the domain of welfare analysis; the topic details the adequacy and role of markets given alternative specifications of the other exogenous factors (preferences/beliefs/endowments). As indicated, much of this analysis of markets concerns settings in which subsets of securities do *not* have an impact on the equilibrium. A truly interesting corollary follows: the central results about security valuation revolve around settings in which (some) securities do not affect (or change) the equilibrium. Thus, paradoxically, many of the valuation formulae in finance, such as the "capital asset pricing model," concern the valuation of securities that have no economic relevance.

3.2. Development of the Basic Competitive Equilibrium Model

Starting from SP (standard problem—Definition 2.2), the following specifies the standard two-date pure exchange economy with fixed information and a securities states tableau A.

The economy consists of $i = 1, \ldots, I$ individuals. (The analysis also uses the notation $i \in I$.) Each individual i has unique personal attributes; thus, one represents the preference ordering of a consumption pattern α_i by

$$V_i(\alpha_i) = \sum_{s \in S} \pi_{is} U_{is}(c_i, w_{is}) = V_i(c_i, z_i A), \tag{3.1}$$

where $\pi_i > 0$. The individual's endowments are given by

$$(\bar{c}_i, \bar{z}_i) \quad \text{or} \quad (\bar{c}_i, \bar{w}_i) \equiv \bar{\alpha}_i. \tag{3.2}$$

As usual, $z_i A = w_i$ and $\bar{z}_i A = \bar{w}_i$. A subscript i representing the ith individual appends the utilities, beliefs, endowments, security holdings, and consumption patterns. This subscript convention applies throughout, and "i" denotes individuals only. Each individual solves his individual-specific SP to arrive at his particular optimal holdings. However, individuals naturally face the same market characteristics (A, P), and these therefore need no subscript annotation.

Feasible allocations require the security holdings summed over individuals not to exceed the exogenously given fixed social totals, where the latter quantities equal the sum of all individuals' endowments. The associated equilibrium restrictions define the *conservation constraints*. Alternatively, the individuals' trades must add up to zero. The constraints are stated algebraically as

$$\sum_{i\in I} (z_{ij} - \bar{z}_{ij}) = 0, \text{ all securities } j \in J, \sum_{i\in I} (c_i - \bar{c}_i) = 0, \tag{3.3}$$

or equivalently,

$$\sum_i z_{ij} = Z_j \equiv \sum_i \bar{z}_{ij}, \quad \text{all } j \in J, \tag{3.4a}$$

and

$$\sum_i c_i = C \equiv \sum_i \bar{c}_i, \tag{3.4b}$$

where $(C,Z) \equiv (C,Z_1, \ldots, Z_J)$ denotes the row vector of exogenous social totals.

The conservation constraints (Eq. (3.4a)) can be expressed also in terms of consumption patterns. Specifically, replace Eq. (3.4a) by

$$\sum_i w_{is} = \sum_i \bar{w}_{is} \equiv W_s > 0, \text{ all } s \in S, \tag{3.5}$$

where $W \equiv (W_1, \ldots, W_S)$ constitutes the row vector of exogenous aggregate consumption supplies across states. One readily verifies the essential equivalence between Eq. (3.4a) and Eq. (3.5). First, any $\{z_i\}_i$ satisfying Eq. (3.4a) implies Eq. (3.5). The observation follows immediately by postmultiplying Eq. (3.4a) by A and by noting that $W = ZA$ holds by definition. Second, although Eq. (3.5) does not imply Eq. (3.4a) generally, given some allocation $\{w_i\}_i$ satisfying Eq. (3.5) there *exists* a corresponding $\{z_i\}_i$ such that Eq. (3.4a) holds. Let z_i, $i = 1, \ldots, I - 1$, be *any* z_i such that $w_i = z_iA$, and put $z_I = Z - (z_1 + \cdots + z_{I-1})$. This allocation fulfills both Eq. (3.4a) and Eq. (3.5), and z_I satisfies $w_I = z_IA$. Thus, only the possibility of linearly dependent securities prevents Eq. (3.5) from implying Eq. (3.4a) directly. But this is of no particular significance.

The W vector may be interpreted loosely as the gross national product (GNP) across states at date-one, and C represents date-zero GNP. The economy exhibits *social* or *aggregate risk* when W_s varies with s. Individual securities may have uncertain payoffs even without social risk (e.g., let $Z = 1$ and $A = I$; then $W = 1$). On the other hand, social risk implies that at least one security has an uncertain payoff pattern.

Some securities, but not all, may have zero total supply, that is, $Z \geq 0$ ($Z = 0$ results in the empirically meaningless $W = 0$). Because of their general interest, the analysis considers zero-supply securities throughout. Two simple real-world examples of zero-supply securities are (i) the private borrowing/lending contract and (ii) option contracts in "puts" and "calls." For all zero-supply securities one individual's (possibly uncertain) monetary gain is another's loss. Zero-supply securities need not be part of any individual's endowments, whereas someone must own securities issued by firms (e.g., stocks and bonds) prior to the trading. Firms' securities therefore ensure positive social consumption totals given that the payoff patterns display limited liability.

One is perhaps more inclined to think of Eq. (3.4a) and Eq. (3.4b) rather than Eq. (3.5) as the conservation constraints. After all, the contractual execution of trades relies on securities, and trading relates only indirectly to the exchange of consumption patterns. Accordingly, a natural initial definition of a pure exchange equilibrium considers individuals' choices of securities.

DEFINITION 3.1. PURE EXCHANGE COMPETITIVE EQUILIBRIUM. *Consider a securities states tableau A and a set of individuals I with MISC preferences/beliefs* $\{V_i\}_i$ *and endowments* $\{(\bar{c}_i, \bar{z}_i)\}_i$. *Then a price vector P and allocation* $\{(c_i, z_i)\}_i$ *constitute a pure exchange equilibrium if, (i),* (c_i, z_i) *maximizes the ith individual's SP (Definition 2.2) and, (ii),* $\{(c_i, z_i)\}_i$ *satisfies the conservation constraints, that is,* $\sum_{i\in I} c_i = \sum_{i\in I} \bar{c}_i \equiv C$ *and* $\sum_{i\in I} z_{ij} = \sum_{i\in I} \bar{z}_{ij} \equiv Z_j$ *all* $j \in J$.

The above statement of an equilibrium emphasizes that the allocation $\{(c_i, z_i)\}_i$ and price vector P are endogenous and that the preferences/beliefs $\{V_i\}_i$, the endowment allocation $\{(\bar{c}_i, \bar{z}_i)\}_i$, and the market structure A are exogenous. The equilibrium outcome thus follows from the prespecified characteristics of the economy. All aspects describing the outcome are endogenous, including individuals' expected utilities.

Combining the above definition with the SP's optimality conditions developed in section 2.3, the necessary and sufficient equilibrium conditions are stated as: find a P and $\{(c_i, z_i)\}_i$ that solve

$$[\partial V_i/\partial z_{ij}]/[\partial V_i/\partial c_i] = P_j \quad i \in I, j \in J \tag{3.6a}$$

$$c_i + z_i \cdot P = \bar{c} + \bar{z}_i \cdot P \quad i \in I \tag{3.6b}$$

$$\sum_i (c_i, z_i) = (C, Z). \tag{3.6c}$$

An equilibrium can be developed and analyzed by focusing explicitly on consumption patterns rather than on securities, i.e., using Eq. (3.5) rather than Eq. (3.4a), and where the equilibrium prices are the implicit prices rather than those of securities. In other words, an individual's optimal choice derives from the perspective of the CCCP instead of the SP. The CCCP approach has advantages beyond its instructive emphasis on consumption patterns and their valuations. Subsequent analysis shows that many theoretical results become more apparent if one analyzes an equilibrium $\{\alpha_i\}_i$ and R instead of $\{(c_i, z_i)\}_i$ and P. The following defines a pure exchange equilibrium using the CCCP as the choice problem.

DEFINITION 3.2. PURE EXCHANGE COMPETITIVE EQUILIBRIUM IN TERMS OF THE CONSTRAINED CONTINGENT COMMODITY PROBLEM. *Consider a securities states tableau A and a set of individuals I with MISC preferences/beliefs* $\{V_i\}_i$ *and endowments* $\{(\bar{c}_i, \bar{w}_i)\}_i \equiv \{\bar{\alpha}_i\}_i \equiv \bar{\alpha}$. *Then an implicit price vector R and allocation* $\{(c_i, w_i)\}_i \equiv \{\alpha_i\}_i \equiv \alpha$ *constitute a pure exchange equilibrium if (i)* α_i *maximizes the ith individual's CCCP (Definition 2.5) with the B matrix being derived from the span of A, and (ii)* α *satisfies the conservation constraints, that is,* $\sum_{i\in I} c_i = \sum_{i\in I} \bar{c}_i \equiv C$ *and* $\sum_{i\in I} w_{is} = \sum_{i\in I} \bar{w}_{is} \equiv W_s$, *all* $s \in S$.

The two equilibrium definitions have a one-to-one relationship in the sense that the matrix A links an equilibrium under Definition 3.1 to one under Definition 3.2, and vice versa. (Of course, the two settings must have equivalent exogenous specifications, that is, in particular, $\bar{w}_i = \bar{z}_i A$.) This one-to-one relationship follows directly from Proposition 2.3 and the equivalence of the conservation constraints (Eq. (3.4a) and (3.5)). Thus, an equilibrium in real terms solves for consumption patterns and related implicit prices, and these variables can be used to recover the financial equilibrium security holdings and security prices. The observations associated with Proposition 2.3 apply no less when one connects the two characterizations of an equilibrium: $w_i = z_i A$ and $P = AR$. Further, given any equilibrium allocation $\{\alpha_i\}_i$, uniqueness in plans $\{(c_i, z_i)\}_i$ occurs if and only if $\{a_j\}_j$ are linearly independent, and a unique R occurs if and only if the market structure A is complete. Also, of course, the matrix B in Definition 3.2 vanishes in the complete markets case, and, notation aside, the equivalence between Definition 3.1 and Definition 3.2 becomes a trivial matter if one puts $A = I$.

Much of the usefulness of the Definition 3.2 equilibrium follows from a subtle yet technically simple observation. Given an equilibrium allocation α, the equilibrium implicit price vector R can be put equal to λ_i, *any* i, where λ_i is the ith individual's equilibrium marginal rates of substitution of consumption vector (i.e., λ_i is evaluated at the equilibrium α_i). This follows since $P = A\lambda_i$, $\lambda_i > 0$, all i, and R satisfies $P = AR$, $R > 0$, only.

The next issue deals with the efficiency of competitive equilibria. One aspect of the problem develops from the standard approach in classical economics. The analysis compares the actual (equilibrium) expected utilities to theoretically feasible benchmarks. The total supplies, (C, Z), still restrict the benchmark allocations, as does the available market matrix A; the allocation of securities to individuals is then conceived to be implemented by some omnipotent but fictitious "planner." An *efficient allocation of securities* maximizes some arbitrarily selected individual's expected utility, the first individual, say, subject to the restrictions: (i) all other individuals reach some prespecified (minimum) levels of expected utilities and (ii) the allocation of securities does not exceed available supplies.

DEFINITION 3.3. CONSTRAINED PARETO EFFICIENCY. *An allocation α is Constrained Pareto Efficient (CPE) with respect to a market structure A (CPE w.r.t. A) if it solves*

$$g(A,v) \equiv \max_{\alpha} V_1(\alpha_1)$$

subject to:

$$\alpha \in G(A) \equiv \left\{\alpha \middle| w_i = z_i A \quad \text{and} \quad \sum_{i \in I} z_i \leq Z, \sum_{i \in I} c_i \leq C\right\}$$

and

$$V_i(\alpha_i) \geq v_i, \qquad i = 2, \ldots, I,$$

where $v \equiv (v_2, \ldots, v_I)$ is a vector of $I - 1$ constants; $G(A)$ defines the set of all allocations consistent with the market structure A and the social totals (C,Z).

The word "constrained" in the definition may seem somewhat equivocal. The more precise language, "w.r.t. A," emphasizes that the constraints qualifying Pareto efficiency pertain to a specific market structure, A. This particularization of markets supplies a critical ingredient that should be kept firmly in mind when one encounters the term CPE.

Allowing the constants $v_2, \ldots, v_I$, which appear in the definition of CPE, to vary over all values for well-defined $g(A,v)$ (that is, the maximization problem has a solution) produces the set of all allocations that satisfy CPE relative to A. Let this set be denoted by $G^*(A)$. The set constitutes a proper subset of $G(A)$, and the notation $G^*(A) \subset G(A)$ is appropriate. Note, however, that the CPE set, $G^*(A)$, in contrast to the set of "technologically" feasible allocations, $G(A)$, depends on $\{V_i\}_i$, although the notation suppresses this dependence. This is another convention to be mindful of.

It is readily seen that if $\alpha' \in G^*(A)$ then, and only then, does no other allocation $\alpha'' \in G(A)$ exist such that

$$V_i(\alpha_i'') \geq V_i(\alpha_i'), \qquad \text{all } i \in I,$$

and where the inequality is strict for at least one individual i. The obvious equivalence between this statement and Definition 3.3 suggests that they should be viewed as two interchangeable definitions of CPE. CPE w.r.t. some A simply means that nobody can be made strictly better off through a reallocation of securities without making at least one other individual strictly worse off; then and only then is the allocation efficient. As an immediate consequence, one obtains

$$g(A,v'') > g(A,v') \text{ if } v'' \leq v'.$$ [1]

The next two propositions demonstrate (i) that every competitive equilibrium allocation achieves CPE w.r.t. its particular market-structure and, the converse, (ii) that an appropriate distribution of endowments supports each CPE allocation as a competitive equilibrium. These two results follow as immediate extensions of the classical equilibrium theory. A well-known and celebrated property of classical equilibrium models is their Pareto efficiency. Similarly, competitive economies can replicate any prespecified Pareto efficient allocation given regular (MISC) preferences. From a classical perspective, (c_i, z_i) defines the "commodity vector," the utility function $V_i(c_i, z_i A)$ provides the preference-ordering for feasible (c_i, z_i), and the Pareto efficiency is relative to allocations of $\{(c_i, z_i)\}_i$.

PROPOSITION 3.1. *Let α be an allocation generated by a competitive equilibrium economy with market structure A; then α satisfies CPE relative to A.*

PROPOSITION 3.2. *Suppose α satisfies CPE relative to A. Then the endowment allocation $\bar{\alpha} = \alpha \in G(A)$ supports α as a competitive equilibrium in an economy with market structure A.*

The proof of the last proposition provides another way of conceptualizing CPE. CPE requires

$$[\partial V_i/\partial z_{ij}]/[\partial V_i/\partial c_i] = [\partial V_1/\partial z_{1j}]/[\partial V_1/\partial c_1] \tag{3.7}$$

for all individuals; the condition also suffices if all $\{V_i\}_i$ are MISC (given that $\sum_i \alpha_i = (C, W)$, of course). Hence, Eq. (3.7) shows the marginal rates of substitution of *securities* (not consumption!), and every CPE allocation equates these across individuals. Alternatively, the necessity and sufficiency of Eq. (3.7) follows since in equilibrium $[\partial V_i/\partial z_{ij}]/[\partial V_i/\partial c_i] = P_j$, and the

[1] In addition to the property $g(A,v') < g(A,v'')$ if $v' \geq v''$, the function $g(A,v)$ also satisfies strict concavity. That is, provided only that $v' \neq v''$ and $0 < k < 1$, one has $kg(A,v') + (1-k) g(A,v'') < g(A, kv' + (1-k)v'')$. To prove this, let α', α'' denote the (optimal) allocations associated with v' and v'', respectively. Let $\alpha_i''' \equiv k\alpha_i' + (1-k)\alpha_i''$ and let $v_i''' \equiv V_i(\alpha_i''')$, $i > 1$. The allocation $\{\alpha_i'''\}_i$ is feasible since A clearly spans α_i''' and $\sum_i \alpha_i''' = (C, W)$. Note next that

$$\begin{aligned} kg(A,v') + (1-k)g(A,v'') &\equiv kV_1(\alpha_1') + (1-k)V_1(\alpha_1'') \leq V(\alpha_1''') \\ &\leq g(A,v''') \leq g(A, kv' + (1-k)v''). \end{aligned}$$

The first inequality follows because V_1 in concave. The second inequality follows since $\{\alpha_i'''\}_i$ is feasible, and g, by definition, maximizes V_1. The third inequality obtains because $v''' \geq kv' + (1-k)v''$, due to concavity of V_i, and g increases as v decreases. Finally, either the first or the third inequality is strict since $\alpha_i' \neq \alpha_i''$ for at least one i.

sets of equilibria and CPE-allocations have a one-to-one correspondence. Note further that P_j derives from the Lagrangean multiplier of the constraint $\sum_i z_{ij} = Z_j$ which enters into the "planner's" optimization problem. In this sense, the security price reflects the scarcity of Z_j.

An additional problem in classical economics deals with the existence of an equilibrium for positive but otherwise arbitrary commodity endowments. The analytical issues are generally somewhat complex, but the discussion need not dwell on those. Since the existence of an equilibrium within the class of models considered requires only relatively weak assumptions, its presumption poses no real hazard. Relying on the conditions sufficient for a unique solution to SP, an equilibrium will exist (although the conditions on the preferences/endowments are not the weakest possible).

PROPOSITION 3.3. *Suppose that the preferences* $\{V_i\}_i$ *are all MISC and* $\alpha_i \geqq 0$. *Suppose further that the endowments satisfy* $\bar{\alpha}_i \geq 0$ *for all* $i \in I$, *where* $\sum_i \bar{\alpha}_i \equiv (C, W) > 0$. *Then a competitive equilibrium exists.*

Given any equilibrium allocation α (or $\{(c_i, z_i)\}_i$), the equilibrium price vector P becomes unique. There are generally no compelling reasons, however, suggesting a unique equilibrium allocation α. Even though the SP with MISC results in a unique α_i for each P, there may be multiple equilibria α, P. Fortunately, in most instances this nonuniqueness of equilibria does not mar the analysis. The analysis of an equilibrium simply relates to one out of the possibly many that could occur. Uniqueness in α, P does not, of course, rule out multiple solutions to $\{(c_i, z_i)\}_i$ and R. As this section noted earlier, an allocation $\{z_i\}_i$ is unique for a given $\{w_i\}_i$ if and only if A excludes linearly dependent securities. And R is unique if and only if (i) markets are complete and (ii) α is unique. These nonuniqueness aspects are without welfare significance, and it makes sense to say that an economy has a unique equilibrium if and only if α (and thus also P) is unique.

3.3. Alternative Market Structures and Economic Efficiency: Constrained Versus Full Pareto Efficiency

The previous chapter observes that a change in the market-structure A may expand an individual's exchange opportunities. This idea extends to a multiperson general equilibrium setting. To be more specific, consider two market structures, A' and A'', and where A' spans a (proper) subspace of A''; then $G(A')$ is a (proper) subset of $G(A'')$, provided that the aggregate consumption supplies remain constant (that is, $(C', W') = (C'', W'') \equiv (C, W)$). A comparative welfare analysis of the two settings would presumably suggest that under some circumstances individuals generally achieve greater welfare in the double-primed economy. Although a precise resolution of this issue demands care when two equilibria are compared, an instructive preliminary observation notes that from the omnipotent "planner's" perspective, at least, no individual should have to be worse off in the double-primed setting. The definition of the function g implies the following obvious relationships.

Proposition 3.4. *Let A' and A'' be two market structures.*

(*i*) *If A' and A'' span the same spaces, then $g(A'',v) = g(A',v)$.*
(*ii*) *If A' spans a strict subspace of the space spanned by A'', then $g(A'',v) \geq g(A',v)$.**

Despite the simplicity of the proposition, a careful delineation of its content is worthwhile.

In conformity with the microanalysis in the previous chapter, first note that the conditions on the market matrices refer only to their spans; other attributes of the markets are of no consequence. Part (i) of Proposition 3.4 conveys this simple message with particular strength.

Second, note that part (ii) of the proposition includes the possibility that $g(A',v) = g(A'',v)$ even when $G(A')$ is a proper subset of $G(A'')$. Although this relationship might conceivably be true for all v, it can also be the case that $g(A',v^1) = g(A'',v^1)$ but $g(A',v^2) < g(A'',v^2)$ for different v^1, v^2 vectors. In other words, the set of allocations in $G(A'')$ but not in $G(A')$ may or may not contain an allocation that dominates one in $G^*(A')$. The factors determining whether this efficiency improvement occurs relate back to all facets of the exogenous variables, that is, the preferences/beliefs $\{V_i\}_i$, the spaces generated by A', A'', the vector of social totals (C, W), and the specification of the vector v.

Third, as indicated, the analysis of the behavior of $g(A'',v) - g(A',v)$ does not by itself deal with the comparative analysis of individuals' expected utilities in two competitive general equilibrium economies with market structures A'' and A', respectively. The point is obvious yet instructive: the outcomes of competitive equilibrium economies depend on the distribution of individuals' endowments, while one uses the planner's optimization problem as a device to solve for the set of efficient outcomes. Given two *equilibrium* outcomes, the signs of $V_i'' - V_i'$ may vary across all i; in contrast, the planner's problem by definition restricts $v_i = V_i'' = V_i'$, $i \geq 2$, and the analysis determines (the sign of) $V_1'' - V_1'$ $(= g'' - g')$. Thus, the comparative equilibrium analysis deals with the two *distributions of expected utilities*, $\{V_i''\}_i$ vs. $\{V_i'\}_i$, generated by the alternative market structures, and these outcomes must be carefully distinguished from the two *distributions of endowed wealth*, $\{\bar{\bar{w}}_i''\}_i$ vs. $\{\bar{\bar{w}}_i'\}_i$, and the (exogenous) *distributions of endowments*, $\{\bar{\alpha}_i''\}_i$ vs. $\{\bar{\alpha}_i'\}_i$. (Section 3.5 provides an extensive analysis.)

Although the planner's optimization problem eschews the issues of (re-)distribution, useful information applicable in the comparison of ("actual") expected utilities in competitive equilibria can be extracted from the behavior of the function g. The two basic possibilities of $g'' > g'$ and $g'' = g'$

for all v bear on the behavior of $\{V_i'' - V_i'\}_i$, where V_i'', V_i' now denote the outcomes of two competitive equilibria. Propositions 3.1 and 3.2 establish the one-to-one correspondence between competitive equilibria and CPE-allocations, and they supply the needed link for such inference. First, suppose that $g'' > g'$ for all v; at least one individual must then be strictly better off in the double-primed competitive economy, no matter what the endowments $\bar{\alpha}''$ and $\bar{\alpha}'$ are. [Proof: If no individual is strictly better off in the double-primed economy, then $g(A'',v'') \leq g(A',v')$ where $v' = (V_2', \ldots, V_I')$, $v'' = (V_2'', \ldots, V_I'')$ and $v' \leqq v''$; but, since g cannot decrease when no element in v increases, $g(A'',v') \leq g(A'',v'')$, and this implies the contradiction $g(A'',v') \leq g(A',v')$.] In the second case, where $g'' = g'$ for all v, no individual is strictly better off unless at least one individual is strictly worse off. (The proof is virtually identical to the previous case.) Although the last assertion is independent of the endowments, note that with identical endowments ($\bar{\alpha}'' = \bar{\alpha}'$) and $g'' = g'$ the two economies support equivalent equilibria: $\alpha'' = \alpha'$.

The above conclusions about individuals' relative well-being in different competitive equilibria are the obvious ones inferred from properties of the function g. To establish sharper and more comprehensive conclusions—possibly by adding restrictions on the exogenous variables—involves more complex analyses. These are fully developed in section 3.5. Particularly noteworthy is that, at least so far, $g'' > g'$ has not ruled out the possibility that some individual(s) is strictly worse off in the double-primed competitive equilibrium. From his (their) point of view, negative welfare effects have not been prevented. Nevertheless, since with a suitable redistribution of endowments no individual *has* to be worse off, a reasonable terminology states that the economies with richer markets lead to *more efficient allocations* (or, given that $g'' = g'$ is a possibility although $G(A'') \supset G(A')$, no less efficient allocations). The use of the word "efficient" reflects a conscious judgment to disregard distributive effects potentially present in the comparison of competitive equilibria. With this perspective, *complete market structures produce the most efficient allocations*. That is, the economic constraints reduce to the omnipresent conservation constraint $\sum_i \alpha_i = (C, W)$. It is therefore clear that g(complete markets, v) $\geq g(A,v)$ for all A and v (and $\{V_i\}_i$). Allocations possessing this maximum efficiency property are of great theoretical interest, and the standard terminology refers to *Pareto Efficient* or, more precisely, to *Fully Pareto Efficient (FPE) allocations*. Its definition follows.

DEFINITION 3.4. FULL PARETO EFFICIENCY. *An allocation α is Fully Pareto Efficient (FPE) if it solves $g(I,v)$ for some v. That is, no α' $\in G(I)$ exists such that*

$$V_i(\alpha_i') \geq V_i(\alpha_i), \quad \textit{all } i \in I,$$

and where the strict inequality obtains for at least one i.

The use of an Arrow-Debreu securities market in the definition is one of convenience. Proposition 3.4, part (i), guarantees that the essence of the definition is market completeness.

In strict technical terms, FPE defines a special case of CPE. Nevertheless, FPE allocations are important because they cannot be improved upon by altering the market structure. This broad optimality property makes alternative characterizations of such allocations interesting and useful.

PROPOSITION 3.5. *An allocation α satisfies FPE if and only if (i) $\sum_i \alpha_i = (C, W)$ and (ii) $[\partial V_i/\partial w_{is}]/[\partial V_i/\partial c_i] \equiv \lambda_{is} = \lambda_{1s}$, $i = 2, \ldots, I$, that is, all individuals have identical marginal rates of substitution of consumption patterns.*

The statement of FPE in terms of the optimality conditions (ii) is one of the most frequently exploited results in financial markets theory; to overrate its significance is difficult. A careful analysis distinguishing between allocations that satisfy CPE, but not FPE, versus those that satisfy FPE is therefore in order. Such a comparison is of particular importance because *complete markets are sufficient but not universally necessary to achieve FPE.* One can concoct $\{V_i\}_i$, v, and incomplete As leading to FPE allocations. At this point one simple example suffices. Consider an equilibrium setting with completely identical individuals ($V_i = V_1$ and $\bar{\alpha}_i = \bar{\alpha}_1$ all $i \in I$). Obviously, exchange becomes superfluous, and the conditions of Proposition 3.5 hold. The conclusion applies regardless of the market structure, so FPE may indeed obtain in an incomplete markets setting. The example seems relatively contrived, but, as will be demonstrated, more alluring cases do exist.

The difference in optimality conditions between CPE and FPE can be described as follows. The condition necessary and sufficient for CPE relative to A, in addition to the obvious one, $\sum_i \alpha_i = (C, W)$, specifies that for each security j

$$[\partial V_i(c_i, z_i A)/\partial z_{ij}]/[\partial V_i(c_i, z_i A)/\partial c_i] \tag{3.8}$$

does not vary with the individual. The proof of Proposition 3.2 demonstrates this, or, alternatively, one can combine Proposition 3.1 and an individual's optimality condition (Eq. (3.6a)). On the other hand, according to Proposition 3.5, FPE specifies that for each state s

$$[\partial V_i(\alpha_i)/\partial w_{is}]/[\partial V_i(\alpha_i)/\partial c_i] \equiv \lambda_{is} \tag{3.9}$$

does not vary with the individual. Equation (3.8) is summarized by $A\lambda_1 = A\lambda_2 = \cdots = A\lambda_I$, and Eq. (3.9) by $\lambda_1 = \lambda_2 = \cdots = \lambda_I$. Since $I\lambda_i = \lambda_i$, FPE indeed defines the restricted special case in which α satisfies CPE relative to I.

The above shows clearly why complete markets lead to condition (ii) in Proposition 3.5. Given that A has full rank, the equilibrium condition $A\lambda_1 =$

$A\lambda_2 = \cdots$ holds only if $\lambda_1 = \lambda_2 = \cdots$. (Elementary linear algebra yields the conclusion.) The case of incomplete markets, however, is ambiguous. One can no longer conclude that $A\lambda_1 = A\lambda_2 = \cdots$ implies $\lambda_1 = \lambda_2 = \cdots$. (This is obvious if $J = 1$ and $S \geq 2$.) Nonetheless, "by chance" or by judicious choice of $\{V\}_i$, v in the planner's problem, the condition $\lambda_1 = \lambda_2 = \cdots$ may be satisfied even for an incomplete A. From a somewhat different perspective, given an FPE $\{(c_i, w_i)\}_i$ *and* some incomplete A that happens to span w_i for all i, one obtains $g(I,v) = g(A,v)$. This works for the identical individuals example: every A spans $w_i = W/I$. Intuitively, the additional constraints associated with incomplete markets may not bind the solution (and the equilibrium). Thus, an allocation that satisfies CPE relative to an incomplete A is also conceivably FPE. To identify conditions such that the equality in $g(I,v) \geq g(A,v)$ applies amounts to an analysis of FPE within settings of incomplete markets.

Summarizing in words, CPE requires all individuals to have identical marginal rates of substitution of *securities*. FPE demands equivalence in the marginal rates of substitution of *consumption patterns*. The latter is a stronger condition because only complete markets and some other specialized settings fulfill FPE, while CPE relative to the underlying markets is a universal equilibrium condition.

Another subtle and powerful observation emerges from the analysis. When the final allocation is FPE, *for whatever reasons*, an assumption that individuals trade in Arrow-Debreu securities loses no generality. The economic intuition behind the observation is that securities in addition to those spanned by A must be exchange and welfare irrelevant since the economy reaches FPE in any event. Only superficially are FPE economies less restrictive than complete markets economies, and this mimics the relationship between complete markets economies and Arrow-Debreu economies. The increased restrictiveness among the three kinds of economies—FPE, complete markets, Arrow-Debreu markets—must be viewed as more apparent than real. Just as an Arrow-Debreu equilibrium can replicate every complete markets equilibrium, *every* FPE equilibrium allocation—even within incomplete markets—can be derived from an otherwise equivalent Arrow-Debreu economy. Definition 3.2 of an equilibrium clarifies the statement. If the A-complementing matrix B is absent because of complete markets, *or* does not bind the optimal CCCP solutions for some equilibrium prices R, then, and only then, does the allocation satisfy FPE, and $\lambda_1 = \lambda_2 = \cdots = R$ provides a solution to the equilibrium implicit prices. In either case, B becomes irrelevant in the analysis. But Definition 3.2 without the matrix B reduces to an Arrow-Debreu economy, so the introduction of such securities does not distort the equilibrium outcome. (The recovery of "actual" security prices and security holdings poses no problem, as discussed in section 3.2.) Of course, to dismiss B from the analysis the matrix must be known to be irrelevant (nonbinding) in advance. That is, prior to the derivation of the equilibrium, one must have enough knowledge about $\{V_i\}_i$, $\bar{\alpha}$ and A (A incomplete) to conclude that the outcome will be FPE.

3.4. Full Pareto Efficiency Within Incomplete Markets

3.4.1. Some general considerations

The question thus arises again: Under what conditions does $g(A,v) = g(I,v)$ hold even though A is incomplete? In the one example supplied, individuals have identical preferences/beliefs/endowments. As suggested previously, the example has extreme properties because any other endowment distribution seemingly invalidates the logic behind the FPE conclusion. Nevertheless, considered in conjunction with Proposition 3.5 and related discussion the example indicates two useful points. First, only relatively restrictive incomplete markets settings lead to FPE. Second, the more interesting cases of FPE within incomplete markets put no restrictions on the endowments; that is, in the planner's problem, $g(A,v) = g(I,v)$ for all v.

The first point suggests that incomplete markets do not suffice for FPE except in special circumstances. To explicate this, the next proposition shows how one constructs a non-FPE equilibrium given *any* incomplete markets.

Proposition 3.6. *Let A be any incomplete markets. Then positive vectors $x_1, x_2, \ldots,$ exist, none of which are equal, such that*

$$Ax_1 = Ax_2 = \cdots$$

Furthermore, given any allocation α and time-additive preferences $\{\rho_i U_i^1 + U_{is}^2\}_{i,s}$, appropriate choice of positive ρ_i, π_i equates the marginal rate of substitution vector λ_i to any prespecified $x_i > 0$.

In other words, given any incomplete A, solutions such that $g(I,v) > g(A,v)$ may occur. This implication is immediate from Propositions 3.5 (the necessity part) and 3.6. A slightly more general but less striking result notes that $\{\rho_i, \pi_i\}_i$ exist such that $g(A'',v) > g(A',v)$ whenever A' spans a strict subspace of A'' (given some (C, W), $\{\rho_i U_i^1 + U_{is}^2\}_{i,s}$ and v).

With incomplete markets any two MRS vectors of consumption can differ unless the setting imposes prior restrictions on preferences/beliefs. More generally, the proposition's second part conveys the idea that the equilibrium MRS vectors $\lambda_1, \lambda_2, \cdots$ possess no particular attributes or relationships beyond what is inherent in $A\lambda_1 = A\lambda_2 = \cdots$ and $\lambda_i > 0$. Additional statements about the structure of $\lambda_1, \lambda_2, \cdots$ are impossible because MISC alone constrains the permissible preferences/beliefs. Thus it follows that diverse beliefs/time-preferences suffice for additional (nonredundant) markets to potentially improve on the risk-sharing efficiency. Loosely speaking, consumption patterns must match beliefs, and with beliefs being diverse and arbitrary FPE requires a rich variety of consumption mixes. For this reason, even when individuals have identical U_i^1 and U_{is}^2, incomplete markets do not generally lead to FPE. Nor does non-time-additive or state dependent utilities make FPE any more likely. In particular, note that $U_{is}^2 = k_{is}\hat{U}_i^2$, where $k_{is} > 0$, constitute perfectly valid state dependent utilities. Probabilities and state dependence now have no mathematical distinctions, thereby implying that restrictions on beliefs serve no purpose unless utilities satisfy state independence.

The general necessity of complete markets for FPE still makes it possible for even arbitrary $\{U_i^1, U_{i,s}^2\}_{i,s}$ to reach FPE within incomplete markets. The principles that prove Proposition 3.6 can be used as readily to demonstrate that FPE within incomplete markets may apply for *specific* v. More precisely, consider any A, time-additive utilities, and a prespecified allocation α; then the identification of some $\{\rho_i, \pi_i\}_i$ and implicitly a v such that $\lambda_1 = \lambda_2 = \cdots$, and thus $g(A,v) = g(I,v)$, poses no difficulties. However, having so fixed $\{\rho_i, \pi_i\}_i$, the preservation of FPE cannot be presumed or expected as v varies. To support FPE within incomplete markets for arbitrary endowments (or v's) clearly requires some kind of restrictions on the permissible heterogeneity in beliefs.

One might conjecture that identical preferences/beliefs suffice for FPE. Unfortunately, this specification does not yield any results for arbitrary endowments. The endowment condition $\bar{\alpha}_i = (C, W)/I$ was critical in the identical individuals example. FPE in incomplete markets therefore involves more complex considerations. Although restrictions on preferences/beliefs alone may suffice for FPE (for arbitrary endowments) in certain extreme cases, the role of the other exogenous factors should not be underrated. The span of the market structure and social totals may also require suitable restrictions. It is possible that $g(I,v) = g(A'',v)$ while $g(I,v) > g(A',v)$, any v, for two distinct incomplete market structures, A'' and A'. Similarly, although the notation defining g suppresses (C, W), the supplies vector could affect conclusions. All aspects influencing individuals' demand functions and market clearing have potential relevance.

3.4.2. The Cases When Preferences Are LRT

It should be fairly evident from the discussion, and the example of completely identical individuals, that FPE within incomplete markets occurs only if demand functions are "sufficiently similar"; that is, the individuals demand mixes of optimal consumption patterns that relate closely to each other. Such circumstances should reduce the need for exchange opportunities. This observation leads to the first general setting in which incomplete markets achieve FPE. If all individuals have LRT preferences with the same slope parameter (β) and identical beliefs, but possibly differ in their intercept parameters (φ_i's) and, of course, endowments, then only two portfolios suffice for FPE: one portfolio allows for risk-free borrowing/lending, and the other portfolio represents the market portfolio. To prove this FPE outcome requires some care, and the Proposition 3.7 that follows supplies a formal proof. Less of a surprise should be that each individual's equilibrium portfolios can be expressed as a linear combination of the risk-free portfolio and the market portfolio. Given the preferences/beliefs/markets specifications, Proposition 2.5 implies that a risk-free portfolio and a second basis portfolio span any one individual's portfolio. Without loss of generality, assume a zero supply risk-free borrowing/lending market. The sum of individuals' *net* private borrowing/lending then equals zero, and the sum of their other security holdings add up to the market portfolio. Accordingly, in equilibrium, the second basis portfolio ends up being proportional to the market portfolio.

PROPOSITION 3.7. *Let A be any market structure that spans the risk-free pattern. Suppose further that individuals have homogeneous beliefs and LRT utilities with identical slope-parameters, β, but generally different φ_i's, $U_i^1(c_i)$'s, and endowments. Then the equilibrium achieves FPE.*

COROLLARY 3.7.1. *If the preferences further satisfy $\varphi_i = 0$ for all i, then $g(A,v) = g(I,v)$ regardless of A.**

In words, under the conditions of the corollary the market portfolio alone ($J = 1$) suffices for FPE; under the proposition's somewhat weaker conditions on individuals' preferences, the opportunity set includes also a risk-free portfolio.

A few simple observations succinctly clarify why the equilibrium allocation does not depend on A (given that A spans 1) and why this allocation achieves FPE. Consider any two markets where $G(A') \subseteq G(A'')$, and let α'' denote the equilibrium allocation relative to A'' for some v. Now, if it so happens that in addition $\alpha'' \in G(A')$, then α'' serves also as an equilibrium allocation in the single-primed setting. This follows since $g(A'',v) \geq g(A',v)$, and the optimal solution in the double-primed setting, by assumption, remains feasible in the single-primed setting. Hence, $\alpha'' = \alpha'$ and $g(A'',v) = g(A',v)$ because the incremental exchange opportunities in the double-primed setting remain unexploited. The same applies to Proposition 3.7: let $A'' = I$ and the explicit analysis of section 2.4 combined with equilibrium conditions implies that $\{1, W\}$ spans w_i'' for all i. Hence, $\alpha' = \alpha''$ given that $G(A') \supseteq G\left(\begin{bmatrix} W \\ 1 \end{bmatrix}\right)$. The reasoning shows that the two-fund separation property *within Arrow-Debreu markets* leads to FPE within incomplete markets (given a risk-free portfolio). Conversely, the proposition cannot hold unless $\{1, W\}$ spans the w_i'' derived within Arrow-Debreu markets. All of this is somewhat ironic since the strengthening of separation to include incomplete markets, as stated in Proposition 2.5, does not facilitate the proof of Proposition 3.7. Yet, Proposition 3.7 is of interest precisely because it admits incomplete markets.

3.4.3. The Cases When Some States Have Identical Aggregate Wealth

The second instance of incomplete markets and an FPE equilibrium is comparatively subtle. The basic idea is that if two states have identical aggregate wealth, then, under suitable restrictions on preferences/beliefs and complete markets, any given individual should consume the same amount in these two states. However, complete markets then exceed the exchange requirements for FPE since no individual wants to hold a portfolio that has different payoffs in the two states. Nobody cares to distinguish between the equivalent aggregate wealth states. More precisely, suppose $W_s = W_t$; one might then consider whether the constraint $w_{it} = w_{is}$ binds the planner's problem within complete markets. If it does not, then as z varies zA need not generate all of the S-dimensional Euclidian space, and FPE can be achieved without complete markets. This raises the question: When is $w_{is} = w_{it}$ a nonbinding constraint regardless of v? An answer to the question identifies conditions on $\{\pi_i\}_i$ and $\{U_{is}\}_{i,s}$ such that $w_{is} = w_{it}$ for all FPE allocations.

Lemma 3.8. *Suppose that s and t are two states such that*

(*i*) $W_s = W_t$;

(*ii*) π_{is}/π_{it} *is the same for all* $i \in I$;

(*iii*) $U_{is}(\cdot,\cdot) = U_{it}(\cdot,\cdot)$ *for all* $i \in I$.

Then $w_{is} = w_{it}$, *all* $i \in I$, *is necessary for FPE.*

The lemma, which (in a somewhat less general form) appears to be attributable to Borch (1960), is of considerable interest in its own right. It provides conditions under which two primitive securities can be merged into one without impinging on the risk-sharing efficiency. For example, suppose that $W_S = W_{S-1}$ and that conditions (ii) and (iii) apply; then the $(S-1) \times S$ market structure

$$\begin{bmatrix} & & 0 & 0 \\ & & \cdot & \cdot \\ I_{S-2} & \cdot & \cdot & \\ & & 0 & 0 \\ 0 & \cdots\ 0 & 1 & 1 \end{bmatrix}$$

reaches the same FPE-equilibrium as a full set of Arrow-Debreu securities. Of course, if $W_S = W_{S-1} = W_{S-2}$, then the three primitive securities S, $S-1$, $S-2$, can be combined into one security, and so forth.[2]

[2] In the extreme $W_1 = \cdots = W_S$ and FPE is always achieved given Lemma 3.8's conditions on preferences/beliefs. The condition on beliefs reduces to homogeneous beliefs. Hence, in an economy with certain aggregate consumption, homogeneous beliefs, and state independent utilities, the efficient sharing of risks ceases to be an issue. Further, in this economy $\lambda_i = k\pi$ for some scalar k; that is, the marginal rates of substitution of consumption vectors are proportional to the probabilities. (In fact, $k = R_F^{-1}$ since $\sum_s \lambda_{is} = R_F^{-1}$.)

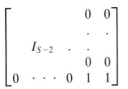

The lemma allows a conclusion about the sufficiency of certain incomplete markets to reach FPE when several states have identical aggregate wealth.

PROPOSITION 3.8. *Suppose that s and t are two states such that*

(i) $a_{js} = a_{jt}$ *for all* $j \in J$;
(ii) π_{is}/π_{it} *is the same for all* $i \in I$;
(iii) $U_{is}(\cdot,\cdot) = U_{it}(\cdot,\cdot)$ *for all* $i \in I$.

Then rank$(A) = S - 1$ *suffices for FPE.**

Having provided sufficient conditions, consider next the conditions' necessity. Regarding the restrictions on utilities and beliefs, it goes almost without saying that these cannot be usefully relaxed. More precisely, condition (i) implies $w_{it} = w_{is}$ all i (and $W_s = W_t$); it follows that if either of the conditions of locally homogeneous beliefs (ii) or local state independence (iii) holds, then the other is necessary for $\lambda_{is} = \lambda_{js}$ to imply $\lambda_{it} = \lambda_{jt} (i,j \in I)$. A more complex question deals with the necessity of the condition (i): $a_{js} = a_{jt}$ for all $j \in J$. The answer is that (i) cannot be weakened even though $W_s = W_t$ by itself may seem sufficient. A demonstration of this demands some circumspection. The following intermediate result helps: $a_{jt} = a_{js}$ is not only sufficient but also necessary to have $w_{it} = w_{is}$ for *all* z_i.[3] Further, according to Lemma 3.8, $w_{it} = w_{is}$ is necessary for FPE. It therefore follows that the only z_i consistent with FPE satisfies $w_{is}(z_i) = w_{it}(z_i)$. But a loss of degrees of freedom occurs without assumption (i) since the last constraint cannot be met automatically otherwise. This prevents full spanning of the remaining states (coordinates). Stated somewhat differently, given conditions (ii) and (iii), $w_{is}(z_i) = w_{it}(z_i)$ imposes a harmless restriction if and only if $a_{jt} = a_{js}$ for all $j \in J$.

An example illustrating the last point may be useful. Let $Z' = 1$ and consider

$$A' = \begin{bmatrix} 1 & 2 & 4 \\ 3 & 4 & 2 \end{bmatrix}.$$

FPE requires that $w_{i2}(z_i) = w_{i3}(z_i)$, and this constraint therefore holds if and only if $z_{i1}2 + z_{i2}4 = z_{i1}4 + z_{i2}2$ or $z_{i1} = z_{i2}$. But this further implies that $w_{i1} = z_{i1} + z_{i2}3 = z_{i2}4$, and hence $w_{i1}/w_{i2} = w_{i1}/w_{i3} = (z_{i1}4/z_{i1}6) = 4/6$ for *all* individuals. Clearly, this consumption mix generally prevents FPE since individuals' state-one utilities/beliefs have not been confined. However, the FPE impossibility vanishes if one replaces A' by A'' where

$$A'' = \begin{bmatrix} 1 & x & x \\ 3 & 6 - x & 6 - x \end{bmatrix},$$

[3] See Proposition 3.14, which Ross (1976a, theorem 4) proves.

and x is any number not equal to 1.5 ($x = 1.5$ implies rank$(A'') = 1$). Let $Z'' = 1$. The social totals remain unchanged, $1A'' = 1A'$, and both markets span two-dimensional spaces. But only the double-primed setting has identical second and third columns. Thus, in that case $w_{i2} = w_{i3}$ for all z_i (regardless of x). Appropriate choice of z_i permits any mix $w_{i1}/w_{i2}(= w_{i1}/w_{i3})$ without violating the FPE condition $w_{i2} = w_{i3}$.

Proposition 3.8 generalizes since the idea is simply that identical columns in A do no harm under suitable conditions on preferences/beliefs. The following useful corollary is immediate.

COROLLARY 3.8.1. *Suppose that*

(*i*) $A = [\bar{A}\bar{A}]$ *and where rank*$(\bar{A}) \equiv \bar{S} = S/2$;
(*ii*) $\pi_{is+\bar{S}}/\pi_{is}$ *is the same for all* $i \in I$, $s = 1, \ldots, \bar{S}$;
(*iii*) $U_{is+\bar{S}}(\cdot,\cdot) = U_{is}(\cdot,\cdot)$ *all* $i \in I$, $s = 1, \ldots, \bar{S}$.

*Then the economy achieves FPE.**

Note that condition (i) implies $a_{js+\bar{S}} = a_{js}$ for all $j \in J$. Hence, the conclusion follows from Propositions 3.4 and 3.8 since the matrix $[II]$ spans the same space as A (I has dimension $S/2$). Of course, this case easily generalizes to $[\bar{A}\bar{A}\bar{A} \cdots]$.

3.4.4. SUMMARY

The two instances of incomplete markets but FPE equilibria (Propositions 3.7 and 3.8) jointly suggest why identical preferences/beliefs, even when combined with state independence or time-additivity, do not strengthen the results. In an economy without social risk (i.e., W is proportional to the unit vector), all individuals hold the market portfolio, given identical beliefs and state independent utilities. This is another direct implication of Lemma 3.8. Although these conditions imply that FPE holds for every market structure, this result does not depend on $V_1 = V_2 = \ldots$ either. On the other hand, given *risky* social aggregates *and* individuals that do not have identical power/logarithmic utilities, FPE allocations are not proportional to the market portfolio for arbitrary endowments. To see this, note that an individual's demand for Arrow-Debreu securities is not proportional to endowed wealth or to invested wealth unless U_i^2 is power/logarithmic (but regardless of the price structure). Hence, individuals demand different *mixes* of consumption depending on their endowed wealth. A market structure of $J = 1$, the market portfolio, then clearly rules out FPE. Similar reasoning applies to demonstrate that adding a borrowing/lending market does not suffice for FPE unless, of course, individuals have LRT utilities with the same slope coefficient. Identical preferences/beliefs "buys" no results because the restriction does not deal with what is critical: the optimal mix of Arrow-Debreu securities as a function of endowed wealth. The optimal mixes of Arrow-Debreu securities are therefore generally unrestricted even when endowments alone differentiate the individuals, and with constrained exchange opportunities FPE cannot be expected.

To recapitulate, FPE obtains under the following circumstances:

(a) Markets are complete; other restrictions on market structure, social totals, endowments, and utilities/beliefs become unnecessary.
(b) Markets are incomplete relative to some states that have identical columns in the market matrix. The only restrictions on utilities/beliefs relate to states with identical columns: utilities are "locally" state independent, and the relative probabilities of these states occurring do not vary with the individual.
(c) A risk-free portfolio exists, beliefs are homogeneous, and utilities are of the linear risk tolerance class with the slope coefficient being identical for all individuals.
(d) Beliefs are homogeneous, and individuals have identical constant relative risk-aversion utilities (i.e., logarithmic or power function utilities).
(e) Cases that rely on specific endowments. The premier example assumes completely identical individuals, including in endowments.

It should be observed that in passing from (a) to (e) the restrictions on the market structure decrease, while those describing the individuals increase. Not surprisingly, a trade-off exists between the two types of restrictions. (The previous chapter's microanalysis of an individual's welfare notes the same phenomenon.)

3.5. Expected Utility Comparisons of Competitive Equilibria with Different Market Structures

The previous section intimated that the expansion of allocative outcomes such that $G(A') \subset G(A'')$ and, somewhat stronger, $g(A'',v) > g(A',v)$, does not by itself permit the conclusion $V_i(\alpha_i'') > V_i(\alpha_i')$ for *all* individuals i in two competitive equilibria using, respectively, the market structures A'' and A'.[4] The inference is inappropriate since the analysis must compare the two equilibrium outcomes $\{V_i'\}_i$ versus $\{V_i''\}_i$ on an individual-by-individual basis. This comparative inquiry makes sense only if one explicitly introduces endowments and their (re-)distribution. In general, the comparison of expected utilities for two competitive equilibria relates to those induced by the respective exogenous specifications $\{V_i\}_i$, A', $\bar{\alpha}'$ and $\{V_i\}_i$, A'', $\bar{\alpha}''$, where $(C',Z'A') = (C'',Z''A'') \equiv (C, W)$ and $\bar{\alpha}' \in G(A')$, $\bar{\alpha}'' \in G(A'')$.

It goes almost without saying that if $\bar{c}_i''/\bar{c}_i'$, $\bar{w}_{is}''/\bar{w}_{is}'$, $s = 1 \ldots, S$ are all small quantities, then individual i is likely to be worse off in the double-primed economy regardless of the other exogenous variables. There is cer-

[4] This section draws on Hakansson (1982).

tainly no reason to expect that $V_i(\alpha_i'') \geq V_i(\alpha_i')$ just because $G(A'') \supseteq G(A')$; the ith individual is simply too endowment-poor in the double-primed economy relative to the single-primed economy, and, from this individual's perspective, the fact that the double-primed economy might perform more efficiently $[g(A'',v) > g(A',v)]$ provides no consolation. Of course, it could be argued that endowment redistributions such that $\bar{\alpha}_i'' \leq \bar{\alpha}_i'$ for some i are "unfair" and "unrealistic," and that comparisons of equilibria permitting such exceptional endowment redistributions necessarily yield results devoid of sharp or interesting insights. To the extent that this objection makes sense, the other extreme seems to be the natural starting point. That is, both economies stipulate equivalent endowments, and the analysis compares two economies identical in all exogenous variables except for the market structure.

DEFINITION 3.5. ENDOWMENT NEUTRALITY. *Two economies, single-primed and double-primed, exhibit endowment neutrality if individuals' endowed consumption patterns remain unchanged:*

$$\bar{\alpha}_i' \equiv (\bar{c}_i', \bar{z}_i'A') = (\bar{c}_i'', \bar{z}_i''A'') \equiv \bar{\alpha}_i'', \qquad \text{all } i \in I.$$

Endowment neutrality focuses on real claims rather than financial claims. The condition $z_i'' = z_i'$ lacks economic content unless $A'' = A'$. But the latter condition makes the comparison of alternative market structures impossible.

The concept of endowment neutrality confines the analysis. Not all $\bar{\alpha}' \in G(A')$ satisfy endowment neutrality since $\bar{\alpha}'$ must be an element in $G(A'')$ as well as in $G(A')$; that is, $\bar{\alpha}' = \bar{\alpha}'' \in [G(A') \cap G(A'')]$. This restricts the permissible endowments unless $G(A') = G(A'')$. However, the set $G(A') \cap G(A'')$ includes all endowments such that each individual owns a fixed fraction of the market portfolio. Specifically, let $(\bar{c}_i', \bar{z}_i') = (k_{1i}C, k_{2i}Z')$ and $(\bar{c}_i'', \bar{z}_i'') = (k_{1i}C, k_{2i}Z'')$ where $\sum_i k_{1i} = \sum_i k_{2i} = 1$, then $\bar{\alpha}_i' = \bar{\alpha}_i'' = (k_{1i}C, k_{2i}W) \equiv \bar{\alpha}_i$ and $\sum_i \bar{\alpha}_i = (C, W)$. Although this comparative equilibrium analysis therefore always allows for endowment neutrality, the procedure does rule out certain endowments. These get rather extreme if A' and A'' generate distinct spaces, and in the limit the only neutral endowments reduce to fractions of the market portfolios. A comprehensive analysis therefore considers both endowment neutrality and unrestricted endowment-redistributions. In what follows, this dual approach—with and without endowment neutrality—will be used when comparing individuals' expected utilities in different settings.

The concept of endowment neutrality cannot be modified by letting individuals' *endowed wealth* equate across settings. The condition $\bar{\bar{w}}_i'' = \bar{\bar{w}}_i'$, all i, is generally impossible to satisfy because $\sum_i \bar{\bar{w}}_i = C +$

$W \cdot R$, and $C + W \cdot R'$ typically does not equal $C + W \cdot R''$ unless the two economies possess at least one common implicit price system. No change in endowed wealth therefore does not imply, and is not implied by, endowment neutrality. Even so, the ways that the endowed wealth distributions bear on individuals' welfare raises an interesting issue, and section 3.7.3 discusses this matter.

The comparison of individuals' expected utilities in two competitive equilibria, double-primed relative to single-primed, leads to four conceivable outcomes: *Pareto-preference,* in which case nobody is worse off and at least one individual is better off; *Pareto-indifference,* in which case everyone is equally well off in either economy; *Pareto-noncomparability,* in which case at least one individual is better off while some other individual(s) is worse off; *Pareto-inferiority,* in which case nobody is better off and at least one individual becomes worse off. These four outcomes partition the set of all comparative outcomes into mutually exclusive and exhaustive categories. The four outcomes will be referred to as *welfare relations*. Their formal definitions follow.

DEFINITION 3.6. WELFARE RELATIONS.

WR1. [α'' *is Pareto-preferred to* α'].

$$V_i(\alpha_i'') \geq V_i(\alpha_i') \text{ all } i \in I, V_i(\alpha_i'') > V_i(\alpha_i') \text{ at least one } i \in I.$$

WR2. [α'' *is Pareto-equivalent to* α']:

$$V_i(\alpha_i'') = V_i(\alpha_i') \text{ all } i \in I.$$

WR3. [α'' *is Pareto-noncomparable to* α']:

$$V_i(\alpha_i'') > V_i(\alpha_i'), V_{i'}(\alpha_{i'}'') < V_{i'}(\alpha_{i'}') \text{ some } i, i' \in I.$$

WR4. [α'' *is Pareto-inferior to* α']:

$$V_i(\alpha_i'') \leq V_i(\alpha_i') \text{ all } i \in I, V_i(\alpha_i'') < V(\alpha_i') \text{ at least one } i \in I.$$

The comparison of market structures involves three possibilities: (i) A' spans the same space as A''; (ii) A' spans a strict subspace of A''; (iii) A' and A'' span spaces neither of which constitutes a subspace of the other, nor are they identical. The three comparisons will be referred to as, respectively, Type I, Type II, and Type III comparisons. More succinctly, one can state these exhaustive and mutually exclusive comparisons as:

Type I: $G(A') = G(A'')$
Type II: $G(A') \subset G(A'')$
Type III: $G(A') \not\subseteq G(A'')$ and $G(A'') \not\subseteq G(A')$

(The analysis need not consider the opposite of Type II since this is merely a question of labeling. However, both WR1 and WR4 must be considered since the outcomes occur as functions of already labeled exogenous specifications.)

The first proposition pertains to Type I comparisons. The question of interest identifies all conceivable welfare relations, with and without endowment neutrality.

PROPOSITION 3.9. *$G(A'') = G(A')$ rules out WR1 and WR4. Further, there exist endowments $\bar{\alpha}''$ and $\bar{\alpha}'$ such that WR3 applies; endowment neutrality implies WR2 if multiple equilibria are disregarded.*

The first part of the result follows immediately from Proposition 3.4(i) since the two allocations α' and α'' satisfy CPE relative to effectively the same set of restrictions. Regarding the second part, the construction of redistributive WR3 outcomes poses no problems either. One shows without difficulty that the planner's problem has a unique solution, thereby ensuring that $\alpha' \neq \alpha''$ is necessary and sufficient for a WR3 outcome. Hence, using Proposition 3.2, there are endowments $\bar{\alpha}'$ and $\bar{\alpha}''$ supporting the distinct allocations α' and α'', respectively. Finally, the definition of a CCCP-equilibrium (Definition 3.2) implies directly that $\alpha' = \alpha''$ if endowment neutrality holds and A', A'' span the same spaces. The statement requires a slight modification if multiple equilibria exist: that case results in a one-to-one correspondence between the two sets of equilibria. (To suggest that WR3 "might occur" for multiple equilibria in spite of endowment neutrality is incorrect. The notion of multiple equilibria means exactly what it says.) Further, note that endowment neutrality suffices for, but is not implied by, a WR2 outcome. Any redistributions of endowments to $\bar{\alpha}'''$ such that $\bar{c}_i' + \bar{w}_i' \cdot R' = c_i''' + \bar{w}_i''' \cdot R'$ sustains the same equilibrium, that is, $R' = R'''$ and $\alpha' = \alpha'''$.

The next proposition deals with Type II comparisons. The results are more surprising than previously and correspondingly also more interesting.

PROPOSITION 3.10. *$G(A') \subset G(A'')$ rules out WR4. Moreover, even under endowment neutrality, beliefs/preferences/endowments configurations $\{V_i\}_i$, $\bar{\alpha}'$, $\bar{\alpha}''$ will always exist such that any one of the three remaining outcomes, WR1, WR2, and WR3, is possible.*

The noteworthy aspect is that endowment neutrality "buys" nothing and does not sharpen the results. This differs from Type I comparisons. For Type II comparisons either WR1 or WR2 or WR3 can take place, with or without endowment neutrality, and Proposition 3.4(ii) obviously excludes Pareto-inferiority (WR4) regardless of the endowments. While one should expect WR3 absent restrictions on the endowment redistribution, the existence of $\{V_i\}_i$, $\bar{\alpha}' = \bar{\alpha}''$ such that one individual becomes worse off in the more efficient double-primed economy is perhaps less apparent. For Type II comparisons, endowment neutrality does *not* prevent the redistribution of *expected utilities*. In a sense, endowment neutrality cannot assure "fairness," and somebody may be worse off in spite of the overall improved economic efficiency. As is partially conveyed in Figure 1, an heuristic argument leading to this conclusion follows three steps:

(i) Choose $\{V_i\}_i$ such that a set of CPE allocations w.r.t. A'' dominates a set of allocations that are CPE relative to A'.

(ii) Choose two CPE allocations $\alpha' \in G^*(A')$ and $\alpha'' \in G^*(A'')$ that satisfy $V_i(\alpha_i'') < V_i(\alpha_i')$ for some i; such allocations must exist since $G^*(A')$ and $G^*(A'')$ can be thought of as two surfaces that separate in $V_1, \ldots, V_I$ space. Further, given step (i), $V_i(\alpha_i') < V_i(\alpha_i'')$ some i.

(iii) The most elaborate step then shows that there exists endowments $\bar{\alpha} \in G(A')$ sustaining *both* equilibria (α' and α''). To accomplish this construction one identifies k_{1i} and k_{2i} within the set of market portfolio endowments, $\bar{\alpha}_i = (k_{1i}C, k_{2i}W)$, $(= \bar{\alpha}_i' = \bar{\alpha}_i'')$ where $\sum_i k_{ji} = 1$. Given any nonequal $W \cdot R'$ and $W \cdot R''$, the constants $\{k_{1i}, k_{2i}\}_i$ suffice to derive whatever endowed wealth distributions $\{\bar{\bar{w}}_i'\}_i$ and $\{\bar{\bar{w}}_i''\}_i$ one needs to sustain α' and α'', respectively.

Similarly to the WR3 demonstration, one can identify neutral endowments $\bar{\alpha}' = \bar{\alpha}''$ sustaining two allocations satisfying $V(\alpha_i'') > V(\alpha_i')$, all $i \in I$, that is, the double-primed outcome Pareto-dominates. An anomalous but frequently exploited case presumes that the *endowments* in the single-primed economy satisfy CPE relative to its market structure. Given endowment neutrality, it follows immediately that either WR1 or WR2 obtains. Nobody trades in the single-primed economy, $\bar{\alpha}' = \alpha'$, and, for every i, α_i' therefore remains a feasible pattern in the double-primed economy. In the

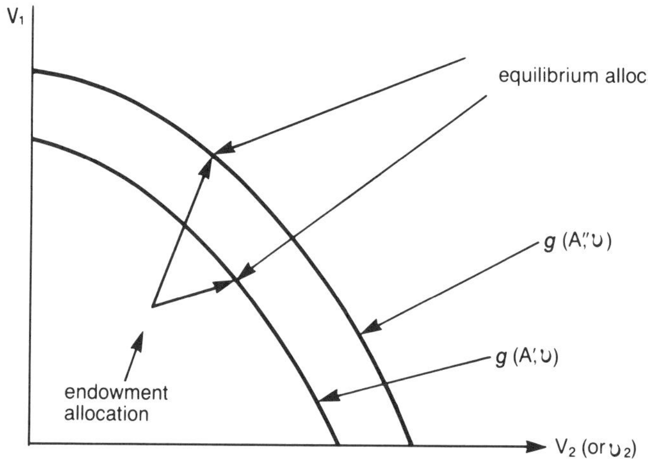

FIGURE 1

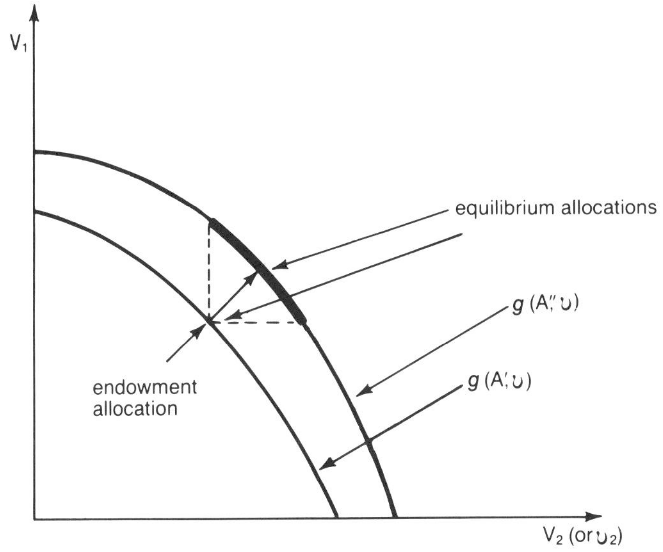

FIGURE 2

double-primed economy an individual trades consumption patterns if, and only if, it makes him strictly better off.[5] Trading occurs generally in the double-primed setting. The inequality

$$g(A', V_2(\alpha_2'), \ldots, V_I(\alpha_I')) < g(A'', V_2(\alpha_2'), \ldots, V_I(\alpha_I')),$$

provides the necessary and sufficient condition for trading. This follows because α'' is CPE relative to A''. Figure 2 depicts these ideas. Further, as the discussion in the previous section makes obvious, the construction of Type II but Pareto-indifferent examples, with or without endowment neutrality, presents no difficulties either.

The results appropriate for Type III comparisons are easy to conjecture. First, it follows immediately from the previous two propositions that if all four kinds of welfare relations can occur, then the comparison is Type III. Neither Type I nor Type II comparisons permit both WR1 and WR4. Second—and this point is more significant—for Type III comparisons appropriate choice of $\{V_i\}_i$ and $\bar{\alpha}'$, $\bar{\alpha}''$ allow any of the four welfare relations, even with endowment neutrality.

PROPOSITION 3.11. *If $G(A'') \not\supseteq G(A')$ and $G(A') \not\supseteq G(A'')$, then beliefs/preferences/endowments configurations $\{V_i\}_i$, $\bar{\alpha}'$, $\bar{\alpha}''$ exist such that any one of the four welfare relations applies. Moreover, endow-*

[5] The necessity follows from Proposition 2.2: SP has a unique optimal α.

ment neutrality does not restrict the possible outcomes or welfare relations.

Similar to Proposition 3.10 and Type II comparisons, endowment neutrality does not limit the conceivable welfare relations for Type III comparisons either. Only for Type I comparisons does endowment neutrality restrict the welfare outcomes. Consequently, one arrives at the following overall conclusion: *Redistributive effects on expected utilities (some individuals are strictly better off while others are strictly worse off) cannot generally be prevented through the imposition of endowment neutrality. The exception suggested for Type I comparisons is of little interest since the conditions* $G(A') = G(A'')$ *and* $\bar{\alpha}' = \bar{\alpha}''$ *imply trivially identical economies by Definition 3.2 of an equilibrium.*

In deriving welfare implications from market structure comparisons, endowment neutrality has proven to be generally unrelated to welfare. If one ignores trivially identical economies, the results convey a "disappointing" impression that anything is possible—even with endowment neutrality—except for what the relative efficiency measure $g(A'',v) - g(A',v)$ implies directly. In the case of Type I comparisons, $g'' - g'$ equals zero, thereby clearly ruling out WR1 and WR4. In the case of Type II comparisons, $g'' - g'$ is nonnegative, and this equally clearly makes WR4 impossible. Beyond this a more precise conclusion about individuals' relative well-being in the two economies generally requires full knowledge of all exogenous variables.

The three propositions of this section demonstrate a one-to-one correspondence between the type of market structure comparison and the set of conceivable welfare relations. Table 1 provides a summary. This conclusiveness has been relatively easy to demonstrate because the analysis considers all conceivable exogenous specifications of (MISC) preferences/beliefs. Nevertheless, for reasons discussed in the previous section, without particular social totals, results cannot be sharpened even if all individuals have

TABLE 1

Market Structure Comparison	Conceivable Welfare Outcomes
Type I:* $G(A') = G(A'')$	WR2 or WR3
Type II: $G(A') \subset G(A'')$	WR1, WR2 or WR3
Type III: $G(A') \not\subseteq G(A'')$ and $G(A'') \not\subseteq G(A')$	WR1, WR2, WR3 or WR4

LEGEND:

WR1 = α'' is Pareto-preferred to α'
WR2 = α'' is Pareto-equivalent to α'
WR3 = α'' is Pareto-noncomparable to α'
WR4 = α'' is Pareto-inferior to α'

* Given endowment neutrality, the two economies are equivalent.

identical preferences/beliefs (and satisfy time-additivity or state independence).

3.6. Schemes That Enrich the Securities-States Tableau and the Risk-Sharing Efficiency

Barring problems associated with the redistribution of expected utilities, the analysis has demonstrated that the greater the spanning space of existing securities, the greater (at least in a weak sense) the welfare.[6] The risk-sharing efficiency relates to the "size" of the space of feasible allocations ($G(A)$), and full Pareto efficiency emerges as the ultimate in risk-sharing efficiency. It would therefore appear to be both reasonable and interesting to inquire into how one might go about enriching a market structure. A successful scheme augments an existing market structure, thereby providing exchange opportunities not previously available. The direct approach to this problem simply introduces primitive securities with zero supply, and individuals then "bet" on the outcome of states. In principle, a full set of Arrow-Debreu securities can augment any market structure. Hence, let A denote any $J \times S$ market structure, and consider the augmented $(J + S) \times S$ market structure

$$A^* = \begin{bmatrix} A \\ I \end{bmatrix};$$

then A^* achieves FPE allocations. The economy has J redundant securities, and individuals can be viewed as not trading their endowments in securities with a positive supply ($Z_j > 0, j = 1, \ldots, J$): trades can be limited to Arrow-Debreu securities of which no individual has any endowment ($Z_j = 0, \bar{z}_{ij} = 0, j = J + 1, \ldots, J + S$). In the frictionless economy modeled, this is conceptually the most straightforward way of reaching FPE. Individuals simply bet among each other on the outcomes of states, thereby successfully dealing with all asymmetries in beliefs, preferences, and endowed consumption patterns.

However, some obvious reasons suggest why the exhaustive proliferation of Arrow-Debreu securities cannot operate in reality. The existence of direct transactions costs acts as one barrier. Some other related problems can be traced to the notion that an economy must use resources to identify and verify state occurrences. These kind of costs affect aggregate supplies negatively, a circumstance that clearly mitigates against the proliferation of zero-supply securities. The introduction of a full set of Arrow-Debreu securities becomes purely a matter of one's imagination, especially since the number of states is probably best viewed as infinite. Thus, one can hardly conceive as a practical matter that individuals develop a prior agreement as

---

[6] This section draws on Ross (1978) and Schrems (1973).

to what constitutes the economy's exhaustive description of states and subsequently agree on the state outcome. (This stretches even the imagination if the number of individuals is large.) Granted, these kinds of objections cannot be resolved within the general pure exchange model considered. The model has exogenous markets without suggesting what securities one should expect. And with endogenous markets the only reasonable upshot would be complete markets since the model presumes that markets and exchanges incur no costs.

In spite of the previous suggestion that markets should be either arbitrarily exogenous or complete, one can raise interesting questions about market enrichment in zero-cost environments. The following argument has at least heuristic merits. The difficulty in augmenting a primary matrix A relates to the complexities associated with state verification. In contrast, the verification of the existing securities' *payoffs* poses no problems. Hence, the analysis focuses on a confined class of (zero-supply) securities usually referred to as *derivative securities:* the payoff of a derivative security depends only on some underlying security's payoff. When the dependence relates to a single primary security's payoff, such as a particular firm's stock price, then the derivative security is *simple.* Similarly, one may also consider *complex* derivative securities, the payoff of which depends on the payoffs of a number of different underlying securities. One straightforward example of the latter lets the derivative security's payoff depend on the payoff of a prespecified portfolio.

Well-known real-world examples of derivative securities are *puts* and *calls* or ("put options" or "call options"). The following describes these securities in a two-date model. Let $a_p \equiv (a_{p1}, \ldots, a_{pS})$ denote the payoff pattern across states of some specific security, or, more generally, of some prespecified portfolio z such that $a_p \equiv zA$, where the subscript "p" denotes portfolio. Relative to this security (portfolio), define the payoff of a call in state s by

$$c_s(a_p;k) \equiv \max\{0, a_{ps} - k\}, \; s = 1, \ldots, S, \tag{3.10}$$

where k is a prespecified constant referred to as the *exercise* price (or *striking* price). One expresses the call's payoff pattern across states by

$$c(a_p;k) \equiv (c_1(a_p;k), \ldots, c_S(a_p;k)) \equiv (\max\{0, a_{p1} - k\}, \ldots, \max\{0, a_{pS} - k\}). \tag{3.11}$$

The notation displays the call's payoffs as a function of the exercise price because the same underlying security can be used for a number of different calls, each with a different exercise price. Not all exercise prices are particularly relevant or interesting, however. When limited liability applies, and $a_p \geq 0$, then $c(a_p;0) = a_p$; a zero exercise price implies that the call merely replicates the underlying security's payoff pattern. More generally, any exercise price satisfying $k \leq \min_{s \in S}\{a_{ps}\}$ leads to $c(a_p;k) = a_p - k1$. The resulting patterns have modest economic interest since a long position in the security (one unit) combined with a short position ($-k$ units) in a risk-free security replicates the payoff pattern $c(a_p;k)$. Under the circumstances the call becomes a redundant security. For large striking prices, the cases $k \geq \max_{s\in S}\{a_{ps}\}$ are of no real interest either since then $c(a_p;k) = 0$. In summary, given a risk-free security, the relationships

$$\min_{s\in S}\{a_{ps}\} < k < \max_{s\in S}\{a_{ps}\} \tag{3.12}$$

impose economically meaningful bounds on the call's exercise price.

One defines a put option relative to a payoff pattern a_p by

$$p_s(a_p;k) \equiv \max\{0, k - a_{ps}\}, \qquad s = 1, \ldots, S, \tag{3.13}$$

where k, again, denotes the exogenous exercise price. The vector $p(a_p;k)$ expresses the put's payoffs across states. For reasons similar to the call, given a risk-free security the put is redundant unless Eq. (3.12) restricts the exercise price.

A long position in a call differs significantly from one in a put. A call pays off only for sufficiently large a_{ps}, and then in proportion to a_{ps}. Conversely, a put pays off if the payoff a_{ps} is sufficiently small, and then in inverse proportion to a_{ps}. In other words, individuals with a "bullish" outlook on the underlying security buy calls, while "bearish" individuals buy the put. This does not imply that a long position in a call equates with a short position in a put: $c(a_p;k) - p(a_p;k) \neq 0$ generally. Nevertheless, Eq. (3.11) and (3.13) for the two derivative securities have much in common; this suggests that if the put and the call have the same exercise prices, then one of them is redundant in conjunction with the other *and* the underlying security. The conjecture is valid given, in addition, the availability of a risk-free portfolio. The literature often refers to this observation as put-call redundancy, although the identification of a redundant security is more general.

PROPOSITION 3.12. *Any one of the four securities* $\{c(a_p;k), p(a_p;k), a_p, 1\}$ *depends linearly on the remaining three:*

$$c(a_p;k) - p(a_p;k) - a_p + k1 = 0.$$

The proposition does not bear on the minimum number of securities needed (and which ones) to generate the space $\{p(a_p;k), c(a_p;k), a_p, 1\}$. The maximum is three, but as the following example illustrates, it may be that only two suffice even when $S > 3$ and k satisfies Eq. (3.12). Let $a_p = (0,2,2,2)$ and $k = 1$; then $c(a_p;k) = (0,1,1,1)$ and $p(a_p;k) = (1,0,0,0)$. The space $\{c(a_p;k), a_p\}$ is the same as $\{a_p\}$, which in turn is a strict subspace of $\{p(a_p;k), a_p\}$. The call becomes redundant and socially useless (Proposition 3.4(i)), while the put has potential social value, that is, it may add to the efficiency of the economy unless other securities already span (1,0,0,0). This occurs when the risk-free security is available; the put pattern (1,0,0,0) is spanned by $\{(1,1,1,1),(0,2,2,2)\}$. In other words, given $\{a_p,1\}$ neither the put nor the call provides any new exchange opportunities.

The example should not be construed as suggesting a general put (or call) redundancy, that is, that the underlying security and a risk-free security span the put (or the call). The example is anomalous not because of the exercise price, but because the security has only two distinct payoffs. The following provides a general and easily verified statement: if the pattern a_p has no less than three distinct payoffs, and k satisfies Eq. (3.12), then and only then are $\{p(a_p;k),a_p,1\}$ (and $\{c(a_p;k),a_p,1\}$) linearly independent. Hence, puts, or calls, potentially improve on the risk-sharing efficiency even when a risk-free security is available.

The example illustrates a second point. The existence of identical payoffs for at least two states, $a_{ps} = a_{pt}$, $t \neq s$, implies that neither puts nor calls of any exercise prices, or combinations of such securities, can discriminate between the states s and t. In other words, if $a_{ps} = a_{pt}$ and w is spanned by $\{p(a_p;k_1), \ldots, p(a_p;k_N), a_p, 1)\}$, then $w_s = w_t$ for any set of exercise prices $k_1, \ldots, k_N$. Obviously, *no* derivative security based on the pattern a_p could possibly discriminate between states with identical payoffs. The *absence* of identical payoffs now takes on particular interest: it is suggestive that a pattern a_p, $a_{ps} \neq a_{pt}$, all $s \neq t$, combined with a sufficient number $(S - 1)$ of puts (or calls), with varying striking prices, should constitute a complete market. The idea is simply that puts (calls) with appropriately spaced exercise prices should be linearly independent of each other.

PROPOSITION 3.13. *Suppose $a_{ps} \neq a_{pt}$ all $s,t \in S (s \neq t)$, and, without loss of generality, arrange states such that $0 \leq a_{p1} < a_{p2} \cdots < a_{pS}$. Then the market structure comprised of securities $\{a_p, p(a_p;a_{p2}), \ldots, p(a_p;a_{pS})\}$ is complete. Moreover, if the restriction $a_{p1} > 0$ is added, then the securities $\{a_p, c(a_p;a_{p1}), \ldots, c(a_p;a_{pS-1})\}$ provide a complete market.*

Two minor remarks are appropriate. First, note that calls cannot generally achieve complete markets unless the condition $a_p > 0$ holds. If $a_{p1} = 0$ then $c(a_p;a_{p1}) = a_p$; the space spanned by the augmented market structure is therefore only $S - 1$ dimensional. The situation does not get remedied through the use of additional calls with non-negative striking prices. One shows easily that for any non-negative constants $k_1, \ldots, k_N$, $\dim\{a_p, c(a_p;k_1), \ldots, c(a_p;k_N)\} \leq S - 1$ given that $a_{p1} = 0$. The problem arises for calls only. In this sense, puts are more powerful than calls. However, a second point modifies the latter statement. The assumption $a_{p1} > 0$ necessary for calls plays no role when the opportunity set includes a risk-free security. This follows from the put-call redundancy of Proposition 3.12 and since puts do not require $a_{p1} > 0$. Hence, $\dim\{a_p, 1, c(a_p;a_{p2}), \ldots, c(a_p;a_{pS-1})\} = S$ and the striking prices all satisfy Eq. (3.12). Similarly, it is also clear that $p(a_p;a_{pS})$, which violates Eq. (3.12), can be replaced by the unit vector so that $\dim\{a_p, 1, p(a_p;a_{p2}), \ldots, p(a_p;a_{pS-1})\} = S$. The notion of puts being "more powerful" than calls must not be overemphasized, since a risk-free security eliminates differences in the market spans of calls versus puts.

The assumption that states and payoffs map one-to-one limits the usefulness of Proposition 3.13. By shifting the focus to the attainment of FPE rather than complete markets, a weakening of the one-to-one condition is possible. Specifically, suppose the options derive from a market portfolio, $a_p \equiv W = ZA$; then the absence of a one-to-one mapping between states and payoffs does no harm to the welfare, provided, of course, that utilities and beliefs satisfy suitable restrictions. Lemma 3.8 supplies the appropriate conditions. This leads to a corollary of Proposition 3.13.

COROLLARY 3.13.1. *Suppose that*

(i) π_{is}/π_{it} *is the same for all* $i \in I$ *if* $W_s = W_t$;
(ii) $U_{is}(\cdot,\cdot) = U_{it}(\cdot,\cdot)$ *for all* $i \in I$ *if* $W_s = W_t$.

Let $\hat{W}_1, \ldots, \hat{W}_K$ *denote the distinct aggregate payoffs. Then the securities* $\{W, p(W;\hat{W}_2), \ldots, p(W;\hat{W}_K)\}$ *achieve FPE.**

The results so far analyze the impact on welfare using options derived from either *one* security or *one* portfolio. A seemingly more powerful strategy to improve on the risk-sharing efficiency would use options—with varying striking prices—on *all* primary securities rather than just one. A particular security may then pay off the same amount in two or more states without impediment, since some other security's payoffs may differ for those states. Of course, given two identical columns, no set of derivative securities would work. The question, then, is whether or not a full set of puts on all primary securities implies a complete market when columns and states have a one-to-one relationship. The answer is negative. Consider the following counterexample; let

$$A = \begin{bmatrix} a_1 \\ a_2 \end{bmatrix} = \begin{bmatrix} 1 & 2 & 1 & 2 \\ 1 & 1 & 2 & 2 \end{bmatrix}.$$

This matrix maps states and columns one-to-one. Augmenting A with a full set of puts, $p(a_1;2)$ and $p(a_2;2)$, yields

$$A^* = \begin{bmatrix} a_1 \\ a_2 \\ p(a_1;2) \\ p(a_2;2) \end{bmatrix} = \begin{bmatrix} 1 & 2 & 1 & 2 \\ 1 & 1 & 2 & 2 \\ 1 & 0 & 1 & 0 \\ 1 & 1 & 0 & 0 \end{bmatrix}$$

The rank of the matrix A^* is less than four because the sum of the first and the fourth columns equals the sum of the second and the third columns. Further, note that a_1 and $p(a_1;2)$ (or a_2 and $p(a_2;2)$) span the unit vector, implying that the addition of a risk-free security to A would not change the conclusion. The introduction of puts with any other striking prices would not change matters either. Hence, the example shows that a full range of simple puts or calls on primary securities generally do not achieve complete markets. As Ross (1976) demonstrates, this conclusion requires only mild assumptions about the primary securities' market structure.

A more sophisticated scheme augments the market structure by deriving the puts from the outcome of a judiciously chosen portfolio. Complex derivative securities based on portfolios other than the market portfolio, as in Corollary 3.13.1, can be considered. Proposition 3.13 suggests the properties such a portfolio ought to have. One wants to find some z such that $a_p(z) \equiv zA$ has no two identical payoffs. As stated previously, no such z can exist when two or more columns in A are identical, since $a_{ps}(z) = a_{pt}(z)$ for all z when columns s and t are identical. Less obviously, however, the absence of two or more identical columns suffices for the existence of a portfolio with distinct payoffs.

PROPOSITION 3.14. *There exists a portfolio z such that $zA \equiv a_p$ with $a_{ps} \neq a_{pt}$, $s \neq t$, $s, t \in S$, if and only if the market structure A has no two identical columns.*

The proposition does not address whether one can find some z such that $a_p(z) \geq 0$ (and $a_{ps}(z) \neq a_{pt}(z)$ when $s \neq t$). Although not particularly straightforward, such portfolios can be shown to exist. This permits a direct application of Proposition 3.13 such that a full set of puts or calls on the payoff pattern of the portfolio leads to a complete market. Nor would $z \geqq 0$ be a binding condition in Proposition 3.14. More generally, it can be shown that "almost any" z implies an $a_p(z)$ with distinct payoffs across states, provided that no two columns in A are identical. (The concept of "almost any" z can be made precise in a measure-theoretic sense; Kose and Arditti [1980] analyze this and related issues.)

The bulk of the discussion in this section focuses on the identification of conditions sufficient for an appropriate set of puts (calls) to achieve FPE. This emphasis should not overshadow that although the ideal of FPE might not be reached, puts and calls on primary securities and on portfolios that approximate the market portfolio enrich the market structure. As a practical matter, this is what makes them important.

Puts (calls) have general properties. No other functions defined on the primary securities generate a space larger than a full set of puts. The construction of Arrow-Debreu securities from three puts (calls) serves as a pertinent illustration. For simplicity, but without substantive loss of generality, assume that $a_{ps+1} - a_{ps} = 1$. One can then easily verify that

$$p(a_p;a_{ps-1}) - 2p(a_p;a_{ps}) + p(a_p;a_{ps+1}) = (c(a_p;a_{ps-1}) \\ - 2c(a_p;a_{ps}) + c(a_p;a_{ps+1})) \tag{3.14}$$

is equivalent to an Arrow-Debreu security paying off one dollar if and only if state s occurs. (If $s = 1$ define $a_{p0} \equiv a_{p1} - 1$; similarly, for $s = S$ define

$a_{pS+1} \equiv a_{pS} + 1$.) More generally, if $a_{ps+1} > a_{ps} > a_{ps-1}$ then one can always find a portfolio $z_1 > 0$, $z_2 < 0$, $z_3 > 0$, depending on $a_{ps+1}, a_{ps}, a_{ps-1}$ only, such that

$$z_1 p(a_p; a_{ps-1}) + z_2 p(a_p; a_{ps}) + z_3 p(a_p; a_{ps+1}) \tag{3.15}$$

is equivalent to an Arrow-Debreu security paying off in state s.[7]

In summary, the possibility that payoff patterns do not distinguish states restrains the power of derivative securities in a welfare context. This limitation obviously applies to any simple or complex derivative securities, and puts and calls serve as illustrations only. A full set of puts on a specific primary security yields a complete market if, and only if, states and the underlying security's payoffs map one-to-one. For complex derivative securities, a full set of puts on an appropriately constructed portfolio generates a complete market if, and only if, states and columns of payoffs map one-to-one. Neither the use of puts as a prototype of a derivative security, nor the use of portfolios as the sole kind of complex derivative securities, can affect previous conclusions. In that sense, this section's results are comprehensive.

3.7. The Theory of Security Valuation

3.7.1. Introduction: welfare and valuation

This section develops the theoretical concepts necessary to analyze the values of securities. Although this topic traditionally has a prominent place in the theory of financial markets—with the apparent rewards being valuation-acronyms such as the "MM," the "CAPM," the "OPM," and the "APT"—the idea that valuation analysis intrinsically relates to welfare is not always fully appreciated. Reasonably *precise* statements about the value of a security, however, require the elimination of much of an economy's potential complexity and ambiguity. But such simplicity is generally not possible unless the setting eliminates ambiguities about the welfare characteristics as well. An extension of this reasoning hypothesizes that welfare and valuation analyses are different sides of the same coin, that is, the identification of the welfare role of a security, or set of securities, is necessary and sufficient to understand how an economy values a security or set of securities.

The observation is not particularly surprising. Prices are determined by the sum of the payoffs across states weighted by their implicit prices. In equilibrium, a statement about the security price structure is a statement about the structure of the implicit prices, where the latter in turn relate back to the equilibrium marginal rates of substitution or consumption patterns. But the matrix A and the implicit prices R, or $\lambda_1, \ldots, \lambda_I$, are precisely

[7] An important paper by Breeden and Litzenberger (1978) exploits Corollary 3.3 and Eq. (3.15) to derive Arrow-Debreu prices from option prices.

those quantities that affect and reflect the welfare characteristics of the economy. When these characteristics are "understood," then, and generally only then, can one expect to be able to say something interesting about P that goes beyond the relationship $P = AR$, $R > 0$. The last relationship by itself has, of course, no content except for the exclusion of arbitrage opportunities. The more substantive question deals with how one may go about deducing sharper insights.

In terms of standard concepts of economics, security values are functions of individuals' preferences/beliefs and other exogenous variables. Since the individuals' demands for securities derive from their preferences/beliefs, the statement is somewhat trite. Nevertheless, this aspect of security valuation is worth keeping in mind. The theoretical implication is that the individuals' exogenously specified preferences/beliefs *always* affect *all* security values. Even so, the analysis must try to disentangle the aggregate demand functions' relationship to the underlying exogenous specifications. The real issue, therefore, becomes the identification of information about the economy such that a parsimonious and reasonably specific function determines the equilibrium values.

The presence of the exogenous variables in the analysis, and resulting valuation formulae, may be either "implicit" or "explicit." In the latter cases the security values derive as explicit functions of preferences/beliefs. The implicit cases, on the other hand, analyze how security values relate to each other regardless of preferences/beliefs.

3.7.2. The Theory of Relative (Arbitrage-Based) Valuation

The idea that the preferences/beliefs may make their presence felt only implicitly can be supported by an illustration of theoretical significance. Consider the issue of pricing a security with a payoff vector that depends linearly on other securities' payoffs. In the absence of arbitrage the redundancy of such a security leads to indeterminate aggregate demand, that is, its demand function is perfectly elastic. The perfect demand elasticity is equivalent to individuals having access to a perfect substitute portfolio. But the pricing of the perfect substitute portfolio is then the only prerequisite to price the redundant security; to express the redundant security's price as a direct function of individuals' preferences/beliefs and other exogenous variables becomes unnecessary. The remaining securities' prices, which determine the price of the linearly dependent security, already fully reflect the exogenous variables. In this sense the other securities' prices provide sufficient information about the economy, and the relationships between the price of the redundant security and the other security prices does not depend on preferences/beliefs. The precise and full version of this observation, including a converse, can be stated as follows.

PROPOSITION 3.15. *Suppose constants* $k_1, \ldots, k_{J-1}$ *exist such that*

(i) $a_J = k_1 a_1 + \cdots + k_{J-1} a_{J-1}$.

Then,

(ii) $P_J = k_1 P_1 + \cdots + k_{J-1} P_{J-1}$.

Conversely, (ii) for all $\{V_i\}_i$ *requires (i).*

The pricing dependence in Proposition 3.15 captures a simple arbitrage relationship. Portfolios having identical payoff patterns cannot differ in value. Thus, if there exists some $z = (z_1, \ldots, z_{J-1}, 0)$ such that $a_J = zA$, then, in the absence of arbitrage, $P_J = a_J \cdot R = zA \cdot R = z \cdot P$; it follows that $P_J = \sum_{j=1}^{J-1} z_j P_j$. The sufficiency part of the proposition is neither surprising nor complex; Proposition 2.1 supplies the key insight for a direct proof.

The necessity part of the proposition is equally important: the preferences/beliefs must be considered in circumstances that exclude arbitrage relationships. Knowing $P_1, \ldots, P_{J-1}$ and A (including a_J) perhaps allows for the calculation of bounds on P_J, but its *exact* determination is impossible without the implicit price system or, alternatively, a presumption of linear dependence. The implicit price system, in turn, has no "reasonable" restrictions beyond positivity; this follows directly from the versatility associated with MISC preferences (recall Proposition 3.6). Accordingly, few general conclusions are available when one compares the relative values of two portfolios, z' and z''.[8] Expanding on Proposition 3.15, only three possibilities exist.

(i) $z'A - z''A = 0$. This case essentially restates the sufficiency part of the proposition, and $z' \cdot P = z'' \cdot P$ for all $R > 0$.

(ii) $z'A - z''A \geq 0$. The portfolio z' dominates z'' stochastically, and $z' \cdot P > z'' \cdot P$ for all $R > 0$.

(iii) $z'A - z''A$ has at least one positive and at least one negative component. Without precise knowledge about the implicit prices, the sign of $z' \cdot P - z'' \cdot P$ is indeterminate. That is, depending on $R > 0$, $z'AR - z''AR$ can be either positive, negative, or zero.

From (ii) and (iii) one infers that a security has a positive price for all implicit prices if, and only if, the payoff pattern satisfies the limited liability condition. This illustrates that little can be said about security values absent the individuals' preferences/beliefs.

[8] The fact that all nonarbitrage prices are theoretically reasonable creates difficulties in empirical tests of the so-called efficient market hypothesis. (The word "efficient" as used here relates to prices properly reflecting information.) Research cannot claim the existence of "superior" nonarbitrage portfolio strategies without a more or less arbitrary maintained hypothesis about what determines portfolio risk.

The relationships stated in Proposition 3.15 can be viewed as irrelevant or important, depending on the perspective one adopts. In the context of welfare analysis the result seems unexciting, since linearly dependent securities have no meaningful function in a no-transactions-costs economy. The Definition 3.2 of an equilibrium emphasizes the irrelevance of linearly dependent securities; their presence is arguably a somewhat pathological characteristic of an economy. (Why would such securities ever exist within the model?) On the other hand, the linear dependence *does* imply a value of the security expressed as a simple linear function of the remaining securities' prices. This arbitrage pricing concept has proven to be useful in a variety of practical valuation settings. One set of useful applications pertains to the valuation of redundant derivative securities, e.g., call and put options. A substantially more subtle set of arbitrage pricing applications reconciles the structure of security prices in two different economies. This section will discuss both implications of Proposition 3.15.

As a first application of the sufficiency part of Proposition 3.15 consider the relationship between the price of a call, P_c, and the price of a put, P_p. Assume that the put and the call have the same exercise price, k, and that both derive from the same underlying security with a pattern a_j and a price P_j. Given also a risk-free security, Proposition 3.12 identifies the linear dependency between the securities' payoff patterns, $c(a_j;k)$, $p(a_j;k)$, a_j, and 1:

$$c(a_j;k) - p(a_j;k) - a_j + k1 = 0. \tag{3.16}$$

Thus, upon applying Proposition 3.15 to Eq. (3.16) it follows that

$$P_c - P_p - P_j + kR_F^{-1} = 0. \tag{3.17}$$

Expression (3.17) is often referred to as put-call parity.[9]

As a second application of Proposition 3.15, consider the pricing of a call option derived from a risky payoff pattern when there are only two states, $a_j \equiv (a_{j1}, a_{j2})$, and, as usual, there is a risk-free security. The risk-free security and risky security jointly span all of two-dimensional space; the call is accordingly redundant. Let $c \equiv (c_1, c_2)$ denote the payoff pattern of the call. Its redundancy implies that two real numbers q_1, q_2 exist such that

$$c = q_1 1 + q_2 a_j. \tag{3.18}$$

In view of Proposition 3.15, Eq. (3.18) thus excludes arbitrage if and only if

$$P_c = q_1 R_F^{-1} + q_2 P_j, \tag{3.19}$$

[9] The observation appears to be due to Kruzienga (1956).

where P_c, P_j denote the prices of the call and the risky security, respectively. By solving for (q_1, q_2) in Eq. (3.18) and substituting into Eq. (3.19), one shows that the value of the call equals

$$P_c = [R_F^{-1}(c_1 a_{j2} - a_{j1} c_2) + P_j(c_2 - c_1)]/(a_{j2} - a_{j1}). \tag{3.20}$$

The explicit introduction of an exercise price, k, makes P_c a simple and direct function of a_j, P_j, R_F, and k. (Merely insert the expressions for c_1 and c_2 as defined by Eq. (3.10).)

The above application of Proposition 3.15 seems exceptional, since the analysis assumes complete markets in the first place. The completeness assumption permits weakening, however. It suffices if the payoff pattern has only two distinct payoffs; the call remains a redundant security, and Eq. (3.20) follows. The generalization illustrates that the call's welfare irrelevance (or linear dependence) drives the valuation formulae (Eq. (3.20)). Completeness of $\{a_j, 1\}$ provides a special case only.

The valuation relationship, Eq. (3.20), derives as easily through the implicit price system. That is, using Proposition 2.1,

$$P_c = c_1 R_1 + c_2 R_2,$$

where R_1 and R_2 solve

$$\begin{bmatrix} R_F^{-1} \\ P_j \end{bmatrix} = \begin{bmatrix} 1 & 1 \\ a_{j1} & a_{j2} \end{bmatrix} \begin{bmatrix} R_1 \\ R_2 \end{bmatrix}.$$

Neither set of derivations requires an explication of the call's exercise price. Nor does the call's derivative nature appear to be particularly relevant. The analysis is valid for any additional security since in a two-state world $\{1, a_j\}$ spans every payoff pattern. Nevertheless, the general approach leading up to Eq. (3.20) has proven useful in the theory of pricing redundant calls because it extends to a T-period environment. In this model the "state-tree" evolves in a binomial fashion, that is, at any point in time the uncertainty over the next time interval is abstracted in two states: the price of the underlying security registers either an "uptick" or a "downtick." A seminal paper by Cox, Ross, and Rubinstein (1979) exploits this approach fully. They derive the celebrated Black-Scholes Option Pricing Model as a limiting argument by letting the up/down ticks be small, while the number of ticks that take place over a (calendar) period is large. In the limit the stock and option prices are observed at all points in time, and the price realization paths are perfectly dependent on each other but uncertain functions of time.

As a third application of Proposition 3.15 and arbitrage pricing, consider the valuation analysis of *forward contracts*. When two parties execute such a contract at date-zero, the buyer transfers no cash to the seller. Instead, the buyer of the security is obligated, unconditionally, to pay some agreed-upon price, at date-*one*; at that point in time the seller also delivers the security. The valuation issue is: What should be the date-one equilibrium forward price? Since the date-one payoff vector of the forward contract is $a_j - P_f 1$, where P_f denotes the forward price, no arbitrage implies that

$$0 = \sum_s (a_{js} - P_f)R_s.$$

The left-hand side equals zero since no cash changes hands at date-zero. But $\sum_s a_{js}R_s = P_j$ and $\sum_s P_f R_s = P_f R_F^{-1}$; thus, to prevent arbitrage, $P_f = P_j R_F$. The forward price simply equals the current price of the security discounted to the future date when the cash payment must be made. In terms of Proposition 3.15, the payoff pattern of the forward contract is spanned by a_j and 1:

$$(a_j - P_f 1) - a_j + P_f 1 = 0,$$

which means that

$$0 - P_j + P_f R_F^{-1} = 0.$$

Essential to the full appreciation of the proposition is the observation that the prices capture individuals' beliefs/preferences indirectly. The relationship $P_{j'} = \sum_{j \neq j'} k_j P_j$, implied by $a_{j'} = \sum_{j \neq j'} k_j a_j$, restricts *relative* prices, and $\{P_j\}_{j \in J, j \neq j'}$, fully incorporates individuals' preferences/beliefs, thereby making it possible to value $P_{j'}$ as a function of remaining security prices. Although the observation is direct and simple, the idea of relative valuation can be adapted without conspicuous focus on no-arbitrage. Consider the problem of comparing and relating the security price vectors across two *different* economies with identical preferences/beliefs. In both economies, of course, the preferences/beliefs determine the security prices. However, when establishing one set of prices the other set of prices may sufficiently reflect the preferences/beliefs; the two price vectors would then relate to each other.[10]

More precisely, let A' and A'' be two market structures, and consider the question of relating the respective equilibrium price vectors, P' and P''. In general, the vectors P' and P'' have no identifiable relationship unless the two economies are identical not only in terms of beliefs/preferences, endowments, and aggregate supplies, but also with respect to the equilibrium consumption patterns, α' and α''. Assuming specifications sufficient for equilibrium equivalence, $\alpha' = \alpha''$, it follows immediately that the equilibrium marginal rates of substitution of consumption patterns are identical, that is,

[10] To establish the relationship between price vectors in economies differing only in their payoff structures is an interesting economic issue. Early on, finance economists raised the question: How does a firm's value change in response to a change in its capital structure? Modigliani and Miller (1958) showed that under certain conditions the answer is "no change in value." The more general analysis that follows subsumes their case.

$\lambda'_{is} = \lambda''_{is} \equiv \lambda_{is}$ all $i \in I$ and $s \in S$. By putting $R = \lambda_i$, and where any i can be chosen, this further implies that

$$P' = A'R \quad \text{and} \quad P'' = A''R. \tag{3.21}$$

The two price vectors P'' and P' relate to each other because the two economies possess a common implicit price system. (Note that $\lambda''_i = \lambda'_i$ all i is only a special case of two economies having a common implicit price system; the point is of interest subsequently.)

A sharper relationship between P'' and P', which goes beyond Eq. (3.21), follows if one further assumes that A' spans a subspace of (possibly equivalent to) A''. Then, and only then, does a $J' \times J''$ matrix T exist such that

$$A' = TA''. \tag{3.22}$$

Using Eq. (3.21) and (3.22), one obtains $TP'' = TA''R = A'R = P'$ so that

$$P' = TP''. \tag{3.23}$$

The conclusion, Eq. (3.23), which thus holds regardless of $\{V_i\}_i$, derives using only (i) $\alpha' = \alpha''$ and (ii) $A' = TA''$. The first assumption is critical because the two economies then have equivalent marginal rates of substitution of consumption vectors, further implying a common implicit price system. The second assumption assures that P' cannot incorporate more information about the equilibrium than P'' (that is, the set of possible P' is a subspace of the set of possible P'', $\{P'' | P'' = A''R, \text{all } R > 0\}$). Hence, the two conditions allow the P'' vector to provide sufficient information about individuals' characteristics in the single-primed economy, and this yields Eq. (3.23).

The relationship $A' = TA''$ is exogenous, so the next question becomes: under what conditions are α' and α'' identical? Propositions 3.4(i) and 3.9 suggest one obvious and direct answer to this question: endowment neutrality combined with spanning equivalence in markets implies equivalent equilibria. Since spanning equivalence also satisfies Eq. (3.22), this leads to Eq. (3.23). The inference Eq. (3.23) from Eq. (3.22) has a central place in financial markets theory; the literature usually refers to the pricing implication as the result of the *Modigliani-Miller Theorem* (the "M-M" Theorem).

PROPOSITION 3.16. *If (i) A' spans the same space as A'' and (ii) endowment neutrality applies, then $P' = TP''$ where the $J' \times J''$ matrix T satisfies $A' = TA''$.**

The conceptual similarity between Propositions 3.15 and 3.16 should be stressed. Both results impose relative pricing restrictions, and preferences/beliefs perform no explicit role in either analysis.

As an illustration of Proposition 3.16 that underscores its close relationship to Proposition 3.15, let $J'' = J' + 1$ and assume that

$$A'' \equiv \begin{bmatrix} A' \\ a''_{J''} \end{bmatrix} \tag{3.24}$$

where some row vector of constants $k \equiv (k_1, \ldots, k_{J'})$ satisfies $a_J'' = kA'$. The security J'' is redundant, and A'' and A' span identical spaces. It further follows that $A'' = TA'$ where

$$T = \begin{bmatrix} I \\ k \end{bmatrix}. \tag{3.25}$$

The last proposition now implies that $P'' = TP'$, or, more concretely, that

$$P''_j = P'_j, \quad j = 1, \ldots, J' \tag{3.26a}$$

and

$$P''_{J''} = \sum_j k_j P'_j. \tag{3.26b}$$

Combining Eq. (3.26a) and (3.26b), one obtains

$$P''_{J''} = \sum_j k_j P''_j. \tag{3.27}$$

Equation (3.27) follows also as a direct application of Proposition 3.15 since $a''_{J''} = \sum_{j \in J'} k_j a''_j$. In words, the pricing of a "newly" introduced redundant security can be solved either via Proposition 3.16, which relates the pricing systems in two "different" economies, or more directly via Proposition 3.15, which prices the "new" security by excluding arbitrage. Both perspectives convey useful insights, and either one may be invoked in discussions of the M-M Theorem. Nevertheless, the literature does not always explicate the significance of endowment neutrality. In Proposition 3.15 endowment neutrality appears irrelevant, but only because the pricing restriction occurs *within* an economy, and not *across* economies. A "within" analysis implicitly fixes the endowments, thereby bypassing Eq. (3.26a) and (3.26b).[11]

It should be apparent that Proposition 3.16 generalizes. As mentioned, to link the two security price vectors the critical step establishes that the two equilibria possess a common implicit price system. Endowment neutrality

---

[11] Note the relevance of Corollary 2.4.1 in the context of Proposition 3.16: the optimal security holdings relate by $z''_i = z'_i T$ where $A' = TA''$. A special case of Corollary 2.4.1 is the so-called "home-made" leverage strategy described in the classic Modigliani and Miller article (1958). If a firm changes its capital structure by issuing bonds and buying back stock, then individuals can undo the increased risk in the equity by selling some stock and lend on private account. The equilibrium consumption patterns and the value of the firm remain unchanged. Choosing such a strategy presents no problems because, in equilibrium, the two portfolios cost the same (i.e., $z'_i \cdot P' = z'_i \cdot TP'' = z''_i \cdot P''$).

combined with spanning equivalence in markets merely makes up one specialized setting yielding $R' = R''$ via the implication $\alpha' = \alpha''$. While endowment neutrality is perhaps not so readily dropped, $\alpha' = \alpha''$ clearly does not require spanning equivalence in markets, since some exchange opportunities may be superfluous. The following generalization of Proposition 3.16 therefore provides a "modern" version of the previous M-M Theorem.

PROPOSITION 3.17. *If (i) $g(A',v) = g(A'',v)$, and (ii) endowment neutrality holds, then the two economies have identical equilibria and a common implicit price system: there exists some R such that $A'R = P'$ and $A''R = P''$. If in addition a matrix T exists such that $A'' = TA'(A' = TA'')$, then $P'' = TP'(P' = TP'')$.**

The proposition's wording stresses the centrality of common implicit prices; its second part, which introduces exogenously related market structures, is subordinated. (Recall that a matrix T satisfying $A' = TA''$ exists if and only if A' spans a subspace of [possibly equivalent to] A''.) Proposition 3.16 permits no similar distinction, since for that case the assumed spanning relationship between A' and A'' precedes the common implicit prices conclusion.

Proposition 3.17 also reflects that a common implicit price system follows directly from Definition 3.2 of an equilibrium. From this equilibrium perspective the "original" M-M Proposition (3.16) is surprisingly veracious: the single- and double-primed economies *define* equivalent economies when A' and A'' span identical spaces (and $\bar{\alpha}' = \bar{\alpha}''$). The "modern" M-M Proposition (3.17) derives from only a slightly more general observation. The spaces generated by the two market matrices are inconsequential as long as they perform the same job, that is, have indistinguishable efficiency implications. Combined with endowment neutrality, this observation then leads directly to equivalence of equilibria and the pricing of consumption patterns.

Proposition 3.17 obviously subsumes LRT preferences. As usual, individuals have identical β-parameters and beliefs, while endowments, φ_i-parameters, and U_i^1 utility functions generally differ. Further, let $A'' = I$, $T = A'$, and where A' spans the risk-free pattern. The conditions of Proposition 3.7 apply so that $g(I,v) = g(A',v)$; one accordingly states the related pricing implication as a corollary of Proposition 3.17.

COROLLARY 3.17.1. *Consider two economies $\{V_i\}_i, A', \bar{\alpha}'$ and $\{V_i\}_i, I, \bar{\alpha}''$ with endowment neutrality and where the market structure A' spans the risk-free pattern. Further, suppose that individuals have homogeneous beliefs and that the preferences are LRT with identical β-parameters. Then $P' = A'P'' = A'R''$.**

This chapter previously stressed that the use of Arrow-Debreu securities entails no loss of generality if one knows that the economy reaches FPE. Proposition 3.7, taken by itself, therefore implies directly Corollary 3.17.1.

The current digression merely interprets the recovery of "actual" security prices from Arrow-Debreu prices as an application of the M-M theorem.[12]

Propositions 3.16 and 3.17 revolve around the intermediate step of identifying conditions for equivalent equilibria. More demanding would be the derivation of an M-M relationship for distinct (or all) equilibria, since such an outcome cannot guarantee a common implicit price system. The required general irrelevance of the equilibrium allocations implies that the endowments can have no effect on implicit prices either. Accordingly, without endowment neutrality any results must use exceptionally strong preferences/beliefs restrictions.

The first setting leading to an M-M proposition without endowment neutrality develops from the observation that a common implicit price system requires only *one* individual to have an unchanged marginal rates of substitution of consumption vector. Further, as one trivially verifies, a λ_i vector is independent of α_i if and only if V_i is linear in α_i. Given the preferences/beliefs

$$V_i = c_i + \sum_s k_s w_{is}, \; k_s > 0,$$

it follows that $\lambda_{is} = k_s$ and the k vector serves as a valid equilibrium implicit price system regardless of other individuals' preferences/beliefs, all endowments and their distribution, the market structure, aggregate supplies, and the final allocation α. The linear preferences individual becomes the "marginal individual," who alone determines the equilibrium prices. However, while a linear V_i satisfies concavity, it is inconsistent with the *strict* concavity required by the MISC assumption. The result is therefore of only limited theoretical interest. (The existence of an equilibrium when V_1 is linear and V_i, $i > 1$, are MISC poses no problems. First, derive α_i, $i > 1$ using $k_1, \ldots, k_S$ as implicit prices. Second, let the allocation α_1 equal the remainder $(C, W) - \sum_{i>1} \alpha_i$. The procedure works because of the nonuniqueness of α_1 in the standard problem, and every α_1 that satisfies $\alpha_1 \cdot k = \bar{\alpha}_1 \cdot k$ is an optimal pattern: $k \equiv (1, k_1, \ldots, k_S)$. The budget equality holds automatically for $i = 1$ since $\alpha_i \cdot k = \bar{\alpha}_i \cdot k$ for all $i > 1$, and $\alpha_1 \cdot k = \left[(C, W) - \sum_{i>1} \alpha_i\right] \cdot k = \left[(C, W) - \sum_{i>1} \bar{\alpha}_i\right] \cdot k = \bar{\alpha}_1 \cdot k$. Of course, insofar as other individuals have linear preferences, an equilibrium exists without a boundary constraint $\alpha_i \geq 0$ only if the linear preferences are identical.)

[12] Corollary 3.17.1 suffices for a frequently invoked claim about nonsynergistic mergers: if two firms merge, then the value of the new firm equals the sum of the firms' premerger values. That is, if $a_j'' = a_1' + a_2'$ then $P_j'' = P_1' + P_2'$. Given $R'' = R'$ the result is immediate. Proposition 2.5 provides a useful interpretation. Given a borrowing/lending market ($a_J = 1$), Proposition 2.5 implies that z_{1i}'/z_{2i}' does not depend on i, and this eliminates the need for having two separate firms. Barring the extreme case of one firm being linearly dependent, Corollary 3.17.1 also essentially provides the necessary conditions.

The second case that permits an implicit price system independent of the endowments' distribution and the equilibrium allocation is much deeper. The underlying idea makes aggregate demands of consumption patterns independent of the endowment distribution by letting *aggregate wealth* determine aggregate demand. Such sufficiency of aggregate wealth follows if each individual's demands for consumption goods are linear in the value of his endowments, $\alpha_{is} = k_{1is} + k_{2s}\bar{\bar{w}}_i$, and where the constants k_{1is}, k_{2s}, as well as $\bar{\bar{w}}_i$, may depend on R; $s = 0,1, \ldots, S$. Summing over individuals' demands implies that for any fixed implicit prices aggregate demands $\left(\sum_i \alpha_{is}\right)$ depend on aggregate wealth $\left(\sum_i \bar{\bar{w}}_i\right)$ which, in turn, does not vary with the endowment distribution since $\sum_i \bar{\bar{w}}_i = C + W \cdot R$. The equilibrium R that equates aggregate demands to exogenous supplies for one endowment distribution also works for any other endowment distribution. The desired M-M result therefore obtains when all individuals have demand functions for α_i that are linear in endowed wealth with $\partial \alpha_{is}/\partial \bar{\bar{w}}_i = k_{2s}$ being identical across individuals. Section 2.4 of the previous chapter developed conditions for demand functions to have this linear form.

PROPOSITION 3.18. *Consider an economy in which individuals have LRT utilities with the same β-parameter, homogeneous beliefs, and $\rho U_i^2 = U_i^1$. Suppose that the market structure A spans the risk-free security. Then the implicit price system is independent of the endowments distribution* (*as well as A*).

The result differs from Corollary 3.17.1 since Proposition 3.18 posits stronger assumptions on the preferences, that is, it includes $\rho U_i^2 = U_i^1$. This condition is necessary for α_i to be linear in endowed wealth. Even so, to prove Proposition 3.18 one can usefully exploit Corollary 3.17.1. The easy and direct proof of Proposition 3.18 first considers the "closed form" Arrow-Debreu markets case. The next step invokes Corollary 3.17.1 which implies directly that Proposition 3.18 subsumes incomplete markets as well. As always, Proposition 2.5 can be bypassed.

The conditions in the proposition are not the weakest possible. A direct inspection of the demand function expressions in Eq. (2.28a) and (2.28b), Chapter 2, which derive within complete markets, reveals that Proposition 3.18 holds even for state- and time-dependent φ_i-parameters when $\beta \neq 0$. The demand for α_{is} as a function of endowed wealth can still be expressed as $\alpha_{is} = k_{1is} + k_{2s}\bar{\bar{w}}_i$. Also, given complete markets, $\beta = 0$ permits heterogeneous beliefs and individual dependent patience parameters. For incomplete markets, however, further analysis shows that these results generalize but partially: φ_i can be time-dependent when $\beta \neq 0$, and the patience parameter can be individual-specific when $\beta = 0$. (The formal statement omits these generalizations because they are relatively pedantic.)

3.7.3. Prices, wealth, and welfare

The next issue deals with converses to the M-M propositions. In comparing two economies that have common implicit prices, what are the welfare implications? Without an assumption about the two market structures, no conclusions are available. A common implicit price system may occur by coincidence (or when one individual has linear V_i), and combining this with Type III market comparison rules out welfare conclusions, even with endowment neutrality. Examples supporting the claim can be constructed. However, given endowment neutrality and a Type II comparison, a little-known converse to the M-M Proposition 3.17 exists.

Proposition 3.19. *Suppose that $A' = TA''$ and that $P' = TP''$ for some $J' \times J''$ matrix T. Suppose further that the two economies satisfy endowment neutrality. Then either WR1 or WR2 obtains, and WR1 (WR2) applies if, and only if, $\alpha' \neq \alpha''(\alpha' = \alpha'')$.*

The proposition subsumes Type I comparisons too, but this is of no interest by itself since WR2 then applies (the proposition merely turns into an incomplete restatement of Proposition 3.16). On the other hand, both the welfare possibilities—WR1 and WR2—may occur with Type II comparisons. The economies of Corollary 3.17.1 exemplify the WR2 cases. WR1 follows generally if one individual has linear V_i, although endowment specific examples consistent with MISC can also be developed.

Proposition 3.19 makes a potential welfare improvement possible by expanding each individual's consumption opportunities. The assumptions on how the payoffs and prices connect imply that the two settings have common implicit prices. The endowed wealth is therefore the same, as are costs of consumption patterns, while the double-primed setting has fewer market restrictions. In essence, Proposition 3.19 casts Proposition 2.4 in an equilibrium context and identifies condition for invariant implicit prices from more basic assumptions about security prices and their payoffs.

As an example of expanded opportunities, suppose $J' = 1$. Then no individual is worse off in the double-primed economy if

$$Z_1'P_1' = \sum_{j \in J''} Z_j''P_j'', \; J'' > 1, \tag{3.28}$$

since the value of the market portfolio is unchanged, but opportunities beyond investing in the market portfolio have opened up. The double-primed economy obviously spans the market portfolio pattern $Z_1'a_1' = W$, and A'' can therefore be viewed as $\{a_1', \text{other security patterns}\}$. And, due to (3.28), R'' sustains the single-primed equilibrium as well. (Proof: $Z_1'A' \cdot R'' = W \cdot R'' = \Sigma Z_j''P_j'' = Z_1'P_1'$, and thus $P' = A'R''$ since Z_1 is a scalar.) More generally, consider

$$A' = A_1 \quad \text{and} \quad A'' = \begin{bmatrix} A_1 \\ A_2 \end{bmatrix}.$$

The matrix A_1 is $J' \times S$ but otherwise arbitrary, and A_2 is any $(J'' - J') \times S$ matrix, $J'' > J'$. Suppose further that $P'_j = P''_j$ for all $j \leq J'$, and let $P''_j, j = J' + 1, \ldots, J''$ be any nonarbitrage prices. It follows that

$$A' = [I:0]A'' \quad \text{and} \quad P' = [I:0]P'',$$

where '0' is a $J' \times (J'' - J')$ matrix with zero entries everywhere; the identity matrix is $J' \times J'$. These pricing/payoff assumptions combined with endowment neutrality meet the conditions of the proposition, and thus no individual is worse off in the double-primed economy.

The above algebra has an interesting interpretation in a more concrete context. Let A_1 be the patterns of securities issued by firms, that is, these securities have positive supply ($Z' > 0$). If A_2 represents the patterns of zero-supply securities, then endowment neutrality is satisfied by the "natural" condition $\bar{z}'_{ij} = \bar{z}''_{ij}, j \leq J'$, and $\bar{z}''_{ij} = 0$ for $j > J'$. Thus, additional zero supply securities harm no individual, provided that their introduction does not affect the prices of firms' (positive-supply) securities. This serves as a welfare justification for the proliferation of markets in puts and calls and other zero-supply securities.

The redistribution of wealth, via a redistribution of endowments, generally has no predictable impact on individuals' welfare, since changes in prices accompany changes in wealth. As economists have long known, given concurrent price changes one cannot predict welfare changes from wealth changes. This observation suggests another important role for endowment-independent implicit prices in welfare analysis. If in addition to (i) $R' = R''$ even though $\bar{\alpha}' \neq \bar{\alpha}''$, (ii) $g(A'',v) = g(A',v)$ for all v, then, for each individual, the signs of $V''_i - V'_i$ and $\bar{\bar{w}}''_i - \bar{\bar{w}}'_i$ are identical. The redistribution of wealth, through a redistribution of endowments, maps into a predictable change in expected utilities. Thus, under the two conditions, aggregate wealth does not change and the notion that an individual's relative wealth indicates his relative welfare becomes meaningful. The conditions (i) and (ii) are necessary as well as sufficient. The necessity of (i) is obvious, since the implicit prices affect both the left-hand side and the right-hand side of the budget constraint in the CCCP. Expressing the point colloquially, securities are relatively cheap in the double-primed economy when $W \cdot R' > W \cdot R''$, so an individual could possibly be better off in the double-primed economy even if his endowed wealth decreases. In fact, $g(A'',v) > g(A',v)$, all v, and $W \cdot R'' < W \cdot R'$ for some $\bar{\alpha}'' = \bar{\alpha}'$ can occur simultaneously, and a decrease in aggregate wealth does not exclude a Pareto improvement. Although tedious, such examples can be constructed. (Of course, if $g(A'',v) = g(A',v)$ for all v and $R'' \neq R'$, then WR3 applies. This follows because $R'' \neq R'$ implies $\alpha' \neq \alpha''$. In this case the sign of $W \cdot R' - W \cdot R''$ clearly has no significance.) The necessity of $g(A'',v) = g(A',v)$ is equally obvious since the change in market opportunities by itself must be welfare irrelevant. This further means that the identical sign relationship between $V_i'' - V_i'$ and $\bar{\bar{w}}_i'' - \bar{\bar{w}}_i'$ for all i takes place (essentially) only under the LRT conditions in Proposition 3.18.

The potential welfare improvement inherent in Proposition 3.19 differs from the scheme used in the context of Proposition 3.10. Without restricting preferences/beliefs, both approaches manipulate assumptions such that an individual is (at least weakly) better off. Yet, as will be shown next, these approaches are only partially similar. The point is central because it demonstrates the two key "tricks" neoclassical models rely on to achieve Pareto improvements.

Define an individual's *consumption opportunity set* by

$$CO_i \equiv \{\alpha_i | c_i + w_i \cdot R \leq \bar{\bar{w}}_i,\ w_i \text{ is spanned by } A\}.$$

The set depends only on A, R and $\bar{\alpha}_i$, and an individual's welfare generally differs when $CO_i'' \equiv CO_i(A'', R'', \bar{\alpha}_i'') \neq CO_i(A', R', \bar{\alpha}_i') \equiv CO_i'$. Let α_i' and α_i'' be the two optimal consumption patterns in the single- and double-primed economy, respectively; then one can conclude that $V_i(\alpha_i'') \geq V_i(\alpha_i')$ if either

I. $CO_i' \subseteq CO_i''$ or
II. $\alpha_i' \in CO_i''$ but possibly $CO_i' \not\subseteq CO_i''$.

Note that case II is weaker than case I; that is, I implies II, but the converse is not true since there may exist nonoptimal α_i that are elements in CO_i' but not in CO_i''. Proposition 3.19 exploits case I: given endowment neutrality, a common implicit price system, and the span of A' being a subspace of the span of A'', one obtains the conclusion $CO_i' \subseteq CO_i''$. The proof of Proposition 3.10 exploits case II: given the assumptions $\alpha_i' = \bar{\alpha}_i'$ and endowment neutrality, it follows immediately that $\alpha_i' \in CO_i''$ (since $\bar{\alpha}_i' \in CO_i''$).

The analysis above highlights parts of the discussion in section 3.5. The general conclusion there was that endowment neutrality, by itself, has no particular welfare implications (except for Type I comparisons). Specifically, $g(A'', v) > g(A', v)$ combined with endowment neutrality did not rule out a WR3 redistribution of expected utilities (Proposition 3.10). *To ensure that no individual is worse off requires additional assumptions.* The two cases explicate the possibilities: *either* there are restrictions on the structure of prices and endowment neutrality (case I), *or* the restrictions on the endowments go beyond endowment neutrality (case II). As Chapter 5 will illustrate, welfare economics frequently uses these two schemes. Other kinds of comparative welfare analysis—not just those involving market structure comparisons—tend to rely on one of the two cases to demonstrate the possibility of a welfare improvement in the economy.[13]

[13] The theory of stockholder production unanimity develops readily from the two cases of welfare improvement. The so-called "ex ante" unanimity result exploits case I, and the "ex post" unanimity result exploits case II. See Ohlson (1985). (The "ex ante" case fixes implicit prices across production plans, and the "ex post" case assumes that share endowments are equilibrium holdings relative to a basic production plan.)

3.7.4. The theory of absolute (preference-based) valuation

The analysis so far deals exclusively with relative security valuation, within or across economies.[14] At this point the study switches to *absolute security valuation*. Expressed briefly, this subject traditionally addresses the following question: given that one views every security as being determined by

$$P_j = f(R_F, E[\tilde{a}_j], \text{risk}_j),$$

then what can be said about the valuation function $f(\cdot,\cdot,\cdot)$ and, further, what defines the appropriate measure(s) of security "risk"? The question departs from certain premises. The beliefs are homogeneous, and the analysis accords considerable status to a security's expected payoff. The argument R_F in $f(R_F,\cdot,\cdot)$ captures the relevance of the time-value of money. A benchmark security with no risk presumably satisfies $P_j = R_F^{-1}E[\tilde{a}_j]$. The question's essence focuses on the need to introduce a variable besides the expected payoff and the risk-free rate to determine the value of a security; this additional variable, if identifiable, ought to be the appropriate measure of security risk. Individuals' preferences/beliefs must now enter into the analysis explicitly, and restrictions on the exogenous variables potentially sharpen the interpretation of the $f(\cdot,\cdot,\cdot)$ expression.

Relying only on basics, one easily derives the general structure of $f(\cdot,\cdot,\cdot)$ from an individual's optimality condition. Define

$$q_{is} \equiv (\lambda_{is}/\pi_{is})R_F.$$

Since optimality requires $P_j = a_j \cdot \lambda_i$ one has

$$P_j = \sum_s a_{js} q_{is} R_F^{-1} \pi_{is} = R_F^{-1} E_i[\tilde{a}_j \tilde{q}_i],$$

where $E_i[\cdot]$ expresses the expectation relative to the ith individual's beliefs. Note next that $E_i[\tilde{q}_i] = 1$ since $\sum_s \lambda_{is} = R_F^{-1}$; hence,

$$E_i[\tilde{a}_j \tilde{q}_i] = E_i[\tilde{a}_j] + cov_i[\tilde{a}_j, \tilde{q}_i],$$

and it further follows that

$$P_j = R_F^{-1}\{E_i[\tilde{a}_j] + cov_i[\tilde{a}_j, \tilde{q}_i]\}, \quad \text{all} \quad i \in I \quad \text{and} \quad j \in J. \tag{3.29}$$

With homogeneous expected payoffs $E_i[\cdot]$ one can drop the subscript i for $cov_i[\cdot,\cdot]$ as well:

$$P_j = R_F^{-1}\{E[\tilde{a}_j] + cov[\tilde{a}_j, \tilde{q}_i]\}. \tag{3.30}$$

The random variable $\tilde{q}_i$ is critical in the identification of security risk and $-\text{risk}_j \equiv cov[\tilde{a}_j, \tilde{q}_i]$. At the same time the $\tilde{q}_i$ variable may seem abstract and

[14] This section draws on Garman (1978) and Rubinstein (1974).

not obviously interpretable.[15] An alternative expression for $\tilde{q}_i$ alleviates these problems. The risk-free rate equals $\left(\sum \lambda_{is}\right)^{-1}$ and $\lambda_{is} = \pi_{is} u_{is}^2(c_i, w_{is})/[\partial V_i/\partial c_i]$. Hence,

$$q_{is} = (\lambda_{is}/\pi_{is}) \left(\sum \lambda_{is}\right)^{-1} = u_{is}^2(c_i, w_{is})/\sum \pi_{is} u_{is}^2(c_i, w_{is}). \tag{3.31}$$

With time-additive and state independent utility and homogeneous beliefs the last expression becomes less unwieldy:

$$q_{is} = u_i^2(w_{is})/E[u_i^2(\tilde{w}_i)]. \tag{3.32}$$

Equations (3.30) through (3.32) provide the information one wants to answer the previously raised question about the nature of the valuation function $f(\cdot,\cdot,\cdot)$. In words, Eq. (3.30) shows that the security's expected payoff adjusted for its riskiness and discounted by the time value of money determines its value. Equation (3.31) and, more clearly, Eq. (3.32) identify the appropriate risk-measure as the covariance between the payoff and the marginal utility of future consumption normalized by its expected value. And individuals agree on a security's risk to the extent that they agree on a security's expected payoff. Thus, even though the $\tilde{q}_i$'s generally differ over individuals because of differences in utilities/beliefs, the analysis shows that $cov_i[\tilde{a}_j, \tilde{q}_i]$ depends only on j and not on i if, and only if, the individuals have homogeneous beliefs about expected payoffs.

It is worthwhile to note that, given homogeneous beliefs and state independent utilities, a constant W implies that the $cov[\tilde{a}_j, \tilde{q}_i]$ are zero. This follows because by Lemma 3.8 and Proposition 3.8, the w_{is} and q_{is} do not vary over states. The payoff $\tilde{a}_j$ can be random for individual securities, but in this no-aggregate-risk economy the securities have no risk either. This conforms nicely with economic intuition. Conversely, a homogeneous-beliefs no-aggregate-risk economy is generally necessary for all the individual securities to have no security risk. This follows because the presence of aggregate risk implies that at least one individual must expose himself to future consumption risk; for this individual $\tilde{q}_i$ is random. One cannot, therefore, expect $cov[\tilde{a}_j, \tilde{q}_i] = 0$ to hold for all j, except for $\tilde{W}$ = constant and for truly pathological state dependent utilities cases.

Although the analysis solves the problem of identifying the structure of the function $f(\cdot,\cdot,\cdot)$, the expressions derived are in no sense more profound than the starting point $P_j = a_j \cdot \lambda_i$. The derivations merely reexpress the basic valuation relationship implied by the individuals' optimality conditions, so that the random variables $\tilde{q}_i$ perform the same function as the λ_i-

[15] Equation (3.29) requires only that the economy excludes arbitrage opportunities. That is, given no-arbitrage opportunities, there always *exists* some positive random variable $\tilde{q}$, $E[\tilde{q}] = 1$, such that the equilibrium values equal (3.29). The notion of security risk as a covariance term subtracted from the expected payoff is therefore general. See Rubinstein (1976) and Garman (1978).

vectors in the valuation expressions. The major use of Eq. (3.30) and (3.32) relates to the possibility of viewing the equilibrium price vector P as a function of the payoffs' probability distribution. Such relationships are particularly relevant for empirical work. For this reason one might want to also focus on the determination of equilibrium *returns*, $\tilde{r}_j \equiv \tilde{a}_j/P_j$. A simple manipulation of Eq. (3.30) leads to

$$E[\tilde{r}_j] - R_F = cov[\tilde{r}_j, -\tilde{q}_i], \quad j \in J. \tag{3.33}$$

The left-hand side of Eq. (3.33) refers to a security's *expected excess return;* this quantity and the security's risk make up two sides of the same coin.

The valuation formulae Eq. (3.30) and (3.33) hold for portfolios no less than for individual securities $\left(\text{proof: } \sum_j z_j P_j = \sum_j z_j (a_j \cdot \lambda_i) = \left(\sum_j z_j a_j\right) \cdot \lambda_i\right)$. The analysis can exploit this portfolio property to eliminate $E[\tilde{u}_i^2]$ and instead relate the security price (or expected return) to the market portfolio's expected return/risk characteristics. Define $P_M \equiv \sum_j Z_j P_j$, and

$$\tilde{r}_M \equiv \tilde{W}/P_M \equiv \tilde{a}_M/P_M = \left(\sum_j Z_j \tilde{a}_j\right)/P_M = \sum_j x_j \tilde{r}_j,$$

where

$$x_j \equiv Z_j P_j / P_M.$$

The x_j's define the relative market value weights, and $\sum_j x_j = 1$. Since Eq. (3.33) holds for portfolios, it follows that

$$E[\tilde{r}_M] - R_F = cov[\tilde{r}_M, -\tilde{q}_i] = \{1/E[\tilde{u}_i^2]\}cov[\tilde{r}_M, -\tilde{u}_i^2].$$

Further,

$$P_j = R_F^{-1}\{E[\tilde{a}_j] + K_i \, cov[\tilde{a}_j, \tilde{u}_i^2]\}, \quad \text{all} \quad j \in J \quad \text{and} \quad j = M,$$

where

$$K_i \equiv 1/E[\tilde{u}_i^2] = -(E[\tilde{r}_M] - R_F)/cov[\tilde{r}_M, \tilde{u}_i^2].$$

Alternatively, in terms of expected excess returns,

$$E[\tilde{r}_j] - R_F = \{cov[\tilde{r}_j, \tilde{u}_i^2]/cov[\tilde{r}_M, \tilde{u}_i^2]\}(E[\tilde{r}_M] - R_F).$$

The covariance ratio inside { } normalizes security j's risk-measure relative to the risk of the market portfolio. The market portfolio has average risk, so that the covariance ratio is above (below) one for securities with above (below) average risk. $\left(\text{Note that } \sum_j x_j \, cov[\tilde{r}_j, \tilde{u}_i^2]/cov[\tilde{r}_M, \tilde{u}_i^2] = 1.\right)$ And all individuals perceive identical relative risk-measures given homogeneous beliefs about expected returns. The analysis builds on no other strong assumptions, and, specifically, the economy may not achieve FPE.

The purpose of financial markets is to allocate aggregate risk, and the valuation analysis implies that in equilibrium *every* individual must bear some of this risk unless he chooses a risk-free consumption pattern. More precisely, let $\tilde{r}^i \equiv \tilde{w}_i / \left(\sum_j z_{ij} P_j\right)$, which defines the ith individual's return on his portfolio, and risk aversion implies that $E[\tilde{r}^i] > R_F$. To prove the latter, use Eqs. (3.32) and (3.33) for a portfolio $\{z_{ij}\}_j$, and note that $cov[\tilde{w}_i, u_i^2(\tilde{w}_i)] = E[(\tilde{w}_i - E[\tilde{w}_i])u_i^2(\tilde{w}_i)] = E[(\tilde{w}_i - E[\tilde{w}_i])(u_i^2(\tilde{w}_i) - u_i^2(E[\tilde{w}_i]))] < 0$; the last inequality follows since $u_i^2(.)$ is a decreasing function and thus $(\tilde{w}_i - E[\tilde{w}_i])(u_i^2(\tilde{w}_i) - u_i^2(E[\tilde{w}_i])) < 0$ except when $\tilde{w}_i = E[\tilde{w}_i]$.[16] The risks the individuals bear, $E[\tilde{r}^i] - R_F$, weighted by their relative market values, add up to aggregate risk as measured by the excess return on the market portfolio. Formally, let $d_i \equiv \bar{I}_i / \sum_i \bar{I}_i \equiv \left(\sum_j z_{ij} P_j\right) \Big/ \left(\sum_j Z_j P_j\right)$, and it follows that

$$\sum_i d_i (E[\tilde{r}^i] - R_F) = E[\tilde{r}_M] - R_F > 0$$

since $d_i > 0$, $\sum_i d_i = 1$, $\sum_i d_i \tilde{r}^i = \tilde{r}_M$, and $\tilde{r}^i \neq R_F$ for at least one i when $\tilde{r}_M$ is random. This application of the valuation formula Eq. (3.33) powerfully illustrates the nature of risk and its allocation in an economy with homogeneous beliefs and risk aversion. (Recall from section 2.2.1 that risk aversion requires state independent utilities. The conclusion does not follow without it.)

Sharper content to the valuation formulae demands the elimination of the subscript "i," that is, the equilibrium reaches FPE. This would seem critical since otherwise all the q_i almost certainly derive as complicated functions of the exogenous variables. The risk-measure lacks concreteness unless the distribution of $\tilde{w}_i$ (and $\tilde{u}_i^2$) is "known" for at least one i. To enrich the valuation formulae's content one needs a parsimonious equilibrium solution, that is, w_i identified as a function of W. This requirement is, of course, generally difficult to satisfy, and FPE by itself eliminates only some of the complexities. However, some well-known special cases—all FPE—yield constructive results.

The most elementary case identifying w_i, and u_i^2, presumes identical individuals. The economy effectively reduces to one that has a single person; in equilibrium the individual consumes (C, W), and $\tilde{u}_i^2$ accordingly equals $u_{\bar{s}}^2(C, \tilde{W}) \equiv u_{\bar{s}}^2(\tilde{W})$ (or $u_{\bar{s}}^2(C/I, \tilde{W}/I)$ if the economy has I identical individuals). Hence, in a single person economy with an observable W ("date-one GNP") the valuation implications become apparent.

PROPOSITION 3.20. *Suppose that the economy consists of only one individual who has state independent preferences. Then, in equilibrium,*

$$P_j = R_F^{-1}\{E[\tilde{a}_j] + \mu \, cov[\tilde{a}_j, u^2(\tilde{W})]\}$$

[16] I am indebted to Hayne Leland for this proof.

where

$$\mu \equiv 1/E[u^2(\tilde{W})] > 0.$$

Furthermore,

$$E[\tilde{r}_j] - R_F = \mu\ cov[\tilde{r}_j, -u^2(\tilde{W})],$$

$$\mu = (E[\tilde{r}_M] - R_F)/cov[\tilde{r}_M, -u^2(\tilde{W})],$$

$$R_F^{-1} = E[u^2(\tilde{W})]/[\partial V/\partial c],$$

*where $\partial V/\partial c$ is evaluated at (C, W).**

The prices above are commonly said to be determined by a "representative individual," and $\tilde{u}^2$ is (proportional to) "marginal social utility" of future consumption. The language perhaps somewhat unfortunately obscures the truly critical feature, namely, the extreme welfare irrelevance of markets. Markets obviously have no economic function unless trading can occur. Note the similarity between Propositions 3.15 and 3.20: both price economically irrelevant securities.

As indicated, empirical finance research focuses traditionally on the structure of returns rather than on prices as they relate to gross payoffs. In deference to this tradition, of significance are conditions that explain a security's expected excess return by the joint probability distribution of the return and the return on the market portfolio. Conditions for such risk/expected excess return relationships are well known, and, interestingly, they make the strict identical individuals assumption unnecessary.

PROPOSITION 3.21. *Suppose that individuals have LRT preferences with identical slope parameter (β) and homogeneous beliefs. Then equilibrium rates of returns are determined by*

$$E[\tilde{r}_j] - R_F = \mu\ cov[\tilde{r}_j, \tilde{r}_M^{-1/\beta}], \quad all \quad j \in J,$$

where

$$\mu \equiv (E[\tilde{r}_M] - R_F)/cov[\tilde{r}_M, \tilde{r}_M^{-1/\beta}],$$

provided that either (i) $\varphi_i = 0$ all i and $\beta > 0$, or (ii) $\beta = -1$ in which case the φ_i may vary with i.

The equilibrium can, of course, also express a security's value:

$$P_j = R_F^{-1}\{E[\tilde{a}_j] - \mu\ cov[\tilde{a}_j, \tilde{r}_M^{-1/\beta}]\}.$$

The admissible heterogeneity of individuals is limited indeed. The isoelastic utilities case permits only individual specific endowments; the quadratic utility case ($\beta = -1$) also permits different φ_i-parameters. Note further that the quadratic utility setting leads to the *Capital Asset Pricing*

Model (CAPM). Thus, in CAPM the risk-measure is proportional to $cov[\tilde{r}_j, \tilde{r}_M]$.[17]

As the proof shows, one key feature that makes the parsimonious valuation formulae possible is the equilibrium implication of portfolio separation: $w_{is} = K_{1i} + K_{2i}W_s$. But this simple relationship by itself helps little unless one can also eliminate or factor out the constants K_{1i}, K_{2i} in the risk-measure. For this reason the proposition excludes the cases in which $\varphi_i \neq 0$ and $\beta \neq -1$. Consider for example generalized power utility; then $u_i^2(w_{is}) = (\varphi_i + K_{1i} + K_{2i}W_s)^{-b}$, and the risk measure $-cov[\tilde{r}_j, \tilde{u}_i^2]$ cannot be simplified further unless either $\varphi_i + K_{1i} = 0$ or $-b = 1$. However, $\varphi_i + K_{1i} = 0$ in the iso-elastic case (i) with $\varphi_i = 0$ (recall that $\varphi_i = 0$ for all i implies $K_{1i} = 0$). The CAPM can be viewed as a knife-edge special setting, since only for $b = -1$ does $\varphi_i + K_{1i} \neq 0$ become irrelevant in $cov[\tilde{r}_j, \tilde{u}_i^2]$ (and K_{2i} factors out).

Results related to LRT utilities with $\beta \neq -1$ and $\varphi_i \neq 0$ are possible if $\rho U_i^2 = U_i^1$ augments the preference specification. Proposition 3.18 exploits this setting and shows that the prices do not depend on the distribution of endowments. This leads to a strengthening of results. Given the additional assumption $\rho U_i^2 = U_i^1$, the equilibrium prices are equivalent to those of a single-person economy in which the individual represents an "average" of the individuals in the original economy. In contrast to the extremely restrictive Proposition 3.20 setting, the notion of a "representative individual" becomes a nonvacuous concept.

PROPOSITION 3.22. *Suppose that individuals have LRT preferences with identical slope parameters, homogeneous beliefs, and* $\rho U_i^2 = U_i^1$. *The equilibrium prices and returns are then equivalent to those of a single-person economy in which preferences are LRT with the same slope parameter and the intercept given by*

$$\hat{\varphi} \equiv \left(\sum_i \varphi_i\right)/I.$$

Per capita supplies replaces aggregate supplies in Proposition 3.20.

Some other, less important, cases suffice for the existence of a representative individual (as a suitable "average" of the individuals in the original economy). These remaining cases relate closely to the discussion that followed Proposition 3.18, and Rubinstein (1974) covers them fully.[18]

---

[17] Removing the assumption of the availability of a risk-free portfolio, the quadratic utility case generalizes to the "zero-beta" CAPM; see Black (1972) and Rubinstein (1973). Portfolio separation still holds in this economy, but surprisingly the equilibrium does not generally achieve FPE. (This follows because $\{1, W\}$ does not generally span w_i; see the discussion that followed Proposition 3.7.) While the second-basis portfolio remains the market portfolio, the first basis portfolio is conveniently put equal to a minimum variance portfolio. In equilibrium, the risk-free security return is replaced by the expected return on a portfolio that does not correlate with the return on the market portfolio.

[18] See also Brennan and Kraus (1976, 1978).

The essence of valuation in Proposition 3.22 is conceptually similar to Proposition 3.20. Both propositions derive valuation formulae that incorporate aggregate wealth in the risk-measure by eliminating all, or close to all, heterogeneity of individuals' characteristics. This reduces the need for exchange to a corresponding degree: Proposition 3.20 depends on no markets ($J \geq 1$), while Proposition 3.22 depends only on the inclusion of a risk-free portfolio in addition to the always available market portfolio. In fact, the welfare irrelevance of (some or all) markets has been a critical feature in all cases that derive valuation formulae (Propositions 3.15, 3.20, 3.21, and 3.22).

The last proposition ends the formal valuation analysis of a two-date economy.[19] The developments have been general in the sense that the propositions hold for arbitrary (but homogeneous) beliefs. One may next ask whether added structure to (π, A), that is, the joint probability-distribution of $\{\tilde{a}_j\}_j$, leads to any interesting results. This question has both a yes and a no answer. It is "no" if the model restricts the state space S to be finite (which has been the maintained assumption throughout). It is "yes" if the finite state space assumption is removed.

To complete the discussion, the two major "yes" cases will be considered briefly.

First, the CAPM obtains if the $\{\tilde{a}_j\}_j$ are jointly normally distributed, even without quadratic preferences (but they must be state independent). Although an economy with normally distributed returns does *not* generally achieve FPE, the reason these securities can be priced is again due to their welfare irrelevance. That is, given that *all* securities' payoffs are jointly normally distributed, in equilibrium the risk-free portfolio and the normally distributed market portfolio serve as basis portfolios. The portfolio separation follows because the joint normality of security payoffs implies that the mean and variance of portfolio payoffs are sufficient parameters for an expected utility evaluation. Further, the CAPM result in this context relies on a curious (and nonobvious) property of jointly normally distributed variables: if $\tilde{a}_j$ and $\tilde{W}$ are jointly normal, then

$$cov[\tilde{a}_j, h(\tilde{W})] = E[h'(\tilde{W})]\, cov[\tilde{a}_j, \tilde{W}], \qquad (3.34)$$

provided that the function h satisfies mild smoothness conditions ($\partial h/\partial W \equiv h'$ here).[20] These two observations suffice for

$$cov[\tilde{a}_j, \tilde{u}_i^2] = \text{constant}_i \times cov[\tilde{a}_j, \tilde{W}],$$

which in turn permits derivation of the CAPM in the same fashion as in the quadratic utility case.

---

[19] The remainder of this chapter deals with a special topic that does not bear on subsequent chapters.

[20] For a proof, see Rubinstein (1976).

Formally, separation in equilibrium implies that

$$w_{is} = K_{1i} + K_{2i}W_s. \tag{3.35}$$

It follows that

$$cov[\tilde{a}_j, \tilde{u}_i^2] = cov[\tilde{a}_j, u_i^2(c_i, K_{1i} + K_{2i}\tilde{W})] = K_{3i} \times cov[\tilde{a}_j, \tilde{W}],$$

where the second equality applies Eq. (3.34); u_i^2 specifies the function h, and K_{3i} is a constant ($K_{3i} \equiv K_{2i} \times E[\partial u_i^2/\partial w_{is}]$).

It may be surprising and nonapparent that the above normally distributed returns CAPM case does not imply a FPE equilibrium. To appreciate this point most readily, consider what happens when one introduces a zero-supply call option on a security. While W still satisfies normality, the call option's payoff pattern is bounded below and clearly cannot do so. Portfolio separation no longer follows, and the call option might well be traded and thereby affect the equilibrium. This then prevents identification of u_i^2 in terms of W. In other words, $g(A,v) = g\left(\begin{bmatrix}1\\W\end{bmatrix}, v\right)$ holds only because *all* the (infinite dimensional) row vectors in A have a joint normal distribution. Other markets do not necessarily sustain the equality, and this makes welfare improvement through zero-supply securities market enrichment possible. But trading in these securities automatically destroys Eq. (3.35), since Eq. (3.35) by itself cannot hold unless combinations of the risk-free portfolio and the market portfolio support the equilibrium.[21]

The second case involves approximate analysis, and a rigorous set of derivations accordingly requires a fairly elaborate machinery. Nevertheless, one can describe the underlying ideas without the mathematical complexities. The distributional assumption specifies that returns (and payoffs) have a linear relationship to a random common factor that can affect all securities, plus a random security-specific component. Formally, assume that

$$\tilde{r}_j = k_{1j} + k_{2j}\tilde{\delta} + \tilde{\varepsilon}_j, \tag{3.36}$$

where the k_{ij}'s are nonstochastic and $cov[\tilde{\varepsilon}_j, \tilde{\varepsilon}_k] = 0, j \neq k$. By convention, $E[\tilde{\delta}] = E[\tilde{\varepsilon}_j] = 0$, which implies the specification $E[\tilde{r}_j] = k_{1j}$. The model's important feature makes the residuals, ε_j, uncorrelated across the securities; further, their distribution does not depend on the common factor $\tilde{\delta}$. Very roughly, Eq. (3.36) is powerful because under appropriate conditions the residuals have no equilibrium relevance; k_{1j} and k_{2j} should then determine a security's expected return/risk equilibrium relationship. To accomplish this

[21] The case of multivariate normality generalizes to multivariate stable ("Pareto-Levy") distributions; see Fama (1971) and Ohlson (1977). More important, note also that continuous time models exploit the distribution properties of returns; see Merton (1973). For a general analysis of return distributions that imply separation, see Ross (1978).

irrelevance one makes the number of securities large, thereby effectively eliminating the residuals' effect on aggregate returns.

The scheme works via a diversification effect. Let x_j denote the relative market value of security j. Then, if J is "large," and the individual x_j's are correspondingly "small," the law of large numbers implies that $\sum_j x_j \tilde{\varepsilon}_j = 0$ (approximately). Hence,

$$\tilde{r}_M \doteq K_1 + K_2\tilde{\delta}, \tag{3.37}$$

that is, $\tilde{\delta}$ correlates almost perfectly with the return on the market portfolio (K_1 and K_2 are $\{x_j\}_j$ weighted averages of $\{k_{1j}\}_j$ and $\{k_{2j}\}_j$, respectively). Suppose further that a "representative" individual, who has state independent utility, determines the prices. Then $\tilde{u}^2 = u^2(C,P_M\tilde{r}_M) = u^2(C,P_M(K_1 + K_2\tilde{\delta}))$; substituting Eq. (3.36) and the last u^2 expression into the (negative) of a security's risk-measure one obtains:

$$\begin{aligned} cov[\tilde{r}_j,\tilde{u}^2] &= cov[k_{1j} + k_{2j}\tilde{\delta} + \tilde{\varepsilon}_j, u^2(C,P_M(K_1 + K_2\tilde{\delta}))] \\ &= k_{2j}\, cov[\tilde{\delta},\tilde{u}^2] \text{ for all } j. \end{aligned}$$

The last equality follows since $\tilde{\varepsilon}_j$ and $\tilde{\delta}$ are independently distributed. In equilibrium the $\{\tilde{\varepsilon}_j\}_j$ are irrelevant because they have no effect on social risk and marginal social utility:

$$\begin{aligned} E[\tilde{r}_j] - R_F = k_{1j} - R_F &= cov[\tilde{r}_j, -\tilde{u}^2] \\ &= -k_{2j}\, cov[\tilde{\delta},\tilde{u}^2] \text{ for all } j = 1,2,\ldots. \end{aligned} \tag{3.38}$$

Similar to the CAPM, Eq. (3.38) expresses a linear relationship between the expected return, k_{1j}, and the "risk," k_{2j}, where k_{2j} is (approximately) proportional to $cov[\tilde{r}_j,\tilde{r}_M]$. (Note that $cov[\tilde{r}_j,\tilde{r}_M] = K_2\, cov[\tilde{r}_j,\tilde{\delta}] = k_{2j}K_2\, var[\tilde{\delta}]$, and $K_2\, var[\tilde{\delta}]$ does not depend on j.) However, the model differs conceptually from the CAPM. The set of assumptions leading to Eq. (3.38) are quite distinct from those used in Proposition 3.21. To further appreciate this point, consider the following generalization of Eq. (3.36) and (3.38). Let k_{2j} and δ be vectors, so that $k_{2j} \cdot \delta$ in Eq. (3.36) represents an inner product. Then, in Eq. (3.38), $-k_{2j} \cdot cov[\tilde{\delta},\tilde{u}^2]$ also denotes an inner product. The last quantity, however, need not be proportional to $cov[\tilde{r}_j,\tilde{r}_M]$.

The irrelevance of the ε_j in equilibrium suggests that the equilibrium relationship $k_{1j} - R_F = k_{2j} \times$ constant also derives via Proposition 3.15. The idea is thus that with $\tilde{\varepsilon}_j \equiv 0$ and

$$\tilde{r}_j = k_{1j} + k_{2j}\tilde{\delta},$$

all the $\tilde{a}_j$ are linear in $\tilde{\delta}$. The risk-free portfolio and the payoff of the market portfolio therefore span each payoff a_j ($= P_j r_j$). Applying the arbitrage pricing machinery of Proposition 3.15, the equilibrium relationship in Eq. (3.38) follows. Of course, this approach to Eq. (3.38) is merely suggestive. It is by no means clear how Proposition 3.15 (and Proposition 2.1) can apply when the $\{\varepsilon_j\}_j$, in fact, do not equal zero. Furthermore, to let J (and S) approach infinity produces its own problems, since one must then generalize Proposition 2.1 to include infinite dimensional cases.[22]

Appendix 3.1 Proofs

Proof of Proposition 3.1: Suppose the allocation (c,z) is not CPE. Then there exists some other feasible allocation (c',z') that dominates (c,z) in a Pareto sense. Further, since individuals maximize their expected utilities,

$$c_i' + z_i' \cdot P \geq \bar{c}_i + \bar{z}_i \cdot P, \qquad \text{all } i \in I,$$

and where the inequality is strict for at least one $i \in I$. Summing over all i one obtains:

$$\sum_i c_i' + \sum_i z_i' \cdot P > C + Z \cdot P,$$

since $(C,Z) = \sum_i (\bar{c}_i, \bar{z}_i)$. But (c',z') must be feasible, i.e., $\sum_i (c_i', z_i') \leqq (C,Z)$, which is impossible given the previously derived strict inequality. The contradiction implies that (c,z) is CPE.

Proof of Proposition 3.2: If α is CPE relative to A then, by definition, the following planner's Lagrangean problem results in α:

$$\max_{\{(c_i,z_i)\}_i \mu \psi} V_1(c_1, z_1 A) - \mu_0\Big(\sum_i c_i - C\Big) - \sum_j \mu_j\Big(\sum_i z_{ij} - Z_j\Big)$$
$$- \sum_{i=2}^{I} \psi_i(v_i - V_i(c_i, z_i A))$$

where $v_i \equiv V_i(\alpha_i)$, and $\mu \equiv (\mu_0, \ldots, \mu_J)$, $\psi \equiv (\psi_2, \ldots, \psi_I)$ define the multipliers. Differentiating with respect to the arguments one obtains the optimality conditions:

$$\partial V_1/\partial c_1 - \mu_0 = 0 \tag{A3.1}$$

$$\partial V_1/\partial z_{1j} - \mu_j = 0,\ j \in J, \tag{A3.2}$$

$$-\mu_0 + \psi_i \partial V_i/\partial c_i = 0,\ i = 2, \ldots, I, \tag{A3.3}$$

$$-\mu_j + \psi_i \partial V_i/\partial z_{ij} = 0,\ j = 1, \ldots, J,\ i = 2, \ldots, I, \tag{A3.4}$$

$$\sum_i (c_i, z_i) = (C,Z) \tag{A3.5}$$

$$-v_i + V_i = 0,\ i = 2, \ldots, I. \tag{A3.6}$$

[22] Dybvig (1983), Grinblatt and Titman (1983), and Ross (1976b) discuss various reasonably simple derivations that result in Eq. (3.38).

Eliminating the multipliers ψ by combining (A3.3) and (A3.4), and combining (A3.1) and (A3.2), one obtains

$$[\partial V_i/\partial z_{ij}]/[\partial V_i/\partial c_i] = \mu_j/\mu_0, j \in J, i \in I. \tag{A3.7}$$

The equilibrium conditions in Eq. (3.6a), (3.6b), and (3.6c) are readily seen to be met for the CPE allocation α: put $P_j = \mu_j/\mu_0$ and Eq. (3.6a) is satisfied; Eq. (3.6b) is satisfied for all $\{P_j\}_j$ since $(c_i, z_i) = (\bar{c}_i, \bar{z}_i)$; Eq. (3.6c) is satisfied because of (A3.5).

Remark: Note that the conditions on $\{V_i\}_i$ must be much stronger in Proposition 3.2 compared to Proposition 3.1. Although MISC is too strong, *some* regularity conditions on $\{V_i\}_i$ are necessary to make (A3.1)–(A3.6) sufficient for an optimum. On the other hand, Proposition 3.1 requires virtually no conditions on $\{V_i\}_i$ (not even transitivity is implied by the proof!).

Proof of Proposition 3.3: The classical framework does not apply automatically since the z_{ij} can be negative without lower bounds. The condition $z_iA \geqq 0$ does not always make the set of available z_i bounded below. To deal with this problem one identifies some other matrix, A', such that

$$\{w_i | w_i = z_iA,\ w_i \geqq 0\} = \{w_i | w_i = z_i'A',\ z_i' \geqq 0\}.$$

The existence of such a matrix A' follows from basic linear algebra. By letting $\bar{z}_i'A' = \bar{z}_iA$ the primed setting is equivalent to the one without. But an equilibrium exists in the primed setting since $z_i' \geqq 0$, consistent with the classical framework. Hence, using Definition 3.2, an equilibrium exists also for the setting without a prime.

Proof of Proposition 3.5: This result is immediate by putting $A = I$ in the proof of Proposition 3.2.

Proof of Proposition 3.6: Let x_1 be any positive vector such that $Ax_1 \neq 0$. Let $\bar{x}$ be any non-null vector satisfying $A\bar{x} = 0$; such a vector exists since A is not of full rank. Let μ be a non-zero real number sufficiently small so that $x_2 = x_1 - \mu\bar{x} > 0$. It follows that $Ax_1 = Ax_2$ although $x_1 \neq x_2$. Define $x(k) \equiv kx_1 + (1 - k)x_2$; the first part of the proposition then follows since $Ax(k) = Ax_1$ where $x(k) > 0$ when $0 < k < 1$, and $x(k)$ varies uniquely with k.

To prove the second part, note that in equilibrium

$$\frac{\pi_{is}u_{is}^2(w_{is})}{\rho_i u_i^1(c_i)} = \lambda_{is},\ s = 1, \ldots, S.$$

Hence, define $\bar{\pi}_{is} \equiv [u_i^1(c_i)/u_{is}^2(w_{is})]\lambda_{is}$, and put $\pi_{is} = \bar{\pi}_{is}\Big/\sum_s \bar{\pi}_{is}$, $\rho_i = \left(\sum_s \bar{\pi}_{is}\right)^{-1}$.

Proof of Proposition 3.7: Initially, assume complete markets. Given the analysis in Section 2.4 (and Proposition 2.5), $w_i = w(\varphi_i, \bar{I}_i)$ can be expressed as

$$w(\varphi_i,\bar{I}_i) = k_1(\varphi_i,\bar{I}_i)1 + k_2(\varphi_i,\bar{I}_i)h$$

where 1 and h are the two basis portfolios. Further, without loss of generality, assume that there exists a risk-free security with zero supply. The aggregate claim on the risk-free basis portfolio, $\sum_i k_1(\varphi_i, \bar{I}_i)$, then equals zero in equilibrium. Hence, since in equilibrium $\sum_i w_i = W$ it follows also that $\sum_i w(\varphi_i, \bar{I}_i) = W = \text{const} \cdot h$; i.e., the second basis portfolio is proportional to the market portfolio. But, given a risk-free portfolio, the two-basis portfolios $\{1, W\}$ are available also within incomplete markets. Hence, the equilibrium remains unchanged.

Remark: The equilibrium relationship $w_i = k_{1i} + k_{2i}W$ expresses a *linear sharing rule*. (A seminal paper by Wilson [1968] considers the optimality of such sharing rules.)

Proof of Lemma 3.8: Let $W_1 = W_2$ and let $\alpha \in G(I)$ be any feasible allocation such that $w_{i1} \neq w_{i2}$ for at least one i. It will be shown that there exists an allocation $\alpha' \in G(I)$ such that $V_i(\alpha_i') \geqq V_i(\alpha_i)$, all $i \in I$, and where the inequality is strict for individuals with $w_{i1} \neq w_{i2}$.

Construct the allocation α' as follows:

$$c_i' = c_i,$$

$$w_{is}' = w_{is}, \text{ all } i \in I \text{ and } s = 3, \ldots, S,$$

$$w_{i1}' = w_{i2}' = k_1 w_{i1} + k_2 w_{i2},$$

where $k_1 \equiv \pi_{1i}/(\pi_{1i} + \pi_{2i})$, $k_2 \equiv \pi_{2i}/(\pi_{1i} + \pi_{2i})$; k_1 and k_2 do not depend on i because of assumption (ii). Further, due to (i), α' is feasible since $k_1 + k_2 = 1$ and $\sum_i w_{i1}' = \sum_i w_{i2}' = k_1 \sum_i w_{i1} + k_2 \sum_i w_{i2} = k_1 W_1 + k_2 W_2 = W_1 = W_2$.

The difference $V_i(\alpha_i') - V_i(\alpha_i) \equiv \Delta_i$ equals

$$\Delta_i = \sum_{s=1,2} \pi_{is} U_i(c_i', w_{is}') - \sum_{s=1,2} \pi_{is} U_i(c_i, w_{is}) \equiv K_{1i} - K_{2i}$$

where $U_i(\cdot,\cdot) \equiv U_{i1}(\cdot,\cdot)$ uses assumption (iii). The second term, K_{2i}, equals

$$K_{2i} = \sum_{s=1,2} \pi_{is} U_i(c_i, w_{is}) = (\pi_{i2} + \pi_{i2})[k_1 U_i(c_i, w_{i1}) + k_2 U_i(c_i, w_{i2})]$$

$$\leqq (\pi_{i1} + \pi_{i2}) U_i(c_i, k_1 w_{i1} + k_2 w_{i2}) = K_{1i}.$$

The inequality $\Delta_i \geq 0$ follows because U_i is strictly concave and $\Delta_i > 0$ iff $w_{i1} \neq w_{i2}$.

Remark: Lemma 3.8 has a well-known extension: if $W_s > W_t$, $U_{is} = U_{it}$, $\pi_{is}/\pi_{it} = \pi_{1s}/\pi_{1t}$, $i = 2, \ldots, I$, then $w_{is} > w_{it}$, *all* i, is a necessary condition for FPE. To prove this, note first that $W_s > W_t$ implies $w_{i's} > w_{i't}$ for at least one individual i'. Second, without difficulty one shows that $\lambda_{i't} = \lambda_{it}$ and $\lambda_{i's} = \lambda_{is}$, which are necessary for FPE (Proposition 3.5), cannot hold when $w_{is} \leq w_{it}$. (Given concavity of U_s, make use of the fact that $u_s^2(c,w_s'') < u_s^2(c,w_s')$ if and only if $w_s'' > w_s'$.)

As a further extension, given homogeneous beliefs and state independent utilities across all states, every FPE allocation can be expressed as $w_{is} = h_i(W_s)$ where $\sum_i h_i(W_s) = W_s$ and h_i is increasing in W_s for all i. (Note that the set of FPE allocations does not depend on the vector of probabilities.)

Proof of Proposition 3.9: Suppose that WR1 is possible. Then, using Proposition 3.1, $g(A'',v'') > g(A',v')$ where $v'' \geqq v'$. But $g(A',v'') = g(A'',v'')$ by Proposition 3.4(i). Hence, $g(A',v'') > g(A',v')$ which is a contradiction since g is a decreasing function in v. WR1 is accordingly ruled out. One proves that WR4 is impossible similarly.

The remainder of the proposition is immediate from Proposition 3.2.

Proof of Proposition 3.10: WR4 is obviously impossible; this follows immediately from the principles used in Proposition 3.9.

To prove WR1 with endowment neutrality, let α' be any allocation that satisfies $\sum_i \alpha_i' = (C, W)$ and $\alpha' \in G(A')$. Using the principles of Proposition 3.6, construct $\{V_i\}_i$ such that α' is CPE relative to A' yet $g(A'',v') > g(A',v')$ where $v_i' = V_i(\alpha_i')$; this poses no problems since it only requires that $A''\lambda_i' \neq A''\lambda_j'$. Let $\bar{\alpha} = \alpha'$. Then WR1 follows since α'' is CPE relative to A'' and $V_i(\alpha_i'') \geq V(\bar{\alpha}_i)$.

WR2 is immediate from the identical-individuals example. (More generally, construct $\{V_i\}_i$ such that $g(I,v') = g(A',v')$.)

Finally, consider WR3 with endowment neutrality. Let $I = 3$; one can then construct an equilibrium such that $\bar{\alpha}_1 = \alpha_1'' \neq \alpha_1'$. Hence, individual 1 is strictly worse off in the double-primed economy even if $g(A'',v') > g(A',v')$ where $v_i' = V_i(\alpha_i')$, $i = 2,3$. (Note that for a Type II comparison with endowment neutrality $g(A'',v') = g(A',v')$ contradicts $\alpha_1'' \neq \alpha_1'$.)

Let α'' be any allocation satisfying $\sum_i \alpha_i'' = (C,W)$, $\alpha'' \in G(A'')$, $\alpha'' \notin G(A')$ but α_1'' is in the span of A'. Using the principles of Proposition 3.6, construct $\{V_i\}_i$ such that α'' is CPE relative to A''. Let $\bar{\alpha}$ be any endowments satisfying $\bar{\alpha} \in G(A')$, $\sum_i \bar{\alpha}_i = (C,W)$, $\bar{\alpha}_1 = \alpha_1''$, and $\bar{c}_2 + \bar{w}_2 \cdot \lambda_1'' = c_2'' + w_2''\lambda_1''$; then $\bar{\alpha}$ sustains α'' as an equilibrium with $R'' = \lambda_1''$. (Note that $\bar{c}_3 + \bar{w}_3 \cdot \lambda_1'' = c_3'' + w_3'' \cdot \lambda_1''$ since $\bar{\alpha}_3 = (C,W) - \sum_{i=1,2} \bar{\alpha}_i$, that is, Walras' law applies.) But the equilibrium in the single-primed economy must be different since $\alpha'' \notin G(A')$, and this generally implies that individual 1 trades in the primed economy; thus $V_1(\alpha_1') > V_1(\bar{\alpha}_1) = V_1(\alpha_1'')$.

Proof of Proposition 3.11: Consider, in turn, WR1, WR2, WR3, and WR4, all with endowment neutrality.

WR1. Let $\bar{a}$ be any vector that A'' spans but A' does not. (For a Type III comparison it is easily shown that such a vector must exist.) Let $\alpha' \in G(A'') \cap G(A')$, $\sum_i \alpha_i' = (C, W)$, be some allocation. Using the principles applied in Proposition 3.6, construct some $\{V_i\}_i$ such that $A'\lambda_i' = A'\lambda_1'$, $i = 2, \ldots, I$, but $\bar{a} \cdot \lambda_i' \neq \bar{a} \cdot \lambda_k'$ for some i,k pair. It follows that $A''\lambda_i' \neq A''\lambda_k'$, i.e., α' is CPE relative to A' but not relative to A''. Put $\bar{\alpha} = \alpha'$ and α' is an equilibrium in the single-primed economy but not in the double-primed. WR1 now follows since $\alpha'' \neq \bar{\alpha} = \alpha'$ and thus $V_i(\alpha_i'') \geq V_i(\bar{\alpha}_i)$.

WR2. Again, use the identical-individuals example.

WR3. Let $I = 3$. Albeit tedious, the idea is to construct $\{V_i\}_i$, via the principles applied in the proof of Proposition 3.6, such that α'', α' are two equilibrium allocations sustained by $\bar{\alpha} \in G(A'') \cap G(A')$ where $\bar{\alpha}_1 = \alpha_1'$, $\bar{\alpha}_2 = \alpha_2''$, $\bar{\alpha}_3 \neq \alpha_3'$, and $\bar{\alpha}_3 \neq \alpha_3''$. (The degrees of freedom in $\{\rho_i, \pi_i, U_{is}^2\}_i$ suffice.) Having done this, the WR3 conclusion is immediate by the usual argument since $\bar{\alpha}_1 \neq \alpha_1''$ and $\bar{\alpha}_2 \neq \alpha_2'$.

WR4. This case is symmetric to WR1.

Proof of Proposition 3.12: Since $\max\{0,x\} = (|x|+x)/2$ it follows that

$$\max\{0, a_{ps} - k\} - \max\{0, k - a_{ps}\} - a_{ps} + k = 0 \text{ for all } s \in S.$$

Proof of Proposition 3.13. The augmented $S \times S$ matrix, A^*, can be written as

$$[a_{js}^*] = \begin{bmatrix} p(a_p; a_{p2}) \\ p(a_p; a_{p3}) \\ \cdot \\ \cdot \\ \cdot \\ p(a_p; a_{pS}) \\ a_p \end{bmatrix}$$

Since $a_p \geq 0$ and $a_{p1} < a_{p2} < \cdots < a_{pS}$, implying $a_{p2} > 0$, it is readily verified that $a_{11}^* > 0$ and $a_{1s}^* = 0$ when $s > 1$. Similarly, one verifies more generally that $a_{js}^* > 0$ if $s = j$ and $a_{js}^* = 0$ if $s > j$. Hence, the diagonal entries in A^* are all positive, and the matrix entries northeast off the diagonal are all zero. Such a matrix has full rank, so markets are complete.

The case of calls is equally straightforward. Write

$$A^* = \begin{bmatrix} a \\ c(a_p;a_{p1}) \\ c(a_p;a_{p2}) \\ \cdot \\ \cdot \\ \cdot \\ c(a_p;a_{pS-1}) \end{bmatrix}.$$

Given $a_{p1} > 0$, and $a_{p1} < a_{p2} < \cdots < a_{pS}$, it is readily shown that $a^*_{js} > 0$ if $j = s$, and $a^*_{js} = 0$ if $j > s$.

Proof of Proposition 3.14. This proof is purely a matter of linear algebra; see Ross (1976a, Proposition 4).

Proof of Proposition 3.15. Without loss of generality, suppose that the redundant security is the Jth one, and thus $a_J = \sum_{j \in J^-} k_j a_j$ for some constants k_j, $j = 1, \ldots, J - 1$; $J^- \equiv \{1, \ldots, J - 1\}$. It follows that $a_J \cdot R = \sum_{j \in J^-} k_j a_j \cdot R = \sum_{j \in J^-} k_j (a_j \cdot R)$. Hence, $P_J = \sum_{j \in J^-} k_j P_j$ since $P_j = a_j \cdot R$, and this proves the sufficiency part.

To prove necessity, note that $P_J = \sum_{j \in J^-} k_j P_j$ implies $\left(a_j - \sum_{j \in J^-} k_j a_j\right) \cdot \lambda_i = 0$ since $P_j = a_j \cdot \lambda_i$. The orthogonality condition must hold for all $\{V_i\}_i$, $\bar{\alpha}$, and this further implies that it must hold for all λ_i since λ_i varies in an unrestricted fashion (except that $\lambda_i > 0$) as $\{V_i\}_i$, $\bar{\alpha}$ vary across all possible settings (in which $\{V_i\}_i$ is MISC and $\bar{\alpha} \in G(A)$). It follows immediately that $a_J = \sum_{j \in J^-} k_j a_j$.

Proof of Proposition 3.18. Without loss of generality, consider Arrow-Debreu markets. The optimal pattern α_i can be expressed as:

$$w_{is}(\bar{\alpha}_i, R) = k_{1s}(\varphi_i, R) + k_{2s}(R)\bar{\bar{w}}_i(\bar{\alpha}_i, R) \quad (s = 0, 1, \ldots, S).$$

This follows from Eqs. (2.19), (2.20), and (2.25) in Chapter 2 (in which $\bar{\bar{w}}_i$ can replace $\bar{I}_i$ since $\rho U_i^2 = U_i^2$; recall the discussion following Eq. (2.33) in Chapter 2). By Definition 3.2 of an equilibrium, the proposition follows if there exists some $R = R'$ that clears markets for all $\bar{\alpha}$. This is equivalent to $\sum_i w_{is}(\bar{\alpha}_i, R')$ being independent of all $\bar{\alpha}$ satisfying $\sum_i \bar{\alpha}_i = (C, W)$. But the latter follows since $\bar{\bar{w}}_i(\bar{\alpha}_i, R) = \bar{c}_i + \bar{w}_i \cdot R$ and thus

$$\sum_i w_{is} = \sum_i k_{1s}(\varphi_i, R') + k_{2s}(R')[C + W \cdot R'] \text{ for all } s = 0, 1, \ldots, S.$$

Remark: Note the critical fact that k_{2s} cannot depend on i, while $k_{1is} = k_{1s}(\varphi_i, R)$ can.

Proof of Proposition 3.19. Let R'' be the implicit price system in the double-primed economy. Then

$$P' = TP'' = TA''R'' = A'R'',$$

where the first and last equalities are direct implications of the assumptions. The second follows from $P'' = A''R''$. Hence, R'' is also an implicit price system in the single-primed economy. Further, the existence of a matrix T such that $A' = TA''$ implies that A' spans a subspace of A''. The remainder of the proposition follows from Proposition 2.4, and the uniqueness of an optimal consumption pattern α_i (Proposition 2.2).

Proof of Proposition 3.21: Refer back to Proposition 3.7 and its proof:

$$w_{is} = k_{1i} + k_{2i} W_s, \quad s = 1, \ldots, S.$$

For case (i) $k_{1i} = 0$ so that $u_i^2(w_{is}) = \hat{k}_{2i} W_s^{-1/\beta}$ when $\hat{k}_{2i}$ is a constant. Further, $cov[\tilde{r}_j, \tilde{u}_i^2] = cov[\tilde{r}_j, \tilde{r}_M^{-1/\beta}] \times \hat{k}_{2i} \times P_M^{-1/\beta}$ for all j including $j = M$. The result now follows since $E[\tilde{r}_j] - R_F = \{cov[\tilde{r}_j, \tilde{u}_i^2]/cov[\tilde{r}_M, \tilde{u}_i^2]\}(E[\tilde{r}_M] - R_F)$ holds as a general expected excess return–relative risk relationship.

Similarly, for case (ii), $u_i^2(w_{is}) = \hat{k}_{1i} + \hat{k}_{2i} W_s$ and $cov[\tilde{r}_j, \tilde{u}_i^2] = cov[\tilde{r}_j, \hat{k}_{1i} + \hat{k}_{2i}\tilde{W}] = cov[\tilde{r}_j, \tilde{r}_M] \times \hat{k}_{2i} \times P_M$.

Remark: Note the peculiar feature of case (ii) (i.e., CAPM). The probability normalized implicit prices, λ_{is}/π_s, are functions *linear* in W_s.

Proof of Proposition 3.22. Refer back to the proof of Proposition 3.18 and Eq. (2.19), (2.20), and (2.25) in Chapter 2. The optimal solution of SP equals

$$w_{is} = w_s(\varphi_i, R, \bar{\bar{w}}_i) = \varphi_i K_{1s}(R) + k_{2s}(R)\bar{\bar{w}}_i, \quad s = 0, 1, \ldots, S.$$

Hence,

$$\sum_i w_{is} = \left(\sum_i \varphi_i\right) K_{1s}(R) + k_{2s}(R)[C + W \cdot R].$$

The result follows by dividing both sides by the number of individuals (I), since one individual with intercept parameter $\left(\sum_i \varphi_i\right)/I$ and endowments $(C, W)/I$ also demands $(C, W)/I$ at the same equilibrium prices as those in the original economy.

Remarks: Proposition 3.21 uses only portfolio separation, while Proposition 3.22 also uses the fact that w_{is} is linear in endowed wealth. (Recall the discussion on pp. 28–29 and 33 in Chapter 2.)

One can specify the composite individual by $\left(\sum_i \varphi_i\right)$, (C, W) rather than $\left(\sum_i \varphi_i\right)/I$, $(C, W)/I$. The implicit prices (and the risk-measure) do not depend on the "normalization" $1/I$.

CHAPTER FOUR

THE MICROANALYSIS OF INFORMATION

4.1. Information in the Portfolio Selection Problem

The headings of the previous two chapters reflect that the information available to individuals does not vary. The analysis simply presumes that individuals impound available information in their probabilities over state occurrences (which includes the perceived state space). But information does not affect the decision problem otherwise, and thus the information cannot bear directly on the analysis of the allocation of risks. The Chapter 3 comparative welfare analysis considers changes in markets and endowment distributions, and the efficiency analysis deals with the impact of markets alone. Intuition suggests that such a focus is too limited, since information should be no less important than markets. The economic justification for security markets stems from the existence of uncertainty and the need to allocate attendant risks; information identifies the perceived uncertainties, and therefore it may also affect the choice of a consumption pattern. A priori there is no reason to presume that markets cannot perform their role differently—and possibly also more efficiently—if individuals have better information about the environment in which decisions are made.[1]

The present chapter models information and evaluates the consequences of information on the individuals' consumption/portfolio selection problem. This microanalysis provides the insights needed for analyzing information in general equilibrium, the subject matter of the final chapter. In other words, Chapters 4 and 5 extend Chapters 2 and 3, respectively. Chap-

[1] The literature is replete with statements to the effect that "information reduces risk" and, in other instances, "information increases risk." Sweeping characterizations of information in these or similar terms are at best misleading.

ters 2 and 4 deal entirely with an individual's decision problem, while Chapters 3 and 5 extend the underlying microanalysis into settings of general equilibrium. Chapter 5 is not surprisingly entitled "General Equilibrium Analysis Under Varying Information."

The general idea of incorporating information into an economic model seems perhaps broad enough to suggest a multiplicity of approaches as far as characterizing information. Fortunately, such is not the case. The formal analysis of information, with which the ensuing section deals fully, follows a standardized framework. In spite of this, information has a multifaceted impact on economic problems; one can identify at least three potentially relevant consequences of information.

(i) The information available determines an individual's environmental knowledge. The observation of a signal—or "event"—virtually by definition changes an individual's conception of the environment. These changes are modeled formally as *probabilistic revisions conditioned on the realized signal.*

(ii) To model the *passage of time* one must model the observation of events. The changing environment in which an individual makes his decisions constitutes the essence of dynamic choice settings under uncertainty. Barring pathological cases, an uncertain change in the environment becomes necessary and sufficient for time to pass.

(iii) *Information may affect individuals' consumption opportunities.* Within the context of an individual choosing current consumption and security holdings, one identifies at least three potentially relevant aspects: (a) information permits an individual to make his plans contingent on the signals observed; (b) the prices of securities typically depend on the signals and the underlying information system; (c) closely related to (ii), the passage of time allows models with trading at several points in time.

Although all three points are valid, it should be stressed immediately that (iii) is by far the most significant factor in evaluating the effects of information. Throughout the analysis the primary and unifying question is: Precisely, how do an individual's consumption opportunities depend on his information? The consistency of this question with the developments in Chapters 2 and 3 is as obvious as it is appealing. The analysis of markets deals with the markets' impact on individual and aggregate consumption opportunities. Information analysis logically mirrors market analysis so that the results in the two areas reinforce each other. Because incomplete information is identical to the imposition of linear constraints on the consumption opportunity sets, analytical results relating to the theory of markets frequently apply to the theory of information as well. Although varying information does introduce new twists due to the "passage of time" phenomenon, the similarity in the roles of information and markets permits theoretical unity. The questions one raises about the effects of information differ little from those that concern markets, and the conditions providing answers are usually relatively easy to anticipate in light of the prior analysis of markets.

4.2. Formal Modeling of Information

Modern economics relies on a standardized framework in its modeling of information. The development here closely follows the succinct and general scheme introduced by Marschak and Radner (1972). There will be one difference, however. Marschak and Radner consider information within a rich variety of decision settings, including complex organizational forms labeled "teams." The analysis here restricts itself to the consumption/portfolio selection problem, that is, the individual faces appropriate extensions of the standard optimization problem introduced in Definition 2.2. Since analysis of financial markets constitutes the ultimate purpose, much is gained by proceeding to this decision problem specificity as soon as practical. Nevertheless, it should be stressed that the mathematical formalization of information (and "signals") does not depend on the decision setting. The scheme is totally general, and it applies in virtually all uncertainty models.

An *information structure,* or *information function,* is a function, η, defined on S that maps into a *signal,* y, for each $s \in S$. Thus, write $y = \eta(s)$. Let Y denote the set of all signals so that $y \in Y$. It is generally convenient to let the signals take on the integer values $y = 1, 2, \ldots, Y$. The convention loses no generality since the labeling of signals is unimportant. Further, similar to the symbol S, the dual use of the symbol Y should be no source of confusion. The standard notation for "the number of elements in a set X" is $|X|$, and for emphasis this notation is occasionally utilized as well ($|X|$ is also commonly said to be the cardinality of a set X).

The definition of an information function simply means that the signal observed is a function of the state that prevails. Although the true state is unknown, given some signal y the remaining uncertainty only admits a more restricted set of possibilities. The idea is usefully formalized. Every information function η *partitions* the state space S into a collection of mutually exclusive but exhaustive subsets: define $S_y \equiv \{s \mid \eta(s) = y, y \text{ fixed}\}$; then $S_y \cap S_{y'} = \phi$ when $y \neq y'$, and $\cup_y S_y = S$. The partition induced by η yields the collection of sets $\{S_1, \ldots, S_Y\}$. Conversely, an information function corresponds to every collection of mutually exclusive and exhaustive sets $\{S_y\}_y$. The set S_y contains the unknown state if and only if the signal y is observed. One frequently refers to a signal y, or a set S_y, as an *event*.

The two extreme partitions are of apparent interest. First, the information function $\eta(s) = s = y$ is *perfect*. The function η is now one-to-one so that the signal reveals the true state. Each set S_y has only one element. Throughout, η^* denotes the perfect information function.

Second, on the other extreme, *no information* applies when $\eta(s) = 1$ for all $s \in S$. The partition $\{S_1\} = \{S\}$ corresponds to the no-information case. For the no-information function the notation η^0 is used.

An information function η'' is (weakly) *more informative* (or *finer*) than η' if and only if the partition generated by η'' is a *subpartition* of the one generated by η'. That is, for each $y' \in Y'$ there exists some subset $\hat{Y}'' \subseteq Y''$, where $\hat{Y}''$ depends on y', such that

$$\bigcup_{y'' \in \hat{Y}''} S_{y''} = S_{y'}.$$

Alternatively, for each $y'' \in Y''$ there exists some $y' \in Y'$, where y' depends on y'', such that

$$S_{y''} \subseteq S_{y'}.$$

The terminology "more informative" captures the essence of a subpartition. If the true state is known to be an element of $S_{y''}$, then it is also known to be an element of $S_{y'}$, $S_{y''} \subseteq S_{y'}$. But the converse does not necessarily hold. Following the observation of any one signal, the unresolved uncertainty is therefore less for η'' than for η'.

The more-informativeness condition is weak when $\eta'' = \eta'$; accordingly, if η'' is more informative than η' and η'', η' are distinct, then η'' is *strictly* more informative than η'. Notice that η^* is no less informative than any other η, and every η is at least as informative as η^0.

A necessary but insufficient condition for η'' being more informative than η' is that $Y'' \geq Y'$. The sufficiency fails because information functions are not generally comparable on the informativeness dimension. (No great economic significance can be attached to the counting of possible signals.) More specifically, no fineness relationship exists between η'' and η' if $S_{y'} \cap S_{y''} \neq \phi$ for some $y' \in Y'$, $y'' \in Y''$ and where neither $S_{y''}$ nor $S_{y'}$ has a subset relationship to the other. In the comparison of information functions, the more-informativeness condition acts as a nontrivial restriction.[2]

The notions of information, signals, and informativeness have been defined without reference to the state and signal probabilities. Nevertheless, the marginal, joint, and conditional probabilities derive from the underlying probability vector $\pi > 0$ defined on S. One verifies the following relationships without difficulty:

$$\pi(y) = \pi(s \in S_y) = \sum_{s \in S_y} \pi(s)$$

[2] For example, if $S''_1 = \{1,2\}$, $S''_2 = \{3,4\}$, $S'_1 = \{1\}$, $S'_2 = \{2,3,4\}$, then $S''_1 \cap S'_2 = \{2\}$ and $S''_1 \not\subset S'_2$, $S'_2 \not\subset S''_1$; η'' and η' clearly do not have a fineness relationship.

$$\pi(s,y) = \begin{cases} \pi(s) & \\ & \text{if} \\ 0 & \end{cases} \quad \begin{matrix} s \in S_y \\ \\ s \notin S_y \end{matrix}$$

$$\pi(s/y) = \begin{cases} \pi(s)/\pi(y) & \\ & \text{if} \\ 0 & \end{cases} \quad \begin{matrix} s \in S_y \\ \\ s \notin S_y \end{matrix}$$

$$\pi(y/s) = \begin{cases} 1 & \\ & \text{if} \\ 0 & \end{cases} \quad \begin{matrix} s \in S_y \\ \\ s \notin S_y \end{matrix}$$

In the usual jargon, the $\{\pi(s)\}_s$ are the *prior* probabilities and the $\{\pi(s/y)\}_{s,y}$ are the *posterior* probabilities.

It may be of some value to note that if y'' and y' are the signals from two different information functions, then

$$\pi(y',y'') = \sum_{s \in S_{y'} \cap S_{y''}} \pi(s).$$

In addition, η'' is more informative than η' if and only if

$$\pi(y',y'') = \pi(y'') \text{ or zero.}$$

Alternatively,

$$\pi(y'/y'') = 0 \text{ or } 1 \text{ for all } y',y''.$$

The $\pi(y/s)$ probabilities equal either zero or one, reaffirming that a given state implies a certain signal. The setup constitutes a simple "true or false" scheme. Such a probabilistic structure at least superficially appears less than completely general. Additional generality would seem possible by allowing $0 < \pi(y/s) < 1$. Unlike the true/false scheme the information function now permits "noisy" as well as "noiseless" signals. However, the suggested generality is more apparent than real. To see this, simply note that $s = 1, \ldots, S$ indexes *all* uncertainty, *including* any "noise" associated with the observation of a signal. The issue reduces to the meaning and definition of a state space. Consider the following: suppose a "basic" state space $\hat{S}$ exists such that $0 < \pi(y/\hat{s}) < 1$ and where $\hat{s} \in \hat{S}$. One can then *define* S such that its typical element is the tuple $(\hat{s},y) = s$ (these elements can be relabled to make $s = 1, \ldots, S$, where $S = |\hat{S}| \times |Y|$). The procedure directly implies that $\pi(y/s)$ equals either zero or one, and this reinstates the simple original "true or false" setup. (Although the appropriate (re-)definition of state space ensures the generality of information being treated as a simple function of the states, the concept of noisy information is still relevant. Chapter 5 considers the precise meaning of noisy information and its implications.)

4.3. Information, the Evaluation of Expected Utility, and Attainable Consumption Patterns

Information has economic significance because plans can be made contingent on observable signals. Modifying the notation of Chapter 2, let c_y, z_{jy}, $y \in Y, j \in J$ denote such a signal contingent plan associated with the information function η. More compactly, write $z_y \equiv (z_{1y}, \ldots, z_{Jy})$ and define a plan by $\gamma(\eta) \equiv \{c_y, z_y\}_y$. A description of the plan thus specifies holdings for all $y \in Y$. On a more fundamental level, since $y = \eta(s)$ every plan $\gamma(\eta)$ may be viewed as a function of the state: $\gamma(\eta) = \{c(\eta(s)), z(\eta(s))\}_s$. With some slight abuse of notation, the "intermediate" function η can be suppressed; one then succinctly denotes a plan by $\{(c(s), z(s)\}_s$ $(= \gamma(\eta))$, although the implicit presence of the information function must be kept firmly in mind. The terse notation is unequivocal as long as the functions $\{c(s), z(s)\}_s$ are understood to be *measurable* relative to the partition associated with the information function η: $c(s) = c(t)$ and $z_j(s) = z_j(t)$, all $j \in J$, whenever $s,t \in S_y$. *The information function puts simple linear restrictions on the degree to which plans may vary across different states.* In other words, for the consumption/portfolio plan to be compatible with the available information, the decision setting must satisfy a set of related linear restrictions. The extreme information functions η^* and η^0 illustrate the point. η^* imposes no restrictions on the functions $\{c(s), z(s)\}_s$, while for η^0 each of these functions map into the same number for all s. Consistent with Chapter 2, $\eta = \eta^0$ makes s-dependent notation on plans superfluous.

A number of essentially equivalent ways states the expected utility associated with a signal contingent plan, $V(\gamma(\eta))$. At the most basic level, V equals

$$V(\gamma(\eta)) = \sum_s \pi(s) U_s \left[c(s), \sum_j a_{js} z_j(s)\right].$$

As mentioned previously, the plan $\{c(s), z(s)\}_s$ must be measurable relative to the partition induced by the function η. To recognize η and measurability explicitly one expresses V as

$$V(\gamma(\eta)) = \sum_s \pi(s) U_s \left[c(\eta(s)), \sum_j a_{js} z_j(\eta(s))\right].$$

Emphasizing the plan's dependency on signals rather than on states leads to the following possibilities:

$$V(\gamma(\eta)) = \sum_y \sum_s \pi(s,y) U_s \left[c_y, \sum_j a_{js} z_{jy}\right]$$

$$= \sum_y \sum_{s \in S_y} \pi(s,y) U_s \left[c_y, \sum_j a_{js} z_{jy}\right],$$

since $\pi(s,y) = 0$ when $s \notin S_y$. Further, since $\pi(s,y) = \pi(y)\pi(s/y)$,

$$V(\gamma(\eta)) = \sum_y \pi(y) \left\{ \sum_{s \in S_y} \pi(s/y) U_s \left[c_y, \sum_j a_{js} z_{jy} \right] \right\}.$$

The expression inside { } represents the *y-conditional expected utility*.

The emphasis so far has been on how signals/states dependent plans map into an expected utility evaluation. The analysis extends to an articulation of the relationship between attainable consumption patterns and information functions. As will be demonstrated, more information effectively loosens the constraints on the available mixes of current and future consumption. The developments require a certain care, however. The market structure also constrains the available future consumption mix, so the disentanglement of information and market structure constraints introduces some complexities. At any rate, the resulting attainability constraints merely identify the minimal "extrabudget" constraints; the specification of an individual's consumption opportunity set in its entirety must await budget constraints modeling.

The effect of information on current consumption is obvious and direct. As demonstrated previously, the S-dimensional vector c must be measurable relative to η, that is, $s, t \in S_y$ implies $c(s) = c(t)$. Clearly, a more informative η imposes fewer linear restrictions on the current consumption vector c.

To identify the restrictions on the date-one consumption vector associated with the (A,η) pair one needs a certain machinery. Assume that η is nondecreasing; an appropriate (re-)labeling of signals ensures no loss of generality. (Thus, $S_1 = \{1,2, \ldots, n_1\}$, $S_2 = \{n_1 + 1, \ldots, n_2\}$ and so forth; $n_1 < n_2 < \ldots$.) This convention about η permits a restatement of the matrix A in terms of Y adjacent submatrices:

$$A = [A_1 \ldots A_y \ldots A_Y].$$

The submatrix A_y "carves out" of A only those columns, indexed by s, for which $s \in S_y$. Accordingly, A_y has J rows, and the number of columns equals the number of elements in the set S_y; that is, A_y is $J \times |S_y|$. In less technical terms, the submatrix A_y defines the relevant payoff matrix after signal y has been observed.

The S-dimensional vector w can be decomposed in a fashion similar to A. Let $\underline{w}_y$ denote the row vector that includes only those elements of w satisfying $s \in S_y$. Then $w = (\underline{w}_1, \ldots, \underline{w}_y, \ldots, \underline{w}_Y)$ since η is nondecreasing. The vector $\underline{w}_y$ has dimension $|S_y|$, and the notation emphasizes that $\underline{w}_y$ is a vector (as opposed to w_s). Armed with these constructs one obtains

$$\underline{w}_y = z_y A_y, \qquad y = 1, \ldots, Y.$$

The attainability of a date-one pattern w accordingly depends on the opportunities available for each y: the matrix A breaks up into adjacent submatrices, and w breaks up into adjacent subvectors. The conditioning of the plan on y, z_y, establishes the connection between A_y and $\underline{w}_y$.

The set of attainable w can be expressed more compactly. Let $\delta(A,\eta)$ denote the matrix resulting from a block-diagonalization of A when η induces the decomposition of A into adjacent submatrices:

$$\delta(A,\eta) \equiv \begin{bmatrix} A_1 & & & & \\ & \cdot & & & \\ & & A_y & & \\ & & & \cdot & \\ & & & & A_Y \end{bmatrix}.$$

The entries off the block-diagonal all equal zero. The matrix $\delta(A,\eta)$ has $J \times Y$ rows and S columns. A vector w is now attainable if and only if there exists some row vector $\underline{z}_1$, with $J \times Y$ elements, such that

$$w = \underline{z}_1 \delta(A,\eta).$$

The vector $\underline{z}_1$ is usefully thought of as the vector resulting from an adjacent ordering of $\{z_y\}_y$ into one "supervector," that is, $\underline{z}_1 \equiv (z_1, \ldots, z_y, \ldots, z_Y) \equiv (z_{jy})_{y,j}$.[3] Hence, *given* (A,η) *the block-diagonalized matrix* $\delta(A,\eta)$ *spans attainable* w. Formally, attainable w are contained in the set

$$C(\delta(A,\eta)) \equiv \{w | w = \underline{z}_1 \delta(A,\eta), \quad \text{all } \underline{z}_1\}.$$

The "span-operator" $C(\cdot)$, which defines the vector space generated by the row vectors in the matrix constituting the operator's argument, will be used throughout.

Similar algebra restates the measurability condition on current consumption. Let 1 and c be S-dimensional vectors, and let $\underline{z}_0 \equiv (z_{01}, \ldots, z_{0Y})$ be a Y-dimensional row vector. Measurability of $\{c(s)\}_s$ relative to η then obtains if and only if c is an element of the set

$$C(\delta(1,\eta)) \equiv \{c | c = \underline{z}_0 \delta(1,\eta), \quad \text{all } \underline{z}_0\}.$$

The set of attainable consumption patterns therefore satisfies the following two conditions:

(i) $c \in C(\delta(1,\eta))$
(ii) $w \in C(\delta(A,\eta))$.

The conditions (i) and (ii) combine conveniently into the requirement that the $2 \times S$ dimensional vector α is in the span of the block-diagonal matrix

$$A_{e,\eta} \equiv \begin{bmatrix} \delta(1,\eta) & 0 \\ 0 & \delta(A,\eta) \end{bmatrix}.$$

---

[3] The notation $(x_{ij})_{j,i}$ denotes a vector $(x_{11}, x_{21}, x_{31}, \ldots, x_{12}, x_{22}, x_{32}, \ldots)$. Note that the order of j,i in $(.)_{j,i}$ determines the definition.

One reads $A_{e,\eta}$ as "the extension of the payoff matrix A given the information function η." The matrix has $Y + J \times Y$ rows and $2 \times S$ columns. Consistent with the number of columns in $A_{e,\eta}$, α has $2 \times S$ elements so one may indeed state that attainable patterns satisfy $\alpha \in C(A_{e,\eta})$.

A numerical example illustrating the derivation of $\delta(A,\eta)$, $\delta(1,\eta)$ and $A_{e,\eta}$ may be useful. Consider

$$A = \begin{bmatrix} 1 & 2 & 3 & 4 & 5 \\ 2 & 3 & 4 & 5 & 6 \end{bmatrix}.$$

Let $\eta(s) = 1$ if $s = 1, 2$, and $\eta(s) = 2$ if $s = 3, 4, 5$. It follows that

$$A_1 = \begin{bmatrix} 1 & 2 \\ 2 & 3 \end{bmatrix}, \; A_2 = \begin{bmatrix} 3 & 4 & 5 \\ 4 & 5 & 6 \end{bmatrix},$$

and

$$\delta(A,\eta) = \begin{bmatrix} 1 & 2 & 0 & 0 & 0 \\ 2 & 3 & 0 & 0 & 0 \\ 0 & 0 & 3 & 4 & 5 \\ 0 & 0 & 4 & 5 & 6 \end{bmatrix}.$$

Further,

$$\delta(1,\eta) = \begin{bmatrix} 1 & 1 & 0 & 0 & 0 \\ 0 & 0 & 1 & 1 & 1 \end{bmatrix}.$$

Hence, the span of the matrix

$$A_{e,\eta} = \begin{bmatrix} 1 & 1 & 0 & 0 & 0 & 0 & 0 & 0 & 0 & 0 \\ 0 & 0 & 1 & 1 & 1 & 0 & 0 & 0 & 0 & 0 \\ 0 & 0 & 0 & 0 & 0 & 1 & 2 & 0 & 0 & 0 \\ 0 & 0 & 0 & 0 & 0 & 2 & 3 & 0 & 0 & 0 \\ 0 & 0 & 0 & 0 & 0 & 0 & 0 & 3 & 4 & 5 \\ 0 & 0 & 0 & 0 & 0 & 0 & 0 & 4 & 5 & 6 \end{bmatrix}$$

generates every attainable consumption vector $\alpha = (c_1, \ldots, c_5, w_1, \ldots, w_5)$.

Note that $C(\delta(A,\eta^0)) = C(A)$ since $\delta(A,\eta^0) = A$; the special no-information case integrates smoothly into the analysis. Furthermore, $C(A) \subseteq C(\delta(A,\eta))$ for every η and A. This observation follows immediately since $z_1 = \ldots = z_y = \ldots = z_Y \equiv z$ implies that $\underline{z}_1\delta(A,\eta) = zA$. The more general relationship asserts that if η'' is at least as informative as η', then

$$C(\delta(A,\eta')) \subseteq C(\delta(A,\eta''))$$

and

$$C(A_{e,\eta'}) \subseteq C(A_{e,\eta''}).$$

A formal proof relies on the same idea as the no-information case. For any $\{z_{y'}\}_{y'}$ put $z_{y''} = z_{y'}$ for all $y'' \in \hat{Y}''$ where $S_{y'} = \bigcup_{y'' \in \hat{Y}''} S_{y''}$; one then verifies easily that $\underline{z}_1'$ and $\underline{z}_1''$ satisfy $\underline{z}_1'\delta(A,\eta') = \underline{z}_1''\delta(A,\eta'')$. Similarly, one can show that $C(A'_{e,\eta}) \subseteq C(A''_{e,\eta})$ if $C(A') \subseteq C(A'')$, any η, so that

$$C(A'_{e,\eta'}) \subseteq C(A''_{e,\eta''})$$

if η'' is at least as informative as η'.

Chapter 2 introduces complete markets because they prompt unrestricted mixes of w. This idea extends naturally to informative information functions.

DEFINITION 4.1. CONDITIONALLY COMPLETE MARKETS. *A market structure A is conditionally complete relative to an information function η if $\delta(A,\eta)$ spans all of S-dimensional space, that is*

$$C(I) = C(\delta(A,\eta)).$$

Of course, conditionally complete markets (CCM) reduce to complete markets in the case $\eta = \eta^0$. Further note that with $\eta \neq \eta^0$ A need not be of full rank for (A,η) to fulfill CCM. As an extreme example, suppose $J = 1$ and $A = [a_1] > 0$, then $([a_1], \eta^*)$ is CCM.

Just as complete markets perform a critical role in the two-date economy without information, conditionally complete markets are of interest in the more general theory. Subsequent analyses frequently rely on this concept.

4.4 Budget Constraints and Standard Problems

The discussion in the previous section demonstrates that more information relaxes the constraints determining the attainable mixes of consumption patterns. A further suggested implication is that more information should be no worse than less. Although such a proposition appeals to common sense, the delineation of appropriate conditions is not completely obvious. An individual's available consumption opportunities also directly relate to his endowments and budget restrictions. The budget restrictions, in turn, depend on prices and how they vary with changes in the information function and signals. With budget restrictions being sensitive to the information functions—which should be expected in a setting of general equilibrium—more information could conceivably make an individual worse off. What actually happens depends upon the relationship between prices and information/signals, and the nature of the budget constraints. As it turns out, several reasonable "standard problems" can be modeled, depending on how one conceptualizes the budget constraints. This section considers three distinct possibilities.

It will be notationally convenient to let "security 0" denote current consumption, and define $J^+ \equiv \{0, 1, \ldots, J\}$. In view of this convention, let

$c_y \equiv z_{oy}$ and $\gamma(\eta) \equiv \{z_{jy}\}_{j\in J^+, y\in Y}$. (Recall that the Y-dimensional vector $(c_y)_y$ is distinct from the S-dimensional vector $(c_s)_s$.) Let P_{jy} denote the price of security j given some signal y, where $j \in J^+$, $y \in Y$, and the related information function is implicit. (The notation $P_{jy}(\eta)$, $z_{jy}(\eta)$ and $y \in Y_\eta$ is less ambiguous but too awkward.)

The simplest possible standard problem, SP-1, extends the SP introduced in Definition 2.2 by letting the individual choose a portfolio $\{z_{jy}\}_{j\in J^+}$ for each y, and for each y there is a separate budget constraint.

DEFINITION 4.2. STANDARD PROBLEM 1. *The individual solves*

$$\max_{\{z_{jy}\}_{j,y}} V(\gamma(\eta))$$

subject to

$$\sum_{j\in J^+} z_{jy}P_{jy} \leq \sum_{j\in J^+} \bar{z}_j P_{jy} \equiv \bar{\bar{w}}_y, \qquad y = 1, \ldots, Y.$$

In Standard Problem 1 (SP-1), the vector $(P_{jy})_{j\in J^+}$ can be rescaled arbitrarily for each y, and leave the consumption opportunity set intact. For example, the security price vector $(1, P_{1y}/P_{0y}, \ldots, P_{Jy}/P_{0y})$ effectively equates the original one. (Even so, the convention $P_{0y} = 1$ is not particularly useful.)

The important property of SP-1 is the disconnectedness of the Y budget constraints: the optimal plan contingent on one particular signal does not relate to the optimal plan for other signals. To be more precise, the choice of $(z_{jy})_{j\in J^+}$ depends on $\{P_{jy}\}_j$ and $\bar{\bar{w}}_y$, but not on $\{P_{jy'}\}_j$ and $\bar{\bar{w}}_{y'}$, $y' \neq y$. Further note that the endowed wealth is generally random because the prices are random. The two observations indicate a curious and confining aspect of SP-1. The individual does not have the opportunity to implement any coordinated plans in *anticipation* of the uncertain forthcoming signal. In a sense, SP-1 simply structures the decision setting into Y disjoint standard problems, and the resolution of signal uncertainty identifies the setting in which the individual finds himself.

However, a modification of the SP-1 consumption/portfolio choice problem is possible so that the anticipation of signals, and their price implications, becomes crucial in the optimal choice. To implement this idea, one allows for a *prior* round of trading in the J^+ securities. Let $\{\hat{P}_j\}_{j\in J^+}$ be the prior round security prices, and let $\hat{z} \equiv (\hat{z}_0, \ldots, \hat{z}_J)$ be the portfolio of prior round security holdings. As stated in the next definition, a second standard problem, SP-2, models two trading rounds.

DEFINITION 4.3. STANDARD PROBLEM 2. *The individual solves*

$$\max_{\{\hat{z}_j\}_j\{z_{jy}\}_{j,y}} V(\gamma(\eta))$$

subject to

$$\sum_{j\in J^+} \hat{z}_j\hat{P}_j \leq \sum_{j\in J^+} \bar{z}_j\hat{P}_j \equiv \bar{\bar{w}},$$

$$\sum_{j\in J^+} z_{jy}P_{jy} \leq \sum_{j\in J^+} \hat{z}_jP_{jy}, \qquad y = 1, \ldots, Y.$$

In words, the "preliminary" portfolio choice, $\hat{z}$, occurs in a prior trading round, and, given some y, the "final" holdings $\{z_{jy}\}_{j\in J^+}$ are chosen in the posterior trading round. Although the posterior round budget constraint is random, the individual *rationally anticipates* what to do under *all* contingencies. The optimization requires the choice of $\hat{z}$ to reflect fully the signal uncertainty. Further, in contrast to SP-1, the choice of $\{z_{jy}\}_{j\in J^+}$ *does* depend on the prices $\{P_{jy'}\}_{j\in J^+}$ $(y' \neq y)$. SP-2 incorporates an element of time passage qualitatively different from SP-1 since the individual has to "plan ahead" in the words' real sense. For this reason, one refers to SP-2 as a *sequential* or *dynamic* consumption/portfolio selection problem.

The introduction of a prior trading round seemingly enlarges an individual's consumption opportunities as compared to SP-1. Subject to the condition that the prices $\{P_{jy}\}_{j,y}$ are (effectively) the same in SP-1 and SP-2, this observation follows immediately since by restricting $\hat{z} = \bar{z}$ SP-2 reduces to SP-1. All policies in SP-1 are thus also available in SP-2, regardless of $\{\hat{P}_j\}_j$. Accordingly, the maximum expected utility of SP-2 is no less than that of SP-1. The potentially greater expected utility of SP-2 relative to SP-1 may be interpreted as a gain due to the possibility of coordinating security holdings across signals.

Generally, SP-1 and SP-2 differ even when the two settings have identical signal-conditioned prices. The solutions and expected utilities should therefore also generally be distinct. However, SP-1 and SP-2 become identical problems under an additional condition on prices. Suppose that the $\{P_{jy}\}_{j,y}$ effectively are nonrandom and independent of y, that is, the relative prices P_{jy}/P_{0y} do not vary with y. To prevent arbitrage in SP-2, the restriction on prices further implies that $\hat{P}_j/\hat{P}_0 = P_{jy}/P_{0y}$. If relative prices do not depend on the signal, then they must be the same prior to the signal. The absence of a price change between the two trading rounds eliminates the need for trading in the first round, and the first-round policy $\hat{z} = \bar{z}$ is consistent with optimality. Consequently, the consumption opportunity sets, and the solutions, of SP-1 and SP-2 are identical.

The SP-1 (SP-2) problem with signal independent prices/wealth is of interest because the individual's information can be thought of as private. As one would expect, more information is no worse than less in a private information setting.

PROPOSITION 4.1. *Let η'' be an information function at least as fine as η'. Suppose further that the information function and signals do not* *affect the security prices in SP-1 (or SP-2). Then*

$V(\alpha'') \geq V(\alpha')$

*where α'' and α' denote the two optimal consumption patterns, respectively.**

The result is a direct implication of the seminal "fineness theorem" due to Marschak and Radner (1972): more information does no harm, provided that the parameters delimiting the opportunity set (prices, wealth) are unaffected. Hence, $CO'' \supseteq CO'$ if η'' is more informative than η'. In the spirit of the fineness theorem, for the result $V'' \geq V'$, V arbitrary, to hold one can also show that η'' needs to be more informative than η'. Such strong restrictions on the information functions can be removed only by confining the set of permissible preference beliefs. (In the extreme, for certain classes of preferences/beliefs every setting results in the same relative expected utility evaluation for any two information/markets pairs; see page 127 and Appendix 5.2.)

At first glance, the developments leading to Proposition 4.1 appear to parallel and possibly generalize those of Chapter 2 and Proposition 2.4: just as more markets potentially improve an individual's welfare, so does more information. The suggestion is not, however, appropriate for SP-1 (SP-2) and Proposition 4.1. At least two arguments mitigate against such an interpretation. First, in the key result of Chapter 2, Proposition 2.4, market enrichment implies greater potential expected utility in a setting constrained by only *one* budget constraint. The SP-1 and SP-2 problems do not have this property, and the enlargement of opportunities in Propositions 2.4 and 4.1 occur for different reasons. Second, in Chapter 2, more markets are weakly preferable to fewer given constant *implicit* prices. The current chapter has not yet introduced implicit prices. Although this omission will be rectified shortly, one may conjecture here that constant implicit prices differs generally from information/signal independent security prices. (Section 5.5 in Chapter 5 shows that constant implicit prices do not imply, but are implied by, the information/signal independence condition of Proposition 4.1.) Moreover, in Proposition 4.1 a weakening of the hypothesis from constant security prices to constant implicit prices is *not* possible. (Section 5.5 discusses this matter also.) One must therefore conclude that the economics leading to Proposition 2.4 develops from reasoning different from that in the "fineness proposition," Proposition 4.1. The broader implication is that the equilibrium analysis in Chapter 5 does not proceed from SP-1. Nor does SP-2 provide the most convenient starting point. This is not to say that SP-1 and SP-2 should be dismissed as theoretically irrelevant in the equilibrium analysis. To the contrary, the next chapter considers both SP-1 and SP-2 in equilibrium, and much of the emphasis deals with SP-2. Nevertheless, a third consumption/portfolio setting will be introduced, the advantages of which stem from its ability to unify the theory. A general framework paralleling Chapter 2, including the identification and usage of implicit prices, departs from a third standard problem.

DEFINITION 4.4. STANDARD PROBLEM 3. *The individual solves*

$$\max_{\{z_{jy}\}_{j,y}} V(\gamma(\eta))$$

subject to

$$\sum_y \sum_j z_{jy} P_{jy} \leq \sum_y \sum_j \bar{z}_j P_{jy} \equiv \bar{\bar{w}}$$

The critical attribute of Standard Problem 3 (SP-3) should be accentuated: the problem has only one budget constraint. The similarity of SP-3 to Chapter 2's SP is as striking as its contrast to SP-1 and SP-2. The SP-3 budget constraint follows from an aggregation of the Y SP-1 constraints, while SP-2 has $Y + 1$ intertwined constraints. The existence of a single constraint permits optimal synchronization of allocations across signals. Because of this, one refers to the SP-3 investment/consumption problem as a fully *signal-coordinated* decision setting.

4.5. The Signal-Coordinated Decision Setting and Implicit Prices

The potential theoretical appeal of SP-3 should not overshadow the fact that the choice setting appears to be contrived and at variance with how one ought to model "real world" signal-dependent trading. In the "real world" the amount of wealth available for consumption/investment changes with time and depends upon the events and decisions made in the past. The idea of one, and only one, portfolio allocation constraint obscures the dynamic element that comes with executing decisions subsequent to, as well as in anticipation of, the observation of events. SP-2 is of interest precisely because it models a dynamic decision environment. The SP-2 model serves as a natural prototype and, arguably, is the only realistic extension of the simple two-date SP setting. SP makes sense only because the individual's information does not change; the generalization SP-2 reflects that time passes because of information, and the individual accordingly needs to revise his portfolio.

However, SP-2 and SP-3 have a common salient feature that justifies the analysis of SP-3: the anticipation of signals necessitates a prior evaluation of the contingent plans' interactive effects across signals. This anticipatory structure of SP-2 and SP-3 is absent in SP-1, since in the latter case the choice of $\{z_{jy}\}_{j \in J^+}$ derives separately for each y. The SP-2 and SP-3 settings have enough in common to make them more similar than different. As a result, the contrived nature and empirical implausibility of SP-3 is less of a problem than what one might at first expect. The next section reconciles SP-

2 with SP-3. Under certain interesting conditions SP-2 and SP-3 end up being completely identical; under all conditions they are "structurally similar," where "structurally similar" can be made usefully precise. Thus, although the remainder of this section discusses SP-3 exclusively, insights obtained facilitate the analysis of SP-2's consumption opportunity set.

Deriving implicit prices for SP-3 involves no great difficulty. There is, however, a slight difference compared to the SP. The SP equals SP-3 given that $\eta = \eta^0$, and it has only one date-zero consumption good. With varying information, which includes perfect information as a special case, one identifies potentially S date-zero consumption goods since date-zero consumption may vary across all states. To handle all conceivable partitions, the analysis must price each of potentially S date-zero goods. In addition, the S-dimensional date-one consumption vector is priced in the usual fashion. Associated with each date is therefore an implicit price vector of dimension S. Denote the two column vectors by $R_0 \equiv (R_{01}, \ldots, R_{0s}, \ldots, R_{0S})$ and $R_1 \equiv (R_{11}, \ldots, R_{1s}, \ldots, R_{1S})$, respectively. Thus, the cost of a unit of date-zero (date-one) consumption in state s equals $R_{0s}(R_{1s})$. For either date, not all consumption mixes are necessarily attainable. Nevertheless, as discussed in Chapter 2, having more prices than the dimensionality of attainable mixes poses no problems.

The conceptualization of a valid vector of implicit prices for an arbitrary information function does not differ from Chapter 2. The exercise that derives the implicit prices basically turns into one of notation. Define $P_y \equiv (P_{1y}, \ldots, P_{Jy})$, $y = 1, \ldots, Y$, as a column vector, and $\underline{P}_1 \equiv (P_1^t, \ldots, P_y^t, \ldots, P_Y^t)^t$ as the column "supervector" obtained by aligning the P_y^t row vectors adjacent to each other. Similarly, for date-zero 'securities' define the Y-dimensional column vector $\underline{P}_0 \equiv (P_{01}, \ldots, P_{0y}, \ldots, P_{0Y})^t$. Let $\underline{P} \equiv (\underline{P}_0^t, \underline{P}_1^t)^t$ be a column vector with $(Y + 1) \times J$ elements. Using a similar scheme, let $\underline{z} \equiv (\underline{z}_0, \underline{z}_1)$ where $\underline{z}_0$ and $\underline{z}_1$ are row vectors as defined in section 4.3. With this notation, one states concisely the budget constraint as

$$\underline{z} \cdot \underline{P} \leq \bar{\bar{w}}(= \bar{\underline{z}} \cdot \underline{P}). \tag{4.1}$$

The tuple $(A_{e,\eta}, \underline{P})$ describes the market characteristics associated with SP-3. Further, since $\alpha = \underline{z}A_{e,\eta}$ it follows that $(R_0^t, R_1^t)^t \equiv R > 0$ constitutes an implicit price vector if and only if

$$\underline{P} = A_{e,\eta}R. \tag{4.2}$$

Substituting Eq. (4.2) into Eq. (4.1) transforms the budget constraint into the available choices of α:

$$\underline{z} \cdot \underline{P} = \underline{z} \cdot A_{e,\eta}R = \alpha \cdot R \equiv c \cdot R_0 + w \cdot R_1 \equiv \sum_s (c_s R_{0s} + w_s R_{1s}) \leq \bar{\bar{w}}, \tag{4.3}$$

provided further that $\alpha \in C(A_{e,\eta})$. ($\bar{\bar{w}} = \bar{\alpha} \cdot R$ where $\bar{\alpha} \equiv \bar{\underline{z}}A_{e,\eta}$.)

The nonuniqueness of R is no cause for concern. The discussion in Chapter 2 still applies. That is, $\alpha \cdot R$ ends up being unique for all valid R when $A_{e,\eta}$ spans α. (Technically, if $A_{e,\eta}R' = A_{e,\eta}R''$ then $\alpha \cdot R' = \alpha \cdot R''$ provided that $\alpha \in C(A_{e,\eta})$.)

Equation (4.2) somewhat obscures the structure of implicit prices. The underlying relationship between $\underline{P}$ and R is brought out more clearly by noting that

$$P_{0y} = \sum_{s \in S_y} R_{0s}, \qquad y = 1, \ldots, Y,$$

that is, $\underline{P}_0 = \delta(1,\eta)R_0$. Further,

$$P_{jy} = \sum_{s \in S_y} a_{js}R_{1s}, \qquad y = 1, \ldots, Y, j = 1, \ldots, J,$$

which one summarizes by $\underline{P}_1 = \delta(A,\eta)R_1$. The most useful normalization of the prices puts $\sum_s R_{0s} = \sum_y \sum_{s \in S_y} R_{0s} = \sum_y P_{0y} = 1$: assign a value of \$1 to one *unconditional* unit of date-zero consumption. (This scheme includes the normalization used in Chapters 2 and 3 as a special case.) The value of a date-one security pattern a_j equals $a_j \cdot R_1 = \sum_s a_{js}R_{1s} = \sum_y \sum_{s \in S_y} a_{js}R_{1s} = \sum_y P_{jy}$, that is, the values of *signal*-contingent claims summed over signals add up to the value of the payoff pattern a_j. The analysis of portfolios yields an identical "sum of the parts equals the whole" conclusion.

As indicated, the structural difference between the SP of Chapter 2 and SP-3 mostly reduces to notation. In the SP, α is $S + 1$ dimensional, while in SP-3 α is $2 \times S$ dimensional. Similarly, the SP has $J + 1$ "direct" choice variables while in SP-3 these variables number $Y \times (J + 1)$. In both settings, the dimensions of the implicit price vector and the security price vector are consistent with the dimensionalities of the consumption/security choices. An important implication emerges: *the results associated with the SP in Chapter 2 extend to SP-3*. As immediate consequences of Propositions 2.1, 2.2, and 2.3, one has:

PROPOSITION 4.2. *SP-3 excludes arbitrage opportunities if and only if there exists a positive implicit price vector R such that $\underline{P} = A_{e,\eta}R$.**

PROPOSITION 4.3. *Given the conditions on V stated in Proposition 2.2, SP-3 has a unique optimal solution α if and only if there is no arbitrage. Further, the optimal plan $\{z_{jy}\}_{j,y}$ is unique if and only if $A_{e,\eta}$ has only linearly independent rows.**

PROPOSITION 4.4. *There exists a CCC-problem equivalent to SP-3.**

The specific structure of $A_{e,\eta}$ sharpens the contents of Propositions 4.2 and 4.3. First, no arbitrage applies if and only if, (i) $\underline{P}_0 > 0$ and (ii) there exists some $R_1 > 0$ such that $\underline{P}_1 = \delta(A,\eta)R_1$. Second, $\underline{z}_0$ is always unique, further implying a unique $\underset{\sim}{z}$ if and only if $\underset{\sim}{z}_1$ is unique. The latter holds if and only if each of the submatrices $\{A_y\}_y$ has only linearly independent rows.

The requirement that α satisfies the budget constraint (Eq. (4.3)) subject to $\alpha \in C(A_{e,\eta})$ can be stated equivalently as a constrained contingent commodity problem. Specifically,

$$\max_{\alpha} V(\alpha)$$

$$s.t.\ \alpha \cdot R \leq \bar{\bar{w}},$$

and

$$\alpha \begin{bmatrix} B_0 & 0 \\ 0 & B_1 \end{bmatrix} = 0.$$

The extrabudget constraints reduce to $cB_0 = 0$ and $wB_1 = 0$. The matrices B_0 and B_1 generate spaces complementary to, respectively, those of $\delta(1,\eta)$ and $\delta(A,\eta)$. That is, $\delta(1,\eta)B_0 = 0$, $\delta(A,\eta)B_1 = 0$, $\dim(B_0) = S - Y$ (since $\dim(\delta(1,\eta)) = Y$), and $\dim(B_1) = S - \dim(\delta(A,\eta))$. It follows that B_0 vanishes if and only if η is perfect; B_1 vanishes if and only if (A,η) is a conditionally complete market. Of course, the presence of B_0, B_1 constraint matrices does not imply that they are always binding. Chapter 3 extensively exploits a similar observation made about SP. Not surprisingly, much of the analysis in Chapter 5 considers this possibility of non-binding constraints.

The most important Chapter 2 extension generalizes Proposition 2.4: enriched markets, *or* enriched information, makes the individual weakly better off. Of course, the statement does not make sense unless one fixes the underlying values in the two settings. Thus, like Proposition 2.4, implicit prices remain constant. The result then follows simply because $C(A''_{e,\eta''}) \supseteq C(A'_{e,\eta'})$ when η'' is at least as informative as η' and $C(A'') \supseteq C(A')$.

PROPOSITION 4.5. *Consider SP-3 with fixed implicit prices. If η'' is at least as informative as η' and $C(A'') \supseteq C(A')$, then*

$$V(\alpha'') \geq V(\alpha')$$

*where α'' and α' denote the two optimal consumption patterns.**

Holding the markets as well as the implicit prices constant, more information is (weakly) better than less.

COROLLARY 4.5.1. *Given any fixed implicit prices and markets in SP-3, more information is weakly preferred to less.**

The proposition and corollary convey the similarity between markets and information in an SP-3 setting. *Both markets and information delineate the set of attainable consumption patterns in terms of linear constraints. An enrichment of either or both relaxes these constraints.*

Only one distinction between markets and information needs elucidation. A change in the information function with fixed markets always changes the SP-3 problem; on the other hand, with fixed information market matrices may differ yet imply the same SP-3: $C(A') = C(A'')$ suffices for $C(A'_{e,\eta}) = C(A''_{e,\eta})$ even though A' may not equal A''. But $\eta'' \neq \eta'$ implies $C(A_{e,\eta''}) \neq C(A_{e,\eta'})$. The latter nonequality applies since $C(\delta(1,\eta'')) = C(\delta(1,\eta'))$ if and only if $\eta'' = \eta'$. Accordingly, Corollary 2.4.1 does not extend directly to varying information. If, however, for some reason $c'' = c'$ in addition to $C(\delta(A'',\eta'')) = C(\delta(A',\eta'))$, then a matrix T exists such that $\delta(A',\eta') = T\delta(A'',\eta'')$ and $\underline{z}''_1 = \underline{z}'_1 T$; furthermore, $V(\alpha'') = V(\alpha')$. The latter means that the optimal portfolio adjusts to replicate the previously optimal date-one consumption pattern.

The LRT utilities results of Chapter 2, Propositions 2.5 and 2.6, extend to SP-3 as well. However, one usefully appends the restriction $\rho U^2 = U^1$. The portfolio separation (in the sense of Proposition 2.5) now relates to $\underline{z} \equiv (\underline{z}_0, \underline{z}_1)$ (or α); without the preference restriction the separation is limited to z_1 (or w). (Chapter 2 makes a virtually identical point.) With the assumption $U \equiv U^2 = U^1/\rho$ one expresses expected utility as

$$V = E[U^1(\tilde{c}) + U^2(\tilde{w})] = \sum_{s=1}^{2S} \hat{\pi}_s U(\alpha_s)$$

where $\hat{\pi}_s \equiv \rho\pi_s$, $\hat{\pi}_{S+s} \equiv \pi_s$, and $U(\alpha_s) = U^1(c_s)$, $U(\alpha_{S+s}) = U^2(w_s)$ $(s \leq S)$. The definition of V does not differ in form from Eq. (2.33) in Chapter 2. Accordingly, the next two propositions are immediate generalizations of Propositions 2.5 and 2.6.

PROPOSITION 4.6. *Consider SP-3 with LRT utilities and* $\rho U^2 = U^1$. *Suppose that* $A_{e,\eta}$ *spans the unit vector. Then there exist two basis portfolios* $\underline{z}'$ *and* $\underline{z}''$ *such that* $\{\underline{z}',\underline{z}''\}$ *span all optimal portfolios as* φ and $\bar{\bar{w}}$ *vary.**

PROPOSITION 4.7. *Consider SP-3 with LRT utilities and* $\rho U^2 = U^1$. *Let* (A'',η'') *and* (A',η') *be two information/market environments that possibly have no common implicit prices but* $1 \cdot R'' = 1 \cdot R'$. *Suppose further that both* $A''_{e,\eta''}$ *and* $A'_{e,\eta'}$ *span the unit vector, and that* $\bar{\bar{w}}' = \bar{\bar{w}}'' \equiv \bar{\bar{w}}$. *Let* α'' *and* α' *denote the two respective optimal patterns. Then the sign of*

$$V(\alpha'') - V(\alpha')$$

remains identical for all φ *and* $\bar{\bar{w}}$.*

Note that an α proportional to the unit vector is attainable if and only if $1 \in C(\delta(A,\eta))$. This follows since $\delta(1,\eta)$ spans $c = 1$.

4.6. The Sequential Decision Setting (SP-2) and Its Relationship to the Signal-Coordinated Decision Setting (SP-3)

4.6.1. General overview

Much of the discussion about SP-3 has been motivated by its purported usefulness in exposing the structure of SP-2.[4] The current section develops the point by analyzing the consumption opportunity set associated with SP-2 in detail. The key insight demonstrates that SP-2 transforms into an SP-3, except that one must generally state some additional attainability constraints delimiting the set of available mixes of consumption patterns. The *structure* of SP-2 is no different from an SP-3. The point will become apparent once it has been established that a vector space $C(\hat{A})$ rather than $C(A_{e,\eta})$ restricts the attainable consumption patterns; $\hat{A}$ is an appropriately constructed matrix, and $C(\hat{A}) \subseteq C(A_{e,\eta})$ where $C(A_{e,\eta})$, of course, defines the space of attainable mixes for SP-3. An important related aspect is that the construction of $\hat{A}$, in contrast to $A_{e,\eta}$, depends on the security prices. Furthermore, one can identify reasonable economic conditions such that $\hat{A}$ is identical to $A_{e,\eta}$, in which case the SP-2 setting is in *all* respects equivalent to the SP-3 setting.

The analysis also identifies the implicit prices in the SP-2 setting, and these prices depend on both the first-round and the second-round security prices. For a number of by now familiar reasons, to derive the implicit prices serves several important purposes. First, effective analysis of how the opportunity set depends on alternative markets and information functions frequently requires that the underlying values of consumption patterns remain the same. This particular issue is complex for SP-2 and, unlike SP-3, one cannot generally assert that more information expands the opportunity set. Second, insofar as one wants to characterize SP-2 as a choice model in which the individual selects consumption patterns directly, these patterns must be priced. Thus, the notion of generalized Arrow-Debreu (complete) markets in SP-2 can be developed only after a derivation of implicit prices.

Given any fixed implicit prices, an individual is no better off in the SP-1 setting than in the SP-2 setting. The overall conclusion, therefore, is that the expected utility reached in the SP-2 setting is bounded by SP-1 at the lower end and by SP-3 at the upper end. This observation greatly aids the Chapter 5 comparative welfare analysis of information and markets for the relatively complex equilibrium models associated with SP-1, SP-2, and SP-3.

---

[4] The extension of the current section to include T-stage, $2 < T < \infty$, trading rounds, dividends across states/dates, and more than two consumption dates poses few problems except for notation (which would have to be quite elaborate). The same applies for the next chapter's equilibrium analysis of SP-2. Hence, the conclusions are far more general than what might appear at first glance.

4.6.2. Attainable Security Holdings

The analysis that follows restates the opportunity set of an SP-2 in a form that makes it directly comparable to an SP-3. In the process, one derives the implicit prices as a function of the security prices $\{\hat{P}_j\}_j$ and $\{P_{jy}\}_{j,y}$.

The choice constraints, which can be assumed binding, are given by

$$\sum_j \hat{z}_j \hat{P}_j = \bar{\bar{w}} \equiv \sum_j \bar{z}_j \hat{P}_j, \tag{4.4}$$

$$\sum_j z_{jy} P_{jy} = \sum_j \hat{z}_j P_{jy}, \quad y = 1, \ldots, Y \tag{4.5}$$

where as before $(\hat{z}_j)_j$ and $(z_{jy})_{jy}$ define the prior and posterior round choice variables. The constraints make economic sense only when they exclude arbitrage opportunities. A necessary condition for no-arbitrage in SP-2 is no-arbitrage in the prior trading round. Hence, invoking Proposition 2.1, Y positive numbers $\{\nu_y\}_y$ exist such that

$$\hat{P}_j = \sum_y P_{jy} \nu_y, \quad j = 0, \ldots, J. \tag{4.6}$$

Define $\hat{\omega}_y \equiv \sum_j \hat{z}_j P_{jy}$, $\bar{\omega}_y \equiv \sum_j \bar{z}_j P_{jy}$, $\hat{\omega} \equiv (\hat{\omega}_y)_y$, and $\underline{\underline{P}} \equiv [P_{jy}]$, a $(J+1) \times Y$ matrix. By substituting Eq. (4.6) into Eq. (4.4) and using the preceding definitions, the constraints Eq. (4.4) and (4.5) are restated as

$$\sum_y \hat{\omega}_y \nu_y = \sum_y \bar{\omega}_y \nu_y = \bar{\bar{w}}, \tag{4.7}$$

$$\sum_j z_{jy} P_{jy} = \hat{\omega}_y, \quad y = 1, \ldots, Y, \tag{4.8}$$

$$\hat{\omega} \in C(\underline{\underline{P}}), \tag{4.9}$$

where $(z_{jy})_{jy}$ and $\hat{\omega}$ comprise the choice variables. Just as the new prices, $\{\nu_y\}_y$, replace $(\hat{P}_j)_j$, the new choice variables $(\hat{\omega}_y)_y$ are in lieu of $(\hat{z}_j)_j$.

The restated SP-2 opportunity set allows a direct interpretation.[5] In the first stage the individual chooses the amount of wealth to spend in each event y, that is, $\hat{\omega}_y$. The price of a unit of $\hat{\omega}_y$ is ν_y, so that the first-stage allocation $(\hat{\omega}_y)_y$ is subject to the budget constraint $\sum_y \hat{\omega}_y \nu_y = \bar{\bar{w}}$. In the second stage the individual decides which securities to hold and how much to consume of the current consumption good in event y. The total expenditures cannot exceed $\hat{\omega}_y$, which was the amount chosen in the first stage. Some

[5] To be sure, note that the $\{\nu_y\}_y$ need not be unique (of course, uniqueness occurs if and only if rank $[\underline{\underline{P}}] = Y$). Nonuniqueness poses no problems, and one can pick any $\{\nu_y\}_y$ that satisfy Eq. (4.6).

$(\hat{\omega}_y)_y$ mixes may be unattainable, however: $\hat{\omega}$ must be in the span of the matrix $\underline{\underline{P}}$ since $\hat{\omega} = \hat{z}\,\underline{\underline{P}}$.

Further simplifications of Eq. (4.7) through (4.9) are possible. Equation (4.8) substituted into Eq. (4.7) results in

$$\sum_j \sum_y z_{jy} P_{jy} \nu_y = \bar{\bar{w}}. \tag{4.10}$$

The spanning condition $\hat{\omega} \in C(\underline{\underline{P}})$ expressed in terms of $(z_{jy})_{jy}$ equals

$$\left(\sum_j z_{jy} P_{jy}\right)_y \in C(\underline{\underline{P}}), \tag{4.11}$$

since $\hat{\omega}_y = \sum_j z_{jy} P_{jy}$.

The quantities $(P_{jy}\nu_y) \equiv \hat{P}_{jy}$ rescale the original prices appearing in the Y second round constraints. This rescaling does not change the consumption/investment opportunities: for each y $\sum_j z_{jy} P_{jy} \leq \sum_j \hat{z}_j P_{jy}$ is equivalent to $\sum_j z_{jy} \hat{P}_{jy} \leq \sum \hat{z}_j \hat{P}_{jy}$, and $\sum_j z_{jy} P_{jy} \leq \hat{\omega}_y$ is equivalent to $\sum z_{jy} \hat{P}_{jy} \leq \hat{\omega}_y \nu_y = \sum_j \hat{z}_j \hat{P}_{jy}$. Stated somewhat differently, a (re-)scaling of the second-round prices to $\hat{P}_{jy}$ such that $\hat{P}_j = \sum_j \hat{P}_{jy}$, all $j \in J^+$, entails no loss of generality. The need for the prices $\hat{P}_{jy}$ stems solely from the "inconvenient" scaling of the original prices. Using the rescaled second-round prices, the constraints Eq. (4.10) and (4.11) reduce equivalently to

$$\sum_j \sum_y z_{jy} \hat{P}_{jy} = \bar{\bar{w}}, \tag{4.12}$$

and

$$\left(\sum_j z_{jy} \hat{P}_{jy}\right)_y \in C(\underline{\underline{\hat{P}}}), \tag{4.13}$$

where $\underline{\underline{\hat{P}}} \equiv [P_{jy}\nu_y]$. The restated opportunity set—which has a single clearly identifiable budget constraint (Eq. (4.12))—is exactly that of SP-3, except for the added constraint (Eq. (4.13)) that places restrictions on the attainable vectors of signal-contingent security holdings. Specifically, as previously, let $\underline{z} = (\underline{z}_0, \underline{z}_1)$, where $\underline{z}_0 = (z_{01}, \ldots, z_{0Y})$ and $\underline{z}_1 = (z_{yj})_{y,j}$, be the $(J + 1) \times Y$ "supervector" of security holdings; then one readily establishes that relative to this supervector the restrictions are linear, that is, the set of $\underline{z}$ satisfying Eq. (4.13) defines a vector space. Accordingly, some matrix, H, must exist such that the set of constraints (Eq. (4.13)) equate the requirement that $\underline{z} \in C(H)$. To recapitulate, an SP-2 (with no-arbitrage) can be restated as an SP-3 if one adds attainability constraints on the contingent security plans.

PROPOSITION 4.8. *Consider a no-arbitrage SP-2 with security prices* $\{\hat{P}_j\}_j$ *and* $\{P_{jy}\}_{j,y}$. *Then positive* $\{\nu_y\}_y$ *exist such that* $\hat{P}_j = \sum_y P_{jy}\nu_y$,

$j = 0, \ldots, J$. Moreover, let $\hat{P}_{jy} \equiv P_{jy}\nu_y$; then the budget constraint

$$\sum_y \sum_j z_{jy}\hat{P}_{jy} \leq \bar{\bar{w}},$$

and an additional vector space constraint on $(z_{jy})_{y,j}$,

$$\Big(\sum_{j\in J^+} z_{jy}\hat{P}_{jy}\Big)_y \in C([\hat{P}_{jy}]),$$

*determine the opportunity set.**

4.6.3. IMPLICIT PRICES AND FURTHER ANALYSIS OF TRADING/CONSUMPTION OPPORTUNITIES

The rescaled second-round prices, $\{\hat{P}_{jy}\}_{y,j}$, relate back to the underlying implicit prices in SP-2. To see this, note that SP-2's first-round budget constraint reduces to Eq. (4.12), and this constraint can be reexpressed in the usual fashion as $\alpha \cdot R \leq \bar{\bar{w}}$. The first-round security prices therefore affect the implicit prices since the second-round and first-round security prices satisfy $\hat{P}_j = \sum_y P_{jy}\nu_y = \sum_y \hat{P}_{jy}$; a change of $\{\hat{P}_j\}_j$, but with $\{P_{jy}\}_{y,j}$ fixed, generally changes the implicit prices. Hence, one values an attainable pattern α by any $(R_0, R_1) > 0$ solving

$$P_{jy}\nu_y = \sum_{s\in S_y} a_{js}R_{1s}, \qquad y = 1, \ldots, Y,$$

and

$$P_{0y}\nu_y = \sum_{s\in S_y} R_{0s}, \qquad y = 1, \ldots, Y.$$

The expressions show that if the analysis departs from some given implicit price vector R, then one scales the security prices conveniently by putting $\nu_y = 1$.

The implicit prices possess the critical property of correctly valuing any payoff pattern acquired in the first round. This can be verified directly. One unit of $\hat{z}_j$ yields a pattern a_j. The value of a_j per implicit prices is $\sum_s a_{js}R_{1s}$; by an outright purchase in the first round it equals $\hat{P}_j$. The two values are the same since $\hat{P}_j = \sum_y \hat{P}_{jy} = \sum_y \sum_{s\in S_y} a_{js}R_{1s} = \sum_s a_{js}R_{1s}$. (For $j = 0$, put $a_j = 1$ and replace R_{1s} by R_{0s}). Similar manipulations yield the same conclusion for portfolios. These kinds of exercises demonstrate that it makes no difference how a particular pattern is acquired. The price paid will be the same regardless of the strategy used (first- vs. second-round or any other attributes describing the portfolio strategy).

Because SP-3 imposes no attainability constraints on $\underline{z}$, it is clear that the consumption patterns available in SP-2 equate to those of an SP-3 if and only if Eq. (4.13) imposes no constraints on $\underline{z}$. Such irrelevance of Eq. (4.13)

applies if, and essentially only if, the row vectors in the matrix $\underline{\underline{\hat{P}}}$ generate the entire space.[6]

COROLLARY 4.8.1. *SP-2 is identical to SP-3 if and only if rank* $[P_{jy}] = rank[\hat{P}_{jy}] = Y$.*

(Using routine matrix algebra, one readily demonstrates that $\underline{\underline{\hat{P}}}$ and $\underline{\underline{P}}$ have the same rank.) The attainability constraints derived from the second-round prices can therefore be neglected if and only if $\underline{\underline{P}}$ spans Y-dimensional space. Because of its theoretical significance, the case deserves a formal definition.

DEFINITION 4.5. DYNAMICALLY COMPLETE MARKETS: *In SP-2, markets are dynamically complete if the row vectors in the matrix of second-round prices* $[P_{jy}]$ *span all of Y-dimensional space.*

The terminology emphasizes that the dynamic nature of the problem does not by itself introduce restrictions on the opportunities. Thus, SP-3 emerges as a benchmark in the analysis of SP-2.

Dynamically complete markets (DCM) may occur in conjunction with conditionally complete markets (CCM). Besides the wealth constraint, the only constraint on consumption patterns the individual faces is the measurability of date-zero consumption. All mixes of signal-contingent date-zero consumption and state-contingent date-one consumption would be available. Conversely, dynamically *in*complete *or* conditionally *in*complete markets make some mixes of $((c_y)_y, w)$ unattainable. DCM and CCM therefore naturally complement each other since they jointly imply, and are implied by, a generalization of the Arrow-Debreu setting introduced in Chapter 2. The sole relevant constraint—the budget constraint—reduces to

$$\sum_y c_y P_{0y} + \sum_s w_s R_{1s} \leq \bar{\bar{w}}.$$

In this environment the individual chooses his contingent consumption patterns directly prior to date-zero, and the prices of interest assign costs to all measurable consumption patterns. Compared to the original SP-2, the above choice environment seems unadorned by its lack of "true" dynamic features as well as "normal" securities. *Nevertheless, the relatively complex sequential consumption/portfolio selection models may reduce to such generalized Arrow-Debreu settings*. The necessary and sufficient condition of CCM/DCM has a simple and direct economic interpretation: because of market completeness at each point in time and in each event, the uncertainty immediately following any one decision point can be dealt with fully.

[6] The Y-dimensional vector $\left(\sum_j z_{jy} P_{jy}\right)_y$ is unconstrained across $\underline{z}$ if, and only if, for each y $P_{jy} \neq 0$ for at least one j. The last condition is assumed to be met throughout.

As one should expect, complete markets imply CCM and DCM. A proof of this poses no difficulties. (CCM is obvious. DCM follows since one can put $\hat{z}_0 = 0$ and let $\omega_y = \sum_{j \in J} \hat{z}_j P_{jy} = \sum_{s \in S_y} R_{1s} q_s$ where $q_s \equiv \sum_{j \in J} \hat{z}_j a_{js}$; further, $(q_s)_s$ is unconstrained given rank$(A) = S$, and thus A generates any mix $(\omega_y)_y$.) More important, CCM/DCM may be fulfilled *without* complete markets. For example, consider $Y = 2$ with $S_1 = \{1, \ldots, (1/2)S\}$, $S_2 = \{(1/2)S + 1, \ldots, S\}$, $A = [\bar{A}\,\bar{A}]$, rank $[\bar{A}] = (1/2)S$, and rank $[\underline{\underline{P}}] = 2$. Although the markets satisfy CCM/DCM, the number of securities need not exceed $(1/2)S$.

What kind of information functions lead to CCM/DCM? In broad terms, this requires "some, but not too much" information. While a refinement of the information function increases the possibility of obtaining CCM, in a rough sense the opposite applies to DCM. The matrix $\underline{\underline{\hat{P}}}$ (or $\underline{\underline{P}}$) can be of rank Y only if $J + 1 \geq Y$. Hence, markets do not satisfy DCM when the number of signals exceeds the number of securities. Further note that the condition $J + 1 \geq Y$ is only necessary, and not sufficient, for DCM since the columns in $\underline{\underline{\hat{P}}}$ may be linearly dependent. Contrary to the case of markets, one cannot conclude that some particular information function implies CCM/DCM. The matrix $\underline{\underline{P}}$ must be dealt with in greater detail, and its analysis falls within the domain of Chapter 5.

Fixing the implicit prices permits a comparison of the consumption opportunity set associated with SP-2 relative to those of SP-1 and SP-3. First, the SP-2 consumption opportunity set has a subset relationship to SP-3 since the budget constraints do not differ, and only SP-2 imposes additional attainability constraints. Second, as noted previously in section 4.4, SP-1's opportunity set is a subset of SP-2's. (The latter followed simply because the extraneous restriction $\hat{z}_j = \bar{z}_j, j \in J^+$, in SP-2 leads to the SP-1 opportunity set.) Let $CO(\text{SP} - n)$ denote the consumption opportunity set for SP-n, $n = 1, 2, 3$; the aforementioned consumption opportunity set relations, plus the boundary cases, are summarized formally as follows.

PROPOSITION 4.9. *Given $\eta \neq \eta^0$ and any fixed implicit price system it follows that*

$$CO(SP-1) \subseteq CO(SP-2) \subseteq CO(SP-3).$$

*The first inclusion sign is an equality if and only if rank $[\underline{\underline{P}}] = 1$; the second inclusion sign is an equality if and only if rank $[\underline{\underline{P}}] = Y$.**

It is important to appreciate that the expected utility of an SP-2 is bounded below by an SP-1 and above by an SP-3. Since either bound may be exact, depending on whether the rank of $\underline{\underline{P}}$ is the minimum or maximum one, SP-2 has characteristics similar to both SP-1 and SP-3, the degree to which depends on the "size" of the space $C(\underline{\underline{P}})$. Upon reflection this result appears straightforward, and it conforms nicely with economic intuition: SP-1, SP-2, and SP-3 permit, respectively, no signal coordination, some signal coordination, and complete signal coordination. Not surprisingly, Proposition 4.9 firmly guides the Chapter 5 equilibrium analysis of SP-2 by comparing the setting to its lower and upper benchmarks.

Further analysis of SP-2 shows that its consumption opportunities may be identified solely in terms of (A,R,η) (and $\bar{\bar{w}}$). In this case, any direct reference to the original observables ($\hat{z}_j, z_{jy}, \hat{P}_j$ and P_{jy}) becomes redundant.

First, following the usual procedure, the budget constraint (Eq. (4.12)) equals $\alpha \cdot R = \bar{\bar{w}}$. Second, the attainability constraints associated with SP-3 apply to SP-2 as well, that is, $\alpha \in C(A_{e,\eta})$. Third, one expresses the left-hand side (L.H.S.) of the posterior round constraints in terms of (α,R) as

$$\sum_{s \in S_y} (c_s R_{0s} + w_s R_{1s}) = \hat{\omega}_y \nu_y, \qquad y = 1, \ldots, Y.$$

Summarizing these equations, one gets

$$\alpha[\delta(R_0^t,\eta) : \delta(R_1^t,\eta)]^t = (\hat{\omega}_y \nu_y)_y,$$

where the right-hand side (R.H.S.) is a row vector constrained by $(\hat{\omega}_y \nu_y)_y \in C([P_{jy}\nu_y])$. The matrix $[P_{jy}\nu_y]$ may also be expressed (somewhat awkwardly) in terms of (A,R,η). Doing so summarizes the SP-2 consumption opportunity set:

(i) $\alpha \cdot R \leq \bar{\bar{w}}$
(ii) $\alpha \in C(A_{e,\eta})$

$$\text{(iii)} \ \alpha \in D(A,\eta,R) \equiv \left\{\alpha \middle| \alpha[\delta(R_0^t,\eta) : \delta(R_1^t,\eta)]^t \in C\left(\begin{bmatrix} 1\delta(R_0^t,\eta)^t \\ A\delta(R_1^t,\eta)^t \end{bmatrix}\right)\right\}.$$

The details of the set (iii) are of no great significance at this point. What needs to be emphasized initially is simply that $D(A,\eta,R)$ is a vector space and that $C(A_{e,\eta}) \cap D(A,\eta,R)$ therefore also results in a vector space. One should expect this in view of Proposition 4.8, which restricts the plans $\underline{z}$ within a vector space. It follows that (ii) and (iii) can be combined: a matrix $\hat{A}$ exists such that the opportunity set can be expressed by

(a) $\alpha \cdot R \leq \bar{\bar{w}}$
(b) $\alpha \in C(\hat{A})$.

The matrix $\hat{A}$ depends at the most on (A,η,R). Naturally, $\hat{A} = A_{e,\eta}$ if and only if (iii) is automatically satisfied, that is, markets are DCM. This is another way of saying that the attainability constraints on plans, Eq. (4.13), transform into the attainability constraint (iii) on consumption patterns.

In sum, although SP-2 has the same general structure as an SP-3 (or SP), a difference obtains because the construction of $\hat{A}$ (or (H)) depends on the implicit prices (or $\{\hat{P}_{yj}\}_{jy}$) as well as (A,η). *In contrast to SP-3 (and SP), the security prices also determine the set that defines the mix of attainable consumption patterns*. This feature provides the critical distinction between SP-2 versus SP-3.

The articulation of SP-2 as a modified SP-3 has the advantage of directly extending many of the SP-3 results to encompass SP-2 as well. For example, sufficient conditions for the existence of a unique optimal consumption pattern follow immediately from Proposition 4.3 (or 2.2.). Also, a CCCP associated with SP-2 must exist, although the dimensionality of the complementary B-matrix does not easily derive in terms of the input A, η, and R. (As opposed to the CCCP associated with SP-3, the complementary matrix is not necessarily block-diagonal.) More important, the insights derived from Proposition 4.8 help to identify the effect of enriched markets or information on the consumption opportunity set. Although $C(A'') \supseteq C(A')$ and η'' finer than η' imply $C(A''_{e,\eta''}) \supseteq C(A'_{e,\eta'})$, the sets $D(A'',\eta'',R)$ and $D(A',\eta',R)$ also need evaluation. Only a partially positive conclusion obtains: $D(A',\eta',R)$ does not have subset relationship to $D(A'',\eta'',R)$ unless either $\eta'' = \eta'$ or $\eta' = \eta^0$. Consequently, the same is true for the set $C(\hat{A}')$ compared to $C(\hat{A}'')$.

PROPOSITION 4.10. *Consider SP-2 with fixed implicit prices. Suppose that $C(A'') \supseteq C(A')$ and that η'' is finer than η'. If $\eta' = \eta^0$ or $\eta'' = \eta'$, then $CO'' \supseteq CO'$. If $\eta'' \neq \eta' \neq \eta^0$, then there exist settings satisfying the condition on markets such that $CO'' \not\supseteq CO'$.*

By inspecting the definition of the set $D(A,\eta,R)$, one can anticipate the reason enriched information does not yield the same conclusion as enriched markets. The role of η clearly differs from the role of A in the set D. However, the proof of Proposition 4.10 does not directly analyze the set D. Instead, it demonstrates a more intuitive result: the set $CO'' \cap C(A_{e,\eta'})$ can be a strict subset of $CO'(= CO' \cap C(A_{e,\eta'}))$. That is, strategies that disregard the incremental information in the more informative setting are not necessarily available in the less informative setting. The individual cannot simply neglect the incremental information in the double-primed setting and thereby replicate everything he can do in the single-primed setting. An exception applies to $\eta' = \eta^0$ because $CO'' \cap C(A_{e,\eta'}) = CO'$. This follows since every first-round choice in SP-2 with η'' is also available in SP (= SP-2 with $\eta = \eta^0$). In general, however, the increase in the number of second-round constraints as η becomes more informative makes coordination across signals more difficult. The SP-1 aspect of SP-2 makes its presence felt: given constant implicit prices, in an SP-1 setting the set $CO'' \cap C(A_{e,\eta'})$ might well be a strict subset of CO'. For example, one constructs such SP-1 settings by letting $A = I$, $S = 2$, $\eta'' = \eta^*$, and $\eta' = \eta^0$.[7] On the other hand, focusing on markets,

[7] If $A = I$, $S = 2$, $\eta'' = \eta^*$, and $\bar{c} \equiv \bar{c}_1 = \bar{c}_2$ the budget constraints

$$c_s R_{0s} + w_s R_{1s} \leq \bar{c} R_{0s} + \bar{w}_s R_{1s}, \; s = 1, 2,$$

determine CO''. Adding the restriction $c_1 = c_2$ one identifies the set $CO'' \cap C(A_{e,\eta''})$. This set is clearly a strict subset of CO':

$$c + \sum_s w_s R_{1s} \leq \bar{c} + \sum_s \bar{w}_s R_{1s}.$$

This follows by simply adding the two equations in the double-primed setting. (Note that $R_{01} + R_{02} = 1$ by convention, and $c \equiv c_1 = c_2$ when $\eta' = \eta^0$.)

$C(A'') \supseteq C(A')$ implies $CO''(SP-1) \supseteq CO'(SP-1)$, given some fixed information function and implicit prices. It should therefore come as no surprise that SP-2 has the same property. In both SP-1 and SP-2, enrichment of markets expands opportunities, while information enrichment may partially eliminate opportunities due to increased difficulties in coordinating plans across signals.

The SP-2 setting is analytically indistinguishable from SP-3 when the conclusions do not depend on the characteristics of the attainability set $C(\hat{A})$ (or $C(A_{e,\eta})$ in SP-3). This suggests that Propositions 4.6 and 4.7, both of which stated implications of LRT utilities in SP-3, extend to an SP-2 setting. Only a slight difficulty is present because the 2S-dimensional vector $\alpha = 1$ must be an element of $C(A_{e,\eta}) \cap D(A,\eta,R)$. The condition $1 \in C(A_{e,\eta})$ needs strengthening unless one assumes DCM. The observation that $1 \in D(A,\eta,R)$ if $1 \in C(A)$ provides the simplest condition; it implies that an α proportional to 1 may be selected in the first trading round.

PROPOSITION 4.11. *Consider SP-2 with LRT utilities and $\rho U^2 = U^1$. Suppose that A spans the unit vector. Then there exist two basis portfolios α' and α'' such that $\{\alpha', \alpha''\}$ span all optimal portfolios as φ and $\bar{\bar{w}}$ vary.**

PROPOSITION 4.12. *Consider SP-2 with LRT utilities and $\rho U^2 = U^1$. Let (A'',η'') and (A',η') be two information/market environments possibly without common implicit prices but $1 \cdot R'' = 1 \cdot R'$. Suppose that the unit vector is spanned by A'' and A' and that $\bar{\bar{w}}'' = \bar{\bar{w}}' \equiv \bar{\bar{w}}$. Let α'' and α' denote the two respective optimal patterns. Then the sign of*

$$V(\alpha'') - V(\alpha')$$

*is the same for all φ and $\bar{\bar{w}}$.**

In view of Proposition 4.9, note that Propositions 4.11 and 4.12 apply for SP-1 settings if prices are signal (and information function) independent.[8] Hence, the fineness condition in Proposition 4.1 can be eliminated if one confines the class of permissible preferences to LRT with fixed β. These preferences, combined with signal-independent prices, imply that all information functions can be ordered expected-utility-wise independently of the parameters $\bar{\bar{w}}$ and φ. As usual, sharper assumptions on the preferences/beliefs lead to sharper conclusions.

Without Proposition 4.8 and the identification of the opportunity set constraints (a) and (b), it would be more difficult to prove the last two results. The power of Proposition 4.8, and the related identification of the problem in terms of implicit prices, stems from its transformation of a dynamic consumption/portfolio selection problem into an equivalent static

[8] Recall that a prior trading round is unnecessary if $\text{rank}[\underline{\underline{P}}] = 1$. This is the case of (effectively) signal independent prices.

problem. The general *structure* of the static problem does not differ fundamentally from the simple standard problem introduced in Chapter 2. That is, the choice problem consists of (a) a budget constraint and (b) extrabudget constraints limiting the consumption patterns (and plans) within some vector space. In the dynamic SP-2 setting, therefore, the only novel aspect pertains to the difficulty of unambiguously identifying the vector space of attainable consumption patterns.

Appendix 4.1. Proofs

Proof of Proposition 4.10. Let $\eta'' = \eta' \equiv \eta$ and suppose that $C(A'') \supseteq C(A')$. The result $CO'' \supseteq CO'$ then follows because (i) $C(A''_{e,\eta}) \supseteq C(A'_{e,\eta})$ and (ii) $D(A'',R,\eta) \supseteq D(A',R,\eta)$. The reason (i) holds was shown in conjunction with SP-3. In a similar fashion, (ii) holds because $C(A'') \supseteq C(A')$ implies $A' = TA''$ for some T, and

$$C\begin{pmatrix} 1\delta(R_0^t,\eta)^t \\ TA''\delta(R_1^t,\eta)^t \end{pmatrix} \subseteq C\begin{pmatrix} 1\delta(R_0^t,\eta)^t \\ A''\delta(R_1^t,\eta)^t \end{pmatrix}.$$

Let η'' be any information function, $\eta' = \eta^0$, and $A'' = A'$. Since $R'' = R'$, it follows immediately that one can put $\hat{P}''_j = \hat{P}'_j$; every plan in the single-primed setting therefore remains available in the double-primed economy.

The above results combine: if $C(A'') \supseteq C(A')$, η'' is at least as fine as η', and $\eta'' = \eta'$ or $\eta' = \eta^0$, then $CO'' \supseteq CO'$.

The proof next considers the negative part of the proposition: if $A'' = A'$ but $\eta'' \neq \eta' \neq \eta^0$, then cases exist such that $CO'' \supseteq CO'$. The result obtains because $CO'' \cap C(A_{e,\eta'}) \subset CO'(= CO' \cap C(A_{e,\eta'})$ is possible.

Consider the following two partitions: $\{S''_1, S''_2, S''_3\}$ and $\{S'_1, S'_2\}$, where $S''_1 = S'_1$, and $S''_2 \cup S''_3 = S'_2$. The information function η'' is strictly finer than $\eta'(\neq \eta^0)$. Assume further without any loss of generality that prices are normalized such that $\hat{P}''_j = \hat{P}'_j = \sum_y P''_{jy} = \sum_y P'_{jy}$, all $j \in J^+$. Let rank$[\underline{\underline{P}}''] =$ rank$[\underline{\underline{P}}'] = 2$; that is, only the single-primed setting satisfies DCM. The condition on ranks introduces no problems. Let $J^+ = 2$, and assume that P'_y, $y = 1,2$ are linearly independent. Let P''_y, $y = 2,3$ be linearly independent, and where $P''_{j1} = P'_{j1}$, $P''_{j2} + P''_{j3} = P'_{j2}$ for $j = 0,1$. This model implies that one can put $R'' = R'$, and the previous normalization and rank conditions are satisfied. (As an example, consider

$$\underline{\underline{P}}' = \begin{bmatrix} 1 & 2 \\ 3 & 5 \end{bmatrix} \text{ and } \underline{\underline{P}}'' = \begin{bmatrix} 1 & 1 & 1 \\ 3 & 1 & 4 \end{bmatrix}\Bigg).$$

In the double-primed setting, the condition that $\alpha \in CO'' \cap C(A_{e,\eta'})$ implies that $z_{j2} = z_{j3}$, all $j \in J^+$. It is shown below that the set of all such restricted plans defines a strict subset of CO'.

The set CO'' is implied by

$$\sum_{y=1}^{3} \sum_{j} z_{jy} P''_{jy} \leq \bar{\bar{w}}''$$

$$\sum_{j} z_{jy} P''_{jy} = \omega_y,\ y = 1,2,3,$$

where $(\omega_1, \omega_2, \omega_3) \in C(\underline{\underline{P}}'')$. Since rank$[\underline{\underline{P}}''] = 2$ and $\omega_2 \neq \omega_3$ for some plans, the last condition is equivalent $\omega_1 = k_2\omega_2 + k_3\omega_3$. If in addition the incremental information is disregarded, $z_{j2} = z_{j3}$, all $j \in J^+$, and the opportunity set reduces to

$$\sum_{J} z_{ji} P''_{j1} + \sum_{j} z_{j2}(P''_{j2} + P''_{j3}) \leq \bar{\bar{w}}$$

$$\sum_{j} z_{j1} P''_{j1} = \sum_{j} z_{j2}(k_2 P''_{j2} + k_3 P''_{j3}).$$

But given $R'' = R'$, it follows that $\bar{\bar{w}}'' = \bar{\bar{w}}'$, $P'_{j1} = P''_{j1}$, and $P'_{j2} = P''_{j2} + P''_{j3}$. Hence, the η'-measurable opportunity set in the double-primed setting equals

$$\sum_{j} z_{j1} P'_{j1} + \sum_{j} z_{j2} P'_{j2} \leq \bar{\bar{w}}'$$

$$\sum_{j} z_{j1} P''_{j1} = \sum_{j} z_{j2}(k_2 P''_{j2} + k_3 P''_{j3})$$

Since the opportunity set in the single-primed economy is defined by the first equation alone (Corollary 4.8.1), the result follows.

Remark: To appreciate the intuition behind the proof of the negative part, consider a *one*-date model, $c \equiv c_y \equiv 0$, with $S > 3$ and incomplete A. In this case $\eta'' = \eta^*$ yields the same opportunity set as $\eta' = \eta^0$! This follows since no meaningful trading can occur in the second round given perfect information: rank$[A_y] = 1$ for all $y = s$. On the other hand, *some* information ($Y = 2$, say) may well strictly enrich the no-information consumption opportunity set.

CHAPTER FIVE

GENERAL EQUILIBRIUM ANALYSIS UNDER VARYING INFORMATION

5.1. Introduction: Information and Equilibrium

This chapter broadens the equilibrium analysis by admitting information.[1] To accomplish such generalization the analysis relies on the previously acquired microanalytic insights about the individual's consumption/portfolio selection problem when information is available. By enriching the simple two-date equilibrium model, one can identify the effects of information and the passage of time. The questions addressed in this chapter generally expand upon those considered in Chapter 3; the chapter develops concepts of economic efficiency (i.e., extensions of CPE and FPE as discussed in sections 3.3 and 3.4), the comparative analysis of conceivable welfare outcomes when information varies (extending section 3.5), and the structure of valuation (extending section 3.7).

Because three different standard problems exist the issues of welfare and valuation cannot be resolved in a simple and direct fashion. Each of the decision settings in the previous chapter can constitute the economic regime that allocates consumption patterns through a competitive equilibrium, so that the multiplicity of economic regimes compels a repeated analysis of efficiency and comparative welfare outcomes, etc. The sequencing followed here reflects that out of the three settings, complete signal coordination (SP-3), renders the best point of departure. As the previous chapter notes, SP-3

[1] The chapter draws upon numerous sources in an eclectic fashion. Aside from the papers cited in the text, basic references are: Arrow (1964), Gale (1982, chapters 2 and 5), Grossman (1977), Kreps (1979), Radner (1968), and Rubinstein (1975). Parts of the analysis reflect my own work (Ohlson and Buckman [1981] and Ohlson [1984]), which addresses information issues first raised by Hirshleifer (1971).

extends the structure of the simple standard problem (SP) with only minor "notational" modifications; accordingly, the equilibrium analysis founded on SP-3 requires no fundamentally new concepts.[2]

Most of the SP-3 analysis deals with a technical issue: Under what conditions on preferences/beliefs/markets does (incremental) information have no effect on the equilibrium? The solution is pivotal for all three equilibrium settings because the analysis of the welfare/valuation characteristics of SP-1 and SP-2 equilibria poses considerable difficulties without a thorough understanding of SP-3 equilibria. It also turns out that one analyzes SP-1 equilibria beneficially prior to the complex and interesting sequential (SP-2) equilibria. The previous chapter on partial equilibrium shows that sequential decision settings have properties falling in between SP-1 and SP-3 settings. To appreciate sequential equilibria, Propositions 4.8 and 4.9 remain central: an individual can only partially coordinate his choice of consumption across signals. As usual, one can therefore justify the analysis of SP-1 and SP-3 equilibria because, if nothing else, their structural characteristics "bracket" sequential equilibria.

Chapter 3 demonstrates that the essence of pure exchange welfare analysis stems from the potential of improving the risk-sharing. This observation is equally valid for models with more complex trading. Similar to the effects arising from enriched markets, a more informative information function potentially has beneficial welfare consequences. Any "zero sum" philosophy is inappropriate whether one analyzes changes in markets or changes in information. Both kinds of changes alter constraints on individuals' opportunities to engage in exchange. Indeed, under appropriate conditions, an enrichment of markets and/or information might well benefit everyone. But the current chapter also introduces a new possibility: *a market/information enrichment can affect everyone adversely*. This conclusion is relevant to SP-1 and SP-2 equilibria, but not to SP-3 equilibria, and it applies to "more markets" as well as to "more information." In the simple two-date SP equilibrium model, no similar adverse effects due to market enrichment stand to reason. (Recall Proposition 3.10.)

The source of the apparent welfare anomaly is not too difficult to identify. Equilibria based on SP-2 or SP-1 settings do not generally possess the clear-cut efficiency properties that assure market/information enrichments to enlarge the set of attainable consumption mixes available in equilibrium. In technical terms, the joint implications of Propositions 3.1 and 3.4(ii) do not generalize for SP-1 and SP-2 because of complexities in determining attainable consumption patterns. Thus, conditions essential for "more being better than less" are absent. One further concludes that for sequential equilibria the workings of the celebrated invisible hand breaks down. Only equi-

[2] For the definitions of SP-1, SP-2, and SP-3, see Definitions 4.2, 4.3, and 4.4, respectively (Chapter 4).

libria based on SP-3 rule out such adverse outcomes, a not-surprising observation since SP-3 relates closely to the simple two-date equilibrium analysis. More generally, welfare conclusions depend on the particulars of the economic regime—SP-1, SP-2, or SP-3—but whether the welfare issue pertains to the role of markets or to information makes little difference. An engaging feature of the analysis is the theoretical unity one obtains for information and market economics.

5.2. Constrained Pareto Efficient Allocations: Equilibria Based on Signal-Coordinated Settings

5.2.1. The Structure of Efficient Allocations

The economy consists of $i = 1, \ldots, I$ individuals. The notation resumes the custom of denoting individuals by the subscript "i"; one accordingly states the ith individual's expected utility as

$$V_i(\alpha_i) \equiv \sum_y \sum_s \pi_i(s,y) U_{is}(z_{ioy}, \sum_{j \in J} z_{ijy} a_{js}).$$

The analysis in Chapter 4, section 4.3, provides other expressions for V_i, some of which will be used occasionally.[3] The only convention reaffirmed is that $\alpha_i \equiv (c_{i1}, \ldots, c_{iS}, w_{i1}, \ldots, w_{iS})$ remains $2 \times S$-dimensional regardless of the information function. The assumption on preferences, MISC (Definition 2.1), applies unless stated otherwise, and $\pi_i(s) > 0$ for all $i \in I$ and $s \in S$. Furthermore, individuals possess *homogeneous information*. The individuals' information functions are thus identical, and this makes an "i" subscript in the notations η_i or y_i superfluous. However, even though the information functions and signals observed do not vary with the individual, the subscript i in $\pi_i(s,y)$ (and $\pi_i(s)$, $\pi_i(s/y)$) cannot be dispensed of since beliefs may be heterogeneous. Individuals observe the same signal but "interpret" the signal differently simply because they may have dissimilar prior beliefs.

Heterogeneous information must not be confused with heterogeneous beliefs. The conditions $\eta_i = \eta_k$ vs. $\pi_i(s) = \pi_k(s)$ are distinct, and, on technical grounds, one of the restrictions does not imply the other. Even so, one can argue that posterior beliefs ought to be identical unless individuals' information differ. Following this line of reasoning, homogeneous prior beliefs seem like a natural assumption. Although this rather philosophical contention may have some merit, it cannot be resolved here. However, it should be noted that heterogeneous information models differ profoundly from homogeneous information models (with or without heterogeneous beliefs). In heterogeneous information settings, concepts of economic behavior and

---

[3] Consistent with Chapter 4, $z_{ioy} \equiv c_{iy}$. Recall further the distinction between c_{iy} and c_{is}: the subscript makes a difference since $y \in Y$ and $s \in S$. Thus, c_{iy} means $c_{iy} = c_{is}$ for all $s \in S_y$.

equilibrium must embody that, in principle, individuals can learn from each other, and the idea of "knowing that someone knows something I don't know" must be factored into individuals' behavior. To deal with the attendant relatively complex equilibrium concepts goes beyond the scope of this book.

While the microanalysis of information suggests three distinct equilibrium regimes, preceding their analysis a useful first step introduces benchmark allocations achievable by the usual omnipotent but fictitious "planner." The discussion of CPE in Section 3.3 motivates this analytical device, and those ideas apply no less here. Hence, the planner's allocation opportunities are constrained (i) by total supplies and (ii) by the "technological" restrictions that now explicitly include the information function as well as the market structure. Formally, one specifies the planner's allocation opportunities $\alpha \equiv \{\alpha_i\}_i \in G(A,\eta)$ by

$$G(A,\eta) \equiv \left\{\alpha \middle| \underline{w}_{iy} = \underline{z}_{iy} A_y, \sum_i z_{iy} \leq Z, \sum_i c_{iy} \leq C, \text{ all } y \in Y\right\}$$

or

$$G(A,\eta) \equiv \left\{\alpha \middle| \alpha_i \in C(A_{e,\eta}), \sum_i \alpha_i \leq (C1, W)\right\}$$

$$\equiv \left\{\alpha \middle| \alpha_i = \underline{z}_i A_{e,\eta}, \sum_i \alpha_i \leq (C1, W)\right\},$$

where 1 is an S-dimensional row vector.[4] The planner has the same information as the individuals. Of course, one associates no beliefs with the planner, especially since the individuals may have heterogeneous beliefs. Since the concept of information does not refer to beliefs (see section 4.2), this perspective entails no logical incompleteness or inconsistency.

Analogous to the simple two-date economy, define the planner's optimization problem by

$$g(A,\eta,v) \equiv \max_{\alpha} V_1(\alpha_1)$$

subject to

$$V_i(\alpha_i) \geq v_i, \; i = 2, \ldots, I,$$

$$\alpha \in G(A,\eta).$$

A natural generalization of the CPE concept introduced in Definition 2.7 is as follows.

DEFINITION 5.1. CONSTRAINED PARETO EFFICIENCY RELATIVE TO (A,η). *An allocation α satisfies CPE relative to (A,η) if it is implied as a solution to $g(A,\eta,v)$ for some v.*

---

[4] For the definitions of A_y, $C(\cdot)$, $A_{e,\eta}$, $\underline{w}_{iy}$, and $\underline{z}_i$, see section 4.3.

Note that the special case of CPE relative to (A,η^0) corresponds to Definition 3.3.

The relationship between CPE and SP-3 equilibria is unambiguous.

PROPOSITION 5.1. *Every SP-3 based equilibrium achieves CPE relative to the specified (A,η)-tuple. Conversely, every such CPE allocation can be replicated in an SP-3 based equilibrium for some distribution of endowments.*[5]*

Definition 3.1 (or 3.2) extends to define an equilibrium in an SP-3 regime. More generally, for each of the three regimes, an equilibrium obtains if and only if (i) signal conditioned security holdings (and consumption patterns) maximize expected utilities and (ii) aggregate demands equal exogenous total supplies. More complex is the question whether SP-1 and SP-2 based equilibria reach CPE. Subsequent sections discuss these two kinds of equilibria in some detail.

Because of the one-to-one correspondence between SP-3 equilibria and CPE, the behavior of the function g bears on the welfare comparisons of alternative SP-3 equilibria. The relevance of the g-function applies to the analysis of SP-1 and SP-2 based equilibria as well, since the I-dimensional vector $(g(\cdot,\cdot,v),v)$ of expected utilities cannot be dominated by any allocation consistent with $\alpha \in G(A,\eta)$. Further, SP-1 and SP-2 reach CPE under certain conditions, and in such cases one may assume that the allocations derive from an SP-3 equilibrium. The last point is analogous to the notion that otherwise similar Arrow-Debreu economies replicate SP-economies achieving FPE.

The next proposition generalizes Proposition 3.4.

PROPOSITION 5.2. *If $C(A'') \supseteq C(A')$ and/or η'' is at least as informative as η', then $g(A'',\eta'',v) \geq g(A',\eta',v)$ for all v.**

Since the proposition includes $A'' = A'$ as a special case, information enrichment never leads to inferior allocations provided that the allocations satisfy CPE. The economic intuition behind the result is simple enough: incremental information allows the planner to do everything he could do previously, plus possibly more, that is, $G(A,\eta'') \supseteq G(A,\eta')$. Evidently, Propositions 5.1 and 5.2 imply that the enrichments of information or markets rule out Pareto-inferior SP-3 equilibria.

The span of the market matrix is, as usual, its sole relevant characteristic. Specifically, if $C(A'') = C(A')$ (i.e., $G(A'',\eta^0) = G(A',\eta^0)$) then $G(A'',\eta) = G(A',\eta)$ for every information function η. (However, $C(A'') \supset C(A')$ implies only that $G(A'',\eta) \supseteq G(A',\eta)$, and the last inclusion relationship can be one of equivalence.) Nevertheless, to keep the exposi-

---

[5] Regarding the converse, note that $\bar{\alpha} \in G(A,\eta^0)$, rather than $\bar{\alpha} \in G(A,\eta)$, causes no problems.

tion straightforward, subsequent discussions generally fix the market structure without mentioning that a constant span of the market structure yields identical conclusions.

In analyzing the function g, of special interest are the two instances in which (i) the market structure imposes no binding restrictions and (ii) the information function imposes no binding restrictions. The first of these two cases generalizes the concept of Full Pareto Efficiency (FPE) introduced in Definition 3.3.

DEFINITION 5.2. FULL PARETO EFFICIENCY RELATIVE TO η. *An allocation α satisfies FPE relative to η if it is implied as a solution to $g(I,\eta,v)$ for some v.*

Hence, one associates with *each* information function a set of FPE allocations. As will be seen, these FPE sets are generally distinct. Further note that CPE allocations can dominate FPE allocations given that the incomplete markets setting uses a strictly more informative information function. That is, $g(A,\eta'',v) > g(I,\eta',v)$ may occur provided that η'' is strictly more informative than η'.

Even in the case of arbitrary preferences/beliefs/endowments, FPE does not require complete markets unless the information function is noninformative. A sufficient condition for FPE relative to η is completeness in the span of the matrix $\delta(A,\eta)$, that is, conditionally complete markets (CCM, Definition 4.1) suffice. (A special case of CCM is perfect information: $\delta(W,\eta^*)$ constitutes an $S \times S$ positive diagonal matrix so that for any markets $C(\delta(A,\eta^*)) = C(I)$ since $C(\delta(A,\eta^*)) \supseteq C(\delta(W,\eta^*)$. More generally, if (A',η') satisfies CCM so does (A'',η'') when $C(A'') \supseteq C(A')$ and η'' is at least as informative as η'.) FPE also requires CCM unless one confines preferences/beliefs. Given that $\delta(A,\eta)$ does not span all of S-dimensional space, one easily constructs preferences/beliefs/endowments such that $g(I,\eta,v) > g(A,\eta,v)$.

With restrictions on preferences/beliefs, FPE can, of course, hold without CCM. Section 3.4 in Chapter 3 identifies conditions such that the simple two-date model achieves FPE within incomplete markets (i.e., the FPE is relative to η^0). The analysis there generalizes with relatively minor and obvious modifications. The allocation restriction on date-one consumption imposed by $w_i \in C(\delta(A,\eta))$, where $C(\delta(A,\eta)) \subset C(I)$, may again not be binding in equilibrium. For example, with identical slope-parameter LRT utilities, homogeneous beliefs, and $1 \in C(\delta(A,\eta))$, the economy reaches FPE relative to η. (The result does not require the assumption $\rho U_i^2 = U_i^1$.) Lemma 3.8 and Proposition 3.8 are also pertinent, bearing in mind only that $\delta(A,\eta)$ rather than A defines the relevant market matrix.

Having considered conditions under which $g(I,\eta,v) = g(A,\eta,v)$, the next issue deals with the equality in $g(A,\eta'',v) \geq g(A,\eta',v)$. More concretely, under what conditions will the planner disregard the incremental information? One addresses this question most effectively by analyzing the dual effects of incremental information. First, information potentially affects the date-one consumption allocation, $\{w_{is}\}_{i,s}$, since the span of $\delta(A,\eta)$ restricts w_i, and $C(\delta(A,\eta'')) \supseteq C(\delta(A,\eta')$ where the subset relationship can be strict. Second, the date-zero consumption allocation, $\{c_{is}\}_{i,s}$, can be affected since c_{is} need not equal c_{it} in states s and t if and only if $s \in S_y$, $t \in S_{y'}$ where $y \neq y'$.

Focusing on date-zero consumption first, the following conditions suffice for a locally nonbinding measurability restriction.

LEMMA 5.3. *Let $\eta \neq \eta^0$ be any information function, and suppose that $\pi_i(y)/\pi_i(y') = \pi_1(y)/\pi_1(y')$ for all $i \in I$ and two signals $y,y' \in Y$. Suppose further that utilities are time-additive. Then $c_{iy} = c_{iy'}$ is necessary for CPE relative to η.*

The conditions, proof, and conclusion of the above result emanate entirely from Lemma 3.8: when two states have the same aggregate date-one supply, Lemma 3.8 implies that two primitive date-one claims can combine into one without adverse efficiency effects. Similarly, Lemma 5.3 exploits the invariance of aggregate supply of date-*zero* consumption across signals, and it follows that the measurability constraint on date-zero consumption is locally nonbinding if $c_{iy} = c_{iy'}$ at the unrestricted optimum. Hence the two signals, y and y', can merge into one without affecting the efficiency of the allocation of $\{c_{is}\}_{i,s}$.

The following example provides an instructive application of Lemma 5.3. Consider $\eta'' \neq \eta^0$ and

(a) $V_i = \sum_y \pi(y) \sum_{s \in S_y} \pi_i(s/y)[U_i^1(c_{is}) + U_{is}^2(w_{is})]$

(b) $A = I$.

Then $g(I,\eta'',v) = g(I,\eta^0,v)$ for all v (and (C,W)). Individuals have homogeneous signal beliefs (see (a)) relative to η'', and thus $c''_{is} = c''_{it}$ all $s,t \in S$ because of Lemma 5.3. Further, given that c''_i does not depend on s, and Arrow-Debreu markets (b), one infers the conclusion since $G(I,\eta^0) = G(I,\eta'') \cap \{c_i$ does not depend on s, all $i \in I\}$. The example demonstrates that an information function may not improve on the set of efficient allocations even when individuals have heterogeneous beliefs.[6]

Lemma 5.3 serves as the first ingredient in the identification of conditions sufficient for incremental information to be useless. The second ingredient implicitly confines preferences/beliefs/markets such that with respect to date-one consumption $\delta(A,\eta)$ relaxes no *binding* restrictions compared to A. Specifically, given (i) homogeneous signal beliefs, (ii) time-additive utili-

[6] Note that $\pi_i(s) = \pi_1(s)$, all $s \in S$, implies $\pi_i(y) = \pi_1(y)$, all $y \in Y$, but the converse is not true unless $\eta = \eta^*$.

ties, *and* (iii) *the condition* $g(\delta(A,\eta),\eta^0,v) = g(A,\eta^0,v)$, one concludes that $g(A,\eta,v) = g(A,\eta^0,v)$. To prove this, first note that $C(\delta(\delta(A,\eta),\eta)) = C(\delta(A,\eta))$.[7] This obviously implies that $g(\delta(A,\eta),\eta,v) = g(A,\eta,v)$. Second, given (i), (ii), and $C(\delta(\delta(A,\eta),\eta) = C(\delta(A,\eta))$, use Lemma 5.3 so that $g(\delta(A,\eta),\eta^0,v) = g(\delta(A,\eta),\eta,v)$. Hence,

$$g(A,\eta,v) = g(\delta(A,\eta),\eta,v) = g(\delta(A,\eta),\eta^0,v) = g(A,\eta^0,v).$$

The first and second equalities follow from the first and second observation, respectively, and the third equality follows from the *condition* (iii).

But the condition (iii), $g(\delta(A,\eta),\eta^0,v) = g(A,\eta^0,v)$, holds if, and generally only if, (A,η^0) suffices for FPE relative to η^0 in the first place. This fact, combined with Lemma 5.3, leads to settings of allocation irrelevant information.

PROPOSITION 5.3. *Suppose that*

(i) *utilities are time-additive*
(ii) *signal beliefs are homogeneous relative to* η
(iii) $g(A,\eta^0,v) = g(I,\eta^0,v)$.

Then

$$g(A,\eta,v) = g(A,\eta^0,v) = g(I,\eta,v).*$$

Thus, under the conditions of the proposition, the optimal allocation of securities, $\{z_{ijy}\}_{i,j,y}$, is simultaneously signal independent and FPE relative to η. The last equality in the proposition follows because (i) and (ii) imply $g(I,\eta^0,v) = g(I,\eta,v)$. With homogeneous beliefs, rather than homogeneous signal beliefs, the allocation is both signal independent and globally optimal: Lemma 5.3 holds for every η, and one obtains $g(I,\eta^*,v) = g(I,\eta^0,v)$. However, to replace homogeneous signal beliefs with homogeneous beliefs would be inappropriate, even as a practical matter. A nonpathological example, presented subsequently, shows that the optimal allocation may not achieve FPE relative to η^* although the conditions of Proposition 5.3 hold.

Chapter 3, section 3.4, provides an extensive discussion of (iii), that is, the conditions under which the allocation reaches FPE (relative to η^0) in

---

[7] To prove this, simply write down the expression for $\delta(\delta(A,\eta),\eta)$. For example, let $Y = 2$ and

$$\delta(A,\eta) = \begin{bmatrix} A_1 & 0 \\ 0 & A_2 \end{bmatrix}.$$

Then

$$\delta(\delta(A,\eta),\eta) = \begin{bmatrix} A_1 & 0 \\ 0 & 0 \\ 0 & A_2 \\ 0 & 0 \end{bmatrix},$$

and clearly $C(\delta(A,\eta)) = C(\delta(\delta(A,\eta),\eta))$.

spite of market incompleteness. Those results apply in the current context as well.

COROLLARY 5.3.1. *Suppose that utilities are LRT, slope parameters and beliefs are identical, and* $1 \in C(A)$. *Then enriched information or markets do not affect the equilibrium*: $g(I,\eta^*,v) = g(A,\eta^0,v)$.*

The LRT cases have exceptional equilibrium properties. No information function—including perfect information—and no markets beyond borrowing/lending can improve upon the efficient allocation of consumption patterns. The general markets/information irrelevance reflects that optimal risk-sharing can be accomplished using a very narrow set of allocations when individuals possess sufficiently similar attributes.

A special but interesting application of Proposition 5.3 has been modeled by Hakansson, Kunkel, and Ohlson (1982 lemma 3). Their analysis highlights the inherent powers of Lemma 3.8 and Corollary 3.8.1.

Consider the market matrix

$$A \equiv [\bar{A} : \bar{A}],$$

where $\bar{A}$ has size $(\frac{1}{2}S) \times (\frac{1}{2}S)$ and rank $\frac{1}{2}S$; A is $(\frac{1}{2}S) \times S$ and also of rank $\frac{1}{2}S$. Markets are therefore incomplete. The columns s and $\frac{1}{2}S + s$ are identical for every $s = 1, \ldots, \frac{1}{2}S$; thus, define the function $t = t(s) \equiv \frac{1}{2}S + s$, where $s \leq \frac{1}{2}S$, and it follows that $a_{js} = a_{jt}$. Let η be such that $Y = 2$ and $S_1 = \{1, \ldots, \frac{1}{2}S\}$, $S_2 = \{\frac{1}{2}S + 1, \ldots, S\}$. (To generalize the example for $Y > 3$ and $A \equiv [\bar{A} : \bar{A} : \cdots]$ presents no difficulties.) Assume time-additive utilities with $U_{is}^2 = U_{it}^2$, $t = t(s)$. The restrictions on beliefs are:

(a) $\pi_i(y)$ does not depend on i
(b) $\pi_i(y/s \text{ or } t(s))$ does not depend on i.

Assumption (a), of course, is nothing but homogeneous signal beliefs. The second condition, (b), one commonly refers to as a homogeneous *information matrix* assumption. The matrix terminology derives from the possibility of reading (b) as $\pi(y/\text{given a particular payoff column in the matrix } \bar{A})$, and the matrix $[\pi(y/s \text{ or } t(s))]$ has Y rows and $\frac{1}{2}S$ columns. In other words, the uncertainty pertains to the column vectors in $\bar{A}$, and the information available characterizes the probability of observing a signal conditioned on the event (s or $t(s)$) which adequately indexes a vector of payoff realizations.

Assumption (b), by itself, has an important implication: the relative probabilities $\pi_i(s)/\pi_i(t)$, $t = t(s)$, are independent of i for every $s = 1, \ldots, S/2$. To see this, first note that

$$\pi(y/s \text{ or } t(s)) = \frac{\pi_i(y,s \text{ or } t(s))}{\pi_i(s) + \pi_i(t(s))} = \begin{cases} \dfrac{\pi_i(s)}{\pi_i(s) + \pi_i(t(s))} \equiv \hat{\pi}^1(s) & y = 1 \\ & \text{if} \\ \dfrac{\pi_i(t(s))}{\pi_i(s) + \pi_i(t(s))} \equiv \hat{\pi}^2(s) & y = 2 \end{cases}$$

Hence, (b) implies that the ratios $\hat{\pi}^1(s)$ and $\hat{\pi}^2(s)$ do not depend on i. Second, the i-independence of $\hat{\pi}^1(s)$ and $\hat{\pi}^2(s)$ carries over to $\pi_i(s)/\pi_i(t(s))$. (This follows because $\hat{\pi}^1(s)$ can be stated as $[\pi_i(s)/\pi_i(t(s))]/\{[\pi_i(s)/\pi_i(t(s))] + 1\}$, and the latter expression is monotonic in the ratio $[\pi_i(s)/\pi_i(t(s))]$.)

But the conditions for Corollary 3.8.1 are now in place. Given the function $t = t(s)$, the columns s and t in A are identical, $U_{is}^2 = U_{it}^2$, and $\pi_i(s)/\pi_i(t) = \pi_1(s)/\pi_1(t)$ all i. Thus, the specification suffices for η^0 allocations to reach FPE relative to η^0 that is, $g(A,\eta^0,v) = g(I,\eta^0,v)$, for all v. The two remaining conditions in Proposition 5.3, (i) and (ii), are also met since signal-beliefs are homogeneous (assumption (a) above), and utilities are time-additive. The incremental information accordingly has no allocation consequence, consistent with the Hakansson, Kunkel, and Ohlson conclusion. The feature stressed here is that their result derives exclusively from Lemma 3.8.

The rather subtle features and implications of the above model must not be overlooked: the analysis shows that incremental information may be irrelevant *although markets are incomplete and beliefs are heterogeneous*. Assumptions (a) and (b), jointly, do not imply homogeneous beliefs. For example, let $S = 6$, $\pi_1 = (0.1, 0.2, 0.1, 0.1, 0.2, 0.3)$, and $\pi_2 = (0.2, 0.1, 0.1, 0.2, 0.1, 0.3)$; then $\pi_1 \neq \pi_2$, and one further verifies without difficulty that (a) and (b) are both satisfied.[8]

Because beliefs can be heterogeneous in the Hakansson, Kunkel, and Ohlson model, of conceivable relevance is the further refinement of the information function. The incremental information (refining η) may have an effect on the optimal allocation of the date-zero good. For example, perfect information and heterogeneous beliefs imply that the optimal allocation of the date-zero good is generally state dependent. This contrasts with the state independent date-zero good allocation in the Hakansson, Kunkel, and Ohlson model; thus the allocation in that model does not necessarily satisfy FPE w.r.t. η^*. To replace homogeneous signal beliefs with homogeneous beliefs in Proposition 5.3 would therefore obscure the local nature of the result. The irrelevance of information pertains only to a *particular* information function compared to no information. Similarly, to replace FPE relative to η^0 with complete markets would obscure that the adequacy of the market structure depends on individuals' beliefs (e.g., condition (b) in the Hakansson, Kunkel, and Ohlson model).

When does a change from η' to any more informative η'' never strictly improve the allocation? The answer to this question has already been indicated. Combining time-additive utilities with homogeneous beliefs (over

[8] The signal probabilities equal to $\pi_i(y = 1) = .4$, $\pi_i(y = 2) = .6$, and the information matrix equals

$$[\pi_i(y/s \quad \text{or} \quad t(s))] = \begin{bmatrix} .5 & .5 & .25 \\ .5 & .5 & .75 \end{bmatrix}.$$

states!) makes incremental information inconsequential if the information function η' suffices for an FPE allocation. The role of incremental information reduces to the enrichment of the span of $\delta(A,\eta)$ since the optimal date-zero good allocation does not depend on signals. Efficiency enhancement through more information becomes impossible once this matrix no longer binds the date-one allocation.

COROLLARY 5.3.2. *Suppose that individuals' utilities are time-additive and that beliefs are homogeneous. Let* $\eta^0,\eta^1,\ldots,\eta^n$ *be a sequence of increasingly informative information functions with* $\eta^n = \eta^*$. *Then* $g(A,\eta^k,v) = g(I,\eta^k,v)$ *implies that*

$$g(A,\eta^m,v) = g(I,\eta^k,v)$$

for all $m \geq k$. *Moreover, with* $W > 0$ *such as k exists.**

The (minimum) magnitude of k obviously depends on the markets and other exogenous specifications. Under the worst of circumstances, one achieves FPE once (A,η^k) satisfies CCM. (The CCM property remains fulfilled for all $m \geq k$). But it should be clear that specific preferences/beliefs may render CCM unnecessarily stringent. For example, given time-additive LRT utilities k needs to be only large enough to ensure that $1 \in C(A_y)$ for all y (i.e., $1 \in C(A_{e,\eta^k})$).

Another more interesting example of FPE relative to η without (A,η) being CCM relies on the idea that the information function $\eta(s) = W_s$ should, under appropriate conditions, be adequate for FPE w.r.t. η regardless of the market structure. That is, knowing the aggregate wealth level suffices for FPE allocations.

PROPOSITION 5.4. *Consider any A and suppose that*

(i) $\pi_i(s)/\pi_i(t)$ *is the same for all* $i \in I$ *if* $W_s = W_t$
(ii) $U_{is}(\cdot,\cdot) = U_{it}(\cdot,\cdot)$ *for all* $i \in I$ *if* $W_s = W_t$
(iii) $\eta(s) = W_s$;

then

$$g(A,\eta,v) = g(I,\eta,v).$$

If one in addition assumes time-additive utilities and homogeneous beliefs, then

$$g(A,\eta,v) = g(I,\eta^*,v).*$$

The first part of the proposition relates directly to Lemma 3.8: assumptions (i) and (ii) imply that every optimal α satisfies $w_{is} = w_{it}$ when $W_s = W_t$, and the conclusion then follows since, given (iii), $\delta(A,\eta)$ spans all distinct levels of aggregate wealth. The second part of the proposition sharpens the result by adding the assumptions, and conclusion, of Corollary 5.3.2.

The last proposition ties in with Corollary 3.13.1, which in turn also derives from Lemma 3.8. Corollary 3.13.1 states that the preferences/beliefs conditions (i) and (ii) in Proposition 5.4 lead to an FPE equilibrium relative to η^0 given the availability of a full set of (put) options on the market portfolio. Thus, to achieve FPE one can either use a full set of options on the aggregate wealth level *or* use perfect information about the same variable.

The point underscores the similarities between markets and information. Both potentially improve on the efficiency of the allocation for the same reason: they relax allocation constraints. The statement applies to markets and information with equal force, except for one qualification. Markets have an effect only on the allocation of the date-one consumption pattern, while in contrast information allows richer date-zero patterns as well as richer date-one patterns. Incremental information therefore has greater potential to improve efficiency than has market enrichment. Specifically, note that, generally, $g(I,\eta'',v) > g(I,\eta',v)$ when η'' is strictly more informative than η', but $g(A'',\eta^*,v) = g(A',\eta^*,v)$ even when $C(A'') \supset C(A')$. This comparative "advantage" of information relative to markets ceases in the case of time-additive utilities and homogeneous beliefs. The frequent utilization of the latter two conditions in the equilibrium analysis of information stems from their inducing full congruity in the theory of markets and the theory of information for CPE allocations.

5.2.2. Efficient allocations and redistributive effects

Up to this point the analysis of the function g relates to the relative efficiency of alternative markets/information specifications. Without difficulty one goes beyond efficiency analysis and considers the conceivable welfare relations associated with comparisons of (A,η) pairs. The similarity of SP-3 equilibria to the SP equilibria allows for generalizations of the (A,η^0) results after few modifications. The only requirement is that Type I, II, and III comparisons must be redefined to embrace distinct information functions as well as distinct market structures.

Type I: $G(A'',\eta'') = G(A',\eta')$; i.e., $C(A'') = C(A')$ and $\eta'' = \eta'$.

Type II: $G(A'',\eta'') \supset G(A',\eta')$; i.e., $C(\delta(A'',\eta'')) \supseteq C(\delta(A',\eta'))$ and η'' is at least as informative as η', and $C(\delta(A'',\eta'')) \neq C(\delta(A',\eta'))$ or $\eta'' \neq \eta'$.

Type III: $G(A'',\eta'') \not\supseteq G(A',\eta')$ and $G(A'',\eta'') \not\subseteq G(A',\eta')$; i.e., all other cases.

Given these modifications, Propositions 3.9, 3.10, and 3.11 remain valid, as is Table 1 (Chapter 3, p. 64). The essence, again, relates to the behavior of $g(A'',\eta'',v) - g(A',\eta',v)$: for Type I comparisons $g'' - g' = 0$, all v; for Type II $g'' - g' \geq 0$ all v; for Type III comparisons the sign of $g'' - g'$ is indeterminate unless the preferences/beliefs have been restricted. Analogous to the discussion in section 3.5, for Type II and III comparisons one can construct settings resulting in Pareto improvement, and for other settings redistributive effects (WR3) on expected utilities can occur. These conclusions apply no less when one adds endowment neutrality.

Time-additive utilities and homogeneous beliefs provide the versatility needed to cope effectively with the complications of having simultaneous variations in information and markets, or information alone. For example, an apparent difficulty exists in showing that Type II comparisons allow for a strict Pareto improvement. With no information, Proposition 3.10 makes the demonstration easy by putting $\alpha' = \bar{\alpha}' = \bar{\alpha}''$; the implication $\alpha_i' \in CO_i''$ prevents individuals from being worse off in the double-primed economy, and $\alpha'' \neq \bar{\alpha}''$ reflects a Pareto improvement. This approach does not work generally if $\eta' \neq \eta^0$. The reason is simple: for SP-3 the endowment allocation must be in the spans of A'_{e,η^0} and A''_{e,η^0} and endowments may not exist that satisfy CPE relative to η'. Thus, to construct a Type II case of Pareto improvement when $C(A'') = C(A')$ and $\eta' \neq \eta^0$ demands some care. One approach selects $\{V_i\}_i$ such that $g(A'',\eta'',v) > g(A',\eta',v) = g(A',\eta^0,v) = g(I,\eta^0,v)$. The first equality follows from time-additive utilities, and homogeneous signal-beliefs relative to η'; the inequality generally holds if beliefs are heterogeneous relative to η''. The assumption $\bar{\alpha}' = \alpha' \in G(A',\eta^0)$, and where α' is CPE relative to (A',η'), now poses no problems, so that Proposition 5.1 combined with endowment neutrality and the inequality $g'' > g'$ imply a strict Pareto improvement. Of course, a second approach selects $\{V_i\}_i$ such that $R'' = R'$, in which case $CO_i' \subseteq CO_i''$ so that $\alpha_i' \in CO_i''$. As one can infer from section 3.7.2, for this to hold it suffices if a single individual has linear utility. But one can also easily construct examples with MISC. No particular reasons suggest the impossibility of a strict Pareto improvement for some prespecified $\{V_i\}_i$, provided that $g'' > g'$ for some v. The point here merely notes that although an SP-3 economy with information is somewhat more complex than one without information, suitable restrictions on preferences/beliefs eliminate virtually all incremental complexities.

5.2.3. The concept of noisy information in the planner's problem

The final part of this section elaborates upon the meaning of preferable information in the planner's problem.[9] Proposition 5.2 states that more information, defined rigorously as a subpartition, leads to a (weak) welfare improvement in the planner's optimization problem. With this concept of preferable information, one attributes the efficiency gains directly to the relaxation of allocation constraints. The requirement for the conclusion may appear excessive, and a natural question is whether an information function can be preferable to some other function without composing a subpartition. Clearly, with *no* restrictions on preferences/beliefs (beyond MISC) or mar-

[9] This section discusses a special topic not referred to subsequently.

kets, the relationship $g(A,\eta'',v) \geq g(A,\eta',v)$ holds only if η'' is more informative than η'. The question therefore needs a more narrow restatement: Can one strengthen Proposition 5.2 by instituting relatively mild regularity conditions on preferences/beliefs/markets? The answer is affirmative.

The general approach develops from the idea that one information function may be less "noisy" than another information function. Combined with relatively mild conditions on preferences/beliefs, one can then state a result much deeper than Proposition 5.2 such that a less noisy information function suffices for (weakly) Pareto-preferable allocations. Yet—and this is indeed the critical point—a less noisy information function does not imply a subpartition. (The converse does hold, however; a more informative function is also less noisy.) What, then, defines (less) noisy information, and under what mild regularity conditions does it yield (weakly) preferable allocations? Section 4.2 in the previous chapter touches briefly on the notion of noisy information. Although the true/false scheme still frames the analysis (i.e., $\pi_i(y/s)$ equals either zero or one), the suggestion there that certain "states" are "more basic" can be exploited. Heuristically, to identify preferable less noisy information the ingredients are:

(i) Signals imply the same *conditional* payoff matrices, and with (sufficiently) state independent utilities the signals per se become irrelevant in the conditional utility evaluations except for their effects on the posterior probability vector and the portfolio. Hence, the payoff realizations define the "more basic states."

(ii) The usefulness of information relates to the joint probability distribution of signals and payoffs.

(iii) One joint probability distribution of signals/payoffs is preferable to another if the signals and the payoffs have a greater statistical association.

Although the points (ii) and (iii) have much intuitive appeal when evaluating information functions, this must not overshadow that the analysis depends critically on the markets and preferences' restriction (i). Note further that interindividual restrictions on the probabilities may be necessary to eliminate inadmissible heterogeneity.

As a simple example of greater (less) statistical association between signals and payoffs, consider the following model. Assume that the joint probabilities of signals and payoffs are common to all individuals and determined by

$$\tilde{y}_j'' = \tilde{a}_j + \tilde{\varepsilon}_{1j},$$

$$\tilde{y}_j' = \tilde{y}_j'' + \tilde{\varepsilon}_{2j},$$

where $\{\varepsilon_{1j}\}_j$ and $\{\varepsilon_{2j}\}_j$ $(j = 1, \ldots, J)$ define sets of pure noise random variables whose distributions do not depend on $\{\tilde{a}_j\}_j$ and $\{\tilde{a}_j,\tilde{y}_j'',\tilde{\varepsilon}_{1j}\}_j$, respectively. The model restricts the payoff matrix since states index all conceivable outcomes of $\{a_j,\varepsilon_{1j},\varepsilon_{2j}\}_j$. States differing only in their realization of

$\{\varepsilon_{1j}, \varepsilon_{2j}\}_j$ have identical column vectors in A. Thus, the payoff matrix can be conceptualized by $A \equiv [\hat{A}\hat{A} \cdots]$, where $\hat{A}$ identifies the matrix of all conceivable payoff realizations. The signal observed from the single-primed (double-primed) information function is the J-vector $y' \equiv (y'_1, \ldots, y'_J)$ ($y'' \equiv (y''_1, \ldots, y''_J)$). Since the single-primed signal derives from the double-primed signal *plus* incremental independent uncertainty, y'' has greater statistical association with $\{\tilde{a}_j\}_j$ compared to y'. One frequently refers to such a relationship as a *garbling* of information. The information function η'' does *not*, however, compose a subpartition of η' since one cannot infer the value of y' from knowing y'' (i.e., $\pi(y'/y'')$ does not equal zero or one).

Note next that for state independent utilities the vector payoff realization constitutes the only *relevant* uncertainty in a conditional utility evaluation. The information function η'' ought to be at least as useful as η' because the incremental uncertainty stemming from $\{\tilde{\varepsilon}_{2j}\}_j$ is totally extraneous and introduces undesirable risk. First, the presence of $\{\tilde{\varepsilon}_{2j}\}_j$ makes the prediction of payoffs less precise, an important matter since such predictions critically affect the optimal allocation of securities. Second, the individuals are risk-averse and have homogeneous beliefs, and this means that any implicit "betting" on the outcome of $\{\tilde{\varepsilon}_{2j}\}_j$ cannot serve any welfare improving purpose. In sum, given the model, one should expect that $g(A,\eta'',v) \geq g(A,\eta',v)$, even though η'' is not as fine as η'.[10]

The above conclusion is indeed correct. However, the formalization (and generalization) of preferable information in the planner's optimization problem demands a fairly laborious machinery. In addition to supplying an appropriate definition of "more of a statistical association," the formal analysis must restrict utilities and payoff matrices such that the relevance of signals stems from their imparting probabilistic revisions in the distribution of payoffs. Neither task is by any means straightforward. Accordingly, the proposition in question, and its proof, appears in an appendix to this chapter.

The appendix further shows that the structure of preferable information in the planner's problem relates closely to a concept of informativeness introduced by Blackwell (1953). The seminal *Blackwell's Theorem*, however, pertains to a single individual's choice problem (which does not have to be a consumption/portfolio setting). The planner's optimization problem has greater complexity than the problems encompassed by Blackwell's Theorem, for two reasons. First, the planner's problem incorporates multiple probability vectors, one for each of the I individuals. The concept of informativeness in Blackwell's Theorem has therefore no direct applicability in the

[10] The accounting literature frequently claims that the fineness theorem and Blackwell's Theorem do not, in general, apply in fixed supplies multiperson settings. Given Proposition 5.2 and Proposition A in Appendix 5.2, such statements are, at best, misleading. Of course, insofar as redistributive effects or inefficient allocations are relevant, the phrase "do not, in general, apply" is correct. However, negative statements of this kind are virtually always true in economics and therefore devoid of insights.

planner's problem if the individuals possess heterogeneous beliefs. The matter is significant. Appendix 5.2 shows that the informativeness condition in the planner's problem allows for limited but nontrivial heterogeneity in individuals' beliefs. And only for homogeneous beliefs do the informativeness conditions on the information function reduce to Blackwell's concept of informativeness. Second, some of the constraints in the planner's problem entwine with probabilities, since each of the $i = 2, \ldots, I$ individuals must reach a prespecified level of (minimum) expected utility. The settings in Blackwell's Theorem do not generically admit such constraints. The conditions and proof of the proposition in Appendix 5.2 do not, therefore, follow immediately from Blackwell's Theorem.

Another important difference relates to the relevance of concavity. While this preference attribute plays no role in Blackwell's Theorem, the appendix shows that in the planner's problem concave preferences are critical.

However, one can make room for a direct application of Blackwell's Theorem in the single-person partial equilibrium consumption/portfolio choice problem. In an SP-1 setting with information/signal independent prices the Blackwell's informativeness condition ranks the information functions the same as expected utility without depending on concavity. Just as the proposition in Appendix 5.2 strengthens Proposition 5.2 by circumscribing individuals' utilities/beliefs/markets, similar but weaker conditions predicate the strengthening of Proposition 4.1.

5.3. Equilibria Based on Settings Without Signal Insurance (SP-1)

The analysis of equilibria based on SP-1 settings focuses on the two usual questions that deal with the economy's welfare. First, what efficiency characteristics are associated with SP-1? Second, what conceivable welfare relations occur in the comparison of alternative markets/information function pairs? These were the two welfare questions raised in the case of SP-3 equilibria, and answers followed relatively easily because of their CPE-feature. In contrast, SP-1 equilibria do not generally reach CPE relative to the underlying (A,η) pair. This simple but critical observation will be discussed in detail; heretofore unencountered difficulties and consequences must be dealt with because of this non-CPE feature.

The analysis of SP-1 prior to SP-2 is advantageous. As suggested, SP-1 has simpler properties than SP-2, and SP-2 derives its unique complexity from being a mixture of SP-1 and SP-3. The analysis of SP-2 equilibria follows in the next section.

An SP-1 equilibrium derives from Y distinct SP equilibria. Given any (A,η) pair one usefully expresses the expected utility of individual i as

$$\max_{\alpha_i} V_i = \sum_{y} \pi_i(y) \max_{z_{iy}} V_{iy},$$

where V_{iy} defines the conditional expected utility:

$$V_{iy} \equiv \sum_{s \in S_y} \pi_i(s/y) U_{is}(z_{ioy}, \sum_j z_{ijy} a_{js}).$$

Each conditional maximization problem restricts available security holdings through the signal-contingent budget constraint:

$$\sum_{j \in J^+} z_{ijy} P_{jy} \leq \sum_{j \in J^+} \bar{z}_{ij} P_{jy}.$$

(Conditions for the existence of an SP-1 equilibrium, $\{P_{jy}\}_{j,y}\{z_{ijy}\}_{i,j,y}$, can be inferred directly from Proposition 3.3.)

The SP-1 equilibria do not generally achieve CPE relative to (A,η) because the equilibrium allocation results from Y disjoint settings. The other side of the coin is the equilibrium's (allocation and prices) independence of the signal probabilities.

PROPOSITION 5.5. *An equilibrium based on an SP-1 setting is independent of the signal probabilities* $\{\pi_i(y)\}_{i,y}$; *the only relevant probabilities are the conditional probabilities* $\{\pi_i(s/y)\}_{i,s,y}$.*

A non-CPE outcome may occur because the $\{\pi_i(y)\}_{i,y}$ affect the expected utility evaluation yet are of no consequence in the allocation of securities and consumption patterns. Stated somewhat differently, the absence of coordination of allocations across signals leads potentially to a suboptimal allocation. The sole appealing attribute about SP-1 equilibria is their *signal efficiency*: given some signal y and related matrix A_y, the *conditional* allocation $\{z_{ijy}\}_{i,j}$ cannot be Pareto improved upon. But the importance of such signal efficiency must not be overrated since it is only necessary and not sufficient for CPE. Conditional expected utilities reflect individuals' welfare but partially, of course, and an efficiency evaluation ultimately must assess the entire allocation $\{z_{ijy}\}_{i,j,y}$.

That SP-1 equilibria typically imply suboptimal allocations because allocations do not coordinate across signals affords ready illustration. Consider a setting in which all individuals possess homogeneous signal-beliefs and time additive utilities. Given these assumptions, CPE requires $\{c_{iy}\}_{i,y}$ to be signal independent (Lemma 5.3). But such an allocation occurs only by coincidence in an SP-1 equilibrium.

The possibility of non-CPE allocations means that the economy does not exploit the risk-sharing opportunities fully. The point becomes most poignant if the trading is unaffected by information in SP-1 but affected in SP-3. One easily constructs such an example. Let the endowments be CPE relative to the no information setting, that is, $\bar{\alpha}$ solves $g(A,\eta^0,v)$ for some v. Suppose further that utilities are time-additive and that $g(A,\eta^0,v) = g(I,\eta^0,v)$. Then the endowments equal the equilibrium holdings in the (A,η) SP-1 economy *regardless of the signal beliefs*. This no-trading outcome follows because $\bar{\alpha}$ would be FPE relative to η were signal-beliefs homogeneous. (Clearly, individuals never trade if endowments achieve FPE relative to η, since trading requires a Pareto improvement.) But the signal beliefs are irrelevant as far as any trading is concerned in SP-1 because of Proposition 5.5. Thus, given heterogeneous signal beliefs one generally obtains $g(A,\eta,v) > g(A,\eta^0,v)$, although the equilibrium in the informative SP-1 economy constitutes a solution to $g(A,\eta^0,v)$.

The absence of coordination of signal-conditioned security allocations across signals potentially has exceptionally adverse welfare effects. In particular, *incremental information may lead to an allocation that makes all individuals strictly worse off.* This possibility may be conceptualized in a number of different ways.

To keep matters simple, suppose that η'' is informative and that $\eta' = \eta^0$. An individual's endowed relative wealth in the η'' = economy, $\bar{\bar{w}}''_{iy} \Big/ \sum_i \bar{\bar{w}}''_{iy}$, varies with y. A negative welfare implication would seemingly follow if the relative wealth is low when $\pi_i(y)$ is large so that $\sum_y \pi_i(y)\left[\bar{\bar{w}}''_{iy} \Big/ \sum_i \bar{\bar{w}}''_{iy}\right] < \bar{\bar{w}}'_i \Big/ \sum_i \bar{\bar{w}}'_i$ for possibly all i. Under the circumstances, every individual ends up with less expected relative wealth in the η'' setting. Recalling that the $\{\pi_i(y)\}_{y,i}$ have no impact on the equilibrium prices, and thus also on endowed wealth, the construction of such a setting should be feasible. The attendant decreases in the individuals' expected wealth in the η''-economy suggest similar effects on expected utilities.

Another apparently negative welfare consequence of an informative SP-1 setting follows because an individual cannot insure his random endowed wealth. From these two related perspectives, (incremental) information potentially causes harmful uncertainty.

Although the literature frequently presents the above arguments because of their heuristic merits, the underlying logic is somewhat precarious. For one thing, endowed (expected) wealth does not bear directly on an individual's welfare (recall the discussion in 3.7.3). As another point, although uninsurable wealth endowments suggest non-CPE allocations, this possibility by itself lacks an indication of the degree or distribution of the efficiency loss. The claim that WR4 outcomes may occur requires more rigorous substantiation.

A direct approach demonstrating Pareto-inferior outcomes aims at the relatively limited usefulness of trading in an SP-1 based equilibrium with information. Suppose that markets are Arrow-Debreu, and let $S = J = I = 2$. Further, let utilities be time-additive and identical for the two individuals, and let beliefs be homogeneous with equally probable states. Compare the information functions $\eta'' = \eta^*$ and $\eta' = \eta^0$. By virtue of Proposition 5.3, $g(I,\eta'',v) = g(I,\eta',v)$ and the η''-economy accordingly rules out a strict Pareto improvement compared to the η'-economy. Suppose further that $W_1 = W_2$, and that $\bar{\alpha}_1 = (C/2, W_1, 0)$, $\bar{\alpha}_2 = (C/2, 0, W_2)$. The symmetry across the two signals implies that for the η'' equilibrium $V''_{i=1,y=1} = V''_{i=2,y=2}$ and $V''_{i=1,y=2} = V''_{i=2,y=1}$. It follows that $V''_{i=1} = V''_{i=2}$ as well as $V'_{i=1} = V'_{i=2}$. Since a Pareto improvement is also impossible, one obtains $V''_i \leq V'_i$, where the equality holds if and only if the double-primed economy results in FPE relative to η''. Such FPE allocations cannot occur because c_{iy} varies with y. To demonstrate this signal dependence, simply exploit that the two individuals are identical in every respect except for their endowments. State-2 claims are worthless given $y = 1$, and individual 2 trades some of his date-zero consumption good in exchange for part of the state-1 claims owned by individual 1. (Given the asymmetric endowments and identical utilities/beliefs, no-trading clearly cannot sustain an equilibrium.) It follows that $c_{i=1,y=1} > C/2$ and $c_{i=2,y=1} < C/2$. The opposite holds for $y = 2$. Hence, the η''-economy does not achieve FPE, and $V''_i < V'_i$ for $i = 1,2$; the η''-outcome is indeed Pareto-inferior (WR4). The suboptimality of trading in the η''-economy becomes evident by comparing it to the trading in the $\eta'(= \eta^0)$-economy. The no-information economy defines a useful benchmark since the trading in that case results in FPE relative to η^0 and, in addition, $g(I,\eta^0,v) = g(I,\eta^*,v)$. Because of the general symmetry across the two states, in a η^0-equilibrium individual 1 trades half of his state-1 claims in exchange for half of individual 2's state-2 claims. The date-zero consumption good does not trade, in sharp contrast to what happens in the η''-economy. In sum, the example demonstrates the following.

PROPOSITION 5.6. *There exist SP-1 economies such that a more informative information function makes all individuals strictly worse off.**

To construct examples leading to Pareto-inferior allocations in SP-1 settings does not demand exceptional assumptions. Restrictions on preferences/beliefs/markets serve no critical purpose. The example is noteworthy only because it highlights suboptimal trading and the absence of an allocative coordination across the different signals. Section 5.5 (Proposition 5.18) provides a more dramatic proposition: in certain cases only WR4 (or WR2) occurs *regardless* of the endowment allocation.

The previous discussion should not be construed to suggest the inevitability of Pareto-inferior (or, at best, Pareto-indifferent) outcomes if the set of FPE allocations does not change with the information functions (i.e., the conditions of Corollary 5.3.2 are met with $k = 0$). Redistributive effects cannot be excluded a priori, and one easily constructs WR3 examples. Nor should the example be interpreted as suggesting that information-enriched SP-1 economies cannot lead to Pareto improvements. Such outcomes are generally possible, provided that $g(A,\eta'',v)-g(A,\eta',v) > 0$ for some v. As a further point, CPE allocations are not intrinsically impossible.

With the "correct" endowments, the allocations will indeed be (CPE) efficient, and with the "incorrect" ones the allocations are inefficient. This conclusion applies whether or not $g(I,\eta'',v)-g(I,\eta^0,v)$ equals zero. Thus, the effects of trading in the η''-economy do not reconcile easily with the outcome of the η^0-economy. The problem is that little can be said about SP-1 equilibria without the endowment specification. The next result articulates the idea in a form which is not the most general one, but it has the advantage of being easy to interpret and prove.

PROPOSITION 5.7. *Consider some preferences $\{V_i\}_i$ and Arrow-Debreu markets. Let α be any signal-efficient allocation relative to some information formation η. Then some $\bar{\alpha} \in G(I,\eta^0)$ exists such that the SP-1 economy supports an equilibrium α.*

FPE allocations are signal-efficient; given complete markets, all FPE allocations are therefore potential equilibrium outcomes.[11] But, on the negative side, signal efficiency is a very weak efficiency concept, and thus a signal-efficient α might well be strictly Pareto-inferior to an allocation implied by $g(I,\eta^0,v)$, some v.

The potential negative welfare consequence of information should be attributed to the SP-1 setting, and not to the information enrichment per se. To emphasize this observation, note that analogous to Proposition 5.6 one can construct fixed-information cases in which the enrichment of *markets* makes all individuals strictly worse off. In other words, even though $C(A'') \supset C(A')$, and $C(\delta(A'',\eta)) \supset C(\delta(A',\eta))$, $\eta \neq \eta^0$, all individuals may be strictly worse off in the double-primed economy.

One develops a scenario as follows. If for each individual i there exists (at least) one y such that $V''_{iy} < V'_{iy}$, then Proposition 5.5 may be applied and appropriate choice of $\{\pi_i(y)\}_{i,y}$ results in the strictly Pareto-inferior outcome $V''_i < V'_i$ for all i. The possibility of each i satisfying $V''_{iy} < V'_{iy}$ for some y is readily conceptualized. Suppose that each individual does not trade for one particular signal in the double-primed economy. For that particular (i,y) pair, $V''_{iy} \leq V'_{iy}$ since the single-primed economy includes $(c''_{iy},\{w''_{is}\}_{s\in Sy}) = (\bar{c}_i,\{\bar{w}_{is}\}_{s\in Sy})$ as an affordable and attainable opportunity. Moreover, the inequality is strict if exchange occurs in the single-primed economy. Although tedious, to work out the details of an example poses in principle few problems since trading almost certainly takes place except for the preselected (i,y)-pairs. (Of course, using this approach the number of individuals must exceed two.)

PROPOSITION 5.8. *There exist SP-1 economies with $\eta \neq \eta^0$ such that an enrichment of markets makes all individuals strictly worse off.**

In sum, Propositions 5.6 and 5.8 jointly illustrate a central message: the essential equivalence between markets and information. An enrichment of either markets or information in an SP-1 setting may lead to a Pareto-

[11] One strengthens the result as follows: if α'' is FPE relative to η'', α' is FPE relative to η', and α'' is Pareto-superior to α', then there exists some $\bar{\alpha} \in G(I,\eta^0)$ that sustains α'' and α' as two SP-1 equilibria.

inferior outcome.[12] For both markets and information one can also show that Pareto-inferior outcomes do not necessarily follow. Examples resulting in any one of the three other welfare relations are easily constructed when $G(A'',\eta'') \supset G(A',\eta')$.

5.4. Equilibria Based on Settings with Sequential Trading (SP-2)

5.4.1. Efficiency analysis

The analyses of SP-3 and SP-1 equilibria provide a useful foundation when one considers the welfare characteristics of the more important SP-2 equilibria.[13] Like an SP-1 but unlike an SP-3 economy, for SP-2 economies one cannot presume allocations to be CPE relative to the underlying (A,η) pair. An exception occurs when the matrix of second round prices, $\underline{\underline{P}}$, satisfies DCM (dynamically complete markets, Definition 4.5). These conclusions follow immediately from Propositions 4.9 and 5.1. Some other useful facts about DCM may be recalled from Chapter 4. First, DCM does not hold when the number of signals is large relative to the number of securities, since DCM requires $Y \leq J + 1$. Second, $Y \leq J + 1$ unfortunately does not suffice for DCM since the matrix $\underline{\underline{P}}$ is endogenous, and the vectors in $\underline{\underline{P}}$ can be linearly dependent. A further complication arises because the space not spanned by the row vectors in $\underline{\underline{P}}$ may be irrelevant. Thus, although DCM suffices for an SP-2 allocation to be CPE relative to (A,η), its necessity and presence depend on exogenous factors.

Since CPE allocations may not always require DCM, one raises a basic question by addressing the following: Even if $Y > J + 1$, what conditions suffice for an SP-2 allocation to reach CPE relative to (A,η), or FPE relative to η? The question has a straightforward answer. The absence of DCM causes no efficiency loss if the first trading round achieves an efficient outcome. Hence, irrelevant information in the sense of $g(A,\eta,v) = g(A,\eta^0,v)$

---

[12] Using Proposition 5.5, one can also show that SP-1 may have several equilibria, yet one equilibrium Pareto dominates some other. Let $Y = 2$, and suppose that *each* signal permits two equilibria (this poses no problems). Denote the implied conditional expected utilities by V_{iy}^k where $k = 1,2$ superscripts the two possible equilibria for each y. Let $I = 2$. Assume that for $i = 1$ $V_{iy}^1 > V_{iy}^2$ for both y. This loses no generality since the four equilibria can be labeled appropriately. Further, this implies that for $i = 2$ $V_{iy}^2 > V_{iy}^1$, $y = 1,2$. (This follows since each conditional allocation satisfies signal efficiency.) Express individual i's expected utility for any of the four equilibria by

$$V_i^{(k_1,k_2)} = \pi_i(y = 1)V_{iy=1}^{k_1} + \pi_i(y = 2)V_{iy=2}^{k_2},\ k_1,\ k_2 = 1,2.$$

If $\pi_{i=1}(y = 2)$ and $\pi_{i=2}(y = 1)$ are both close to zero, then it is readily seen that $V_i^{(1,2)} > V_i^{(2,1)}$ for both i. (Hart [1975] develops the conclusion in a somewhat different economy. The idea here is the same.)

[13] As previously observed, the importance of SP-2 derives from its constituting the natural prototype multiperiod extension of the simple SP equilibria.

Proving the existence of an SP-2 equilibrium raises considerable difficulties. See Werner (1985).

implies a CPE equilibrium relative to (A,η), as well as (A,η^0), and no trading occurs in the second trading round.

PROPOSITION 5.9. *Suppose that* $g(A,\eta,v) = g(A,\eta^0,v)$. *The SP-2 based equilibrium is then CPE relative to* (A,η). *Moreover, no individual needs to trade in the second trading round.**

The proof follows from a subtle but by now familiar argument: the elimination of markets and exchange opportunities causes no change in the equilibrium, provided that the optimal strategy remains feasible. Thus, an SP-3 equilibrium with a signal independent securities' allocation also supports an SP-2 equilibrium.

Proposition 5.3 covers cases satifying Proposition 5.9. Specifically, homogeneous signal beliefs, time-additive utilities, and $g(A,\eta^0,v) = g(I,\eta^0,v)$ suffice for the information, and the second trading round, to be irrelevant. Any SP-2 setting consistent with the three conditions therefore reaches FPE relative to η.

Barring relatively strong restrictions on preferences/beliefs (or endowments)—such as the LRT utilities setting of Corollary 5.1, or the Hakansson, Kunkel, and Ohlson model—the condition $g(A,\eta,v) = g(A,\eta,{}^0v)$ generally requires complete markets. However, complete markets imply that $\underline{\underline{P}}$ satisfies DCM, and the assumptions of time-additivity and homogeneous signal-beliefs merely render a second round of trading superfluous.

PROPOSITION 5.10. *In an SP-2 economy complete markets imply dynamically complete markets; the equilibrium achieves FPE.*

Thus, complete markets compel the equivalence of SP-2 and SP-3 economies, and allocations satisfy FPE relative to the underlying information function. Complete markets therefore retain their essence in SP-2 equilibria: individuals can contract on all measurable contingencies, and their opportunity constraints can be equivalently expressed as

$$\sum_y c_{iy} P_{oy} + \sum_s w_{is} R_{1s} \leq \bar{\bar{w}}_i (\equiv \bar{\alpha} \cdot R).$$

The price paid for such a strong conclusion is that the dynamic feature of the SP-2 economy introduces no richness or new features to the analysis. Similarly, any conception of "real-world" securities in this environment becomes at best contrived. In the case of an SP-2 setting with complete markets or, more generally, an FPE-equilibrium, one might as well assume individuals to implement their trading in an SP-3 setting with Arrow-Debreu securities. This benchmark aspect of Arrow-Debreu markets is precisely what makes them so important—and limited—in economic theory.

It is worth noting that complete markets perform efficiently because they give rise to DCM/CCM, and, unlike Proposition 5.9, focusing on the trading serves no useful purpose. Although the first round has an abundance of securities, this does not eliminate the need for a second round of trading. The conclusion follows because the first-round choice of $\hat{c}_i$ cannot depend on y, while a second trading round permits c_{iy} to vary with y as is required generally for FPE relative to $\eta(\neq \eta^0)$.

One easily constructs an incomplete markets SP-2 equilibrium that does not result in a CPE allocation relative to an underlying (A,η) pair. A setting with $Y > J + 1$ generally suffices. In a multiple individuals SP-2 setting with arbitrary preferences/beliefs, one must expect the absence of DCM to entail additional binding constraints compared to an SP-3 equilibrium. The possibility of non-CPE equilibria makes the following question interesting: Whether or not markets satisfy DCM, does there exist some efficiency characterization of SP-2 equilibria? A possible answer, of course, acknowledges the signal efficiency of the equilibrium. However, this characterization does not adequately address the question. An SP-2 equilibrium enjoys at least partial signal insurance because of the presignal trading round, and the concept of signal efficiency does not incorporate this feature. A sharper efficiency concept originates from an observation first presented in the previous chapter. Section 4.6 notes the similarity between the SP-2 and the SP-3 choice settings; the key difference relates to the fact that in SP-2 $\underline{\underline{P}}$, as well as (A,η), constrains the attainable mixes of consumption patterns. But SP-2 is otherwise structurally identical to an SP-3. One infers that an SP-2 equilibrium satisfies a CPE property *relative to the set of attainable patterns.*

To be precise, consider some *specific* SP-2 equilibrium, and let $\hat{A}$ denote the matrix such that $C(\hat{A})$ determines the vector space of attainable consumption patterns. Section 4.6.3 demonstrates the existence of such an $\hat{A}$-matrix.[14] The discussion there also emphasizes that $\hat{A}$ depends on $\underline{\underline{P}}$ as well as (A,η). Now, given the matrix $\hat{A}$ that derives from some specific SP-2 equilibrium, define the planner's optimization problem as:

$$h(\hat{A},v) = \max_{\alpha} V_1(\alpha_1)$$

subject to

$$V_i(\alpha_i) \geq v_i, \; i = 2, \ldots, I,$$

$$\alpha_i \in C(\hat{A}),$$

$$\sum_{i=1}^{I} \alpha_i \leqq (C1,W).$$

There then exists some v^* such that the solution implied by $h(\hat{A},v^*)$ replicates the SP-2 equilibrium. This conclusion is unproblematic and immediate

[14] To recapitulate, section 4.6.3 shows that a matrix $\hat{A}$ exists such that SP-2's consumption opportunity set is equivalent to (a) $\alpha_i \cdot R \leq \bar{\alpha}_i \cdot R$, and (b) $\hat{A}$ spans $\alpha_i : \alpha_i \in C(\hat{A})$.

from the discussion in Chapter 2, section 2.3. It therefore makes economic sense to say that "sequential equilibria are constrained Pareto efficient." However, the classical welfare analysis does not generalize entirely, because not all solutions implied by $h(\hat{A},v)$ as v varies are replicable by SP-2 equilibria through a variation in endowments. That is, for SP-2 economies the second part of Proportion 5.1 has no counterpart, and there exists no converse to the efficiency property. Ideally one would like to make some statement to the effect that every solution to the planner's problem with a fixed $\hat{A}$ can be replicated through appropriate allocation of endowments. But this cannot be done generally unless $\underline{\underline{P}}$ is DCM for arbitrary endowments (complete markets eliminate the problem; see Proposition 5.10). The source of the problem is obvious: $\hat{A}$ depends on the span of $\underline{\underline{P}}$ which in turn depends on endowments.[15]

In summary, an SP-2 equilibrium results in a CPE-allocation relative to an identifiable vector space. But this property does not embed the same "quality" as the classical analysis because the vector space is generally endogeneous and depends on endowments.

5.4.2. Analysis of welfare relations

The next issue concerns the analysis of conceivable welfare relations for sequential equilibria. As a first observation, to construct examples in which incremental information, or enriched markets, lead to any one of the WR1, WR2, or WR3 outcomes entails no difficulties when $Y \leq J + 1$. DCM follows generally unless one specifies the preferences/beliefs/markets/endowments to deliberately impart linear dependence in the $\underline{\underline{P}}$ matrix. From this perspective it follows that welfare outcomes in SP-3 economies also apply in SP-2 for the three types of markets/information comparisons. However, since markets need not be DCM in SP-2, one cannot conclude that WR1, WR2, and WR3 comprise the only possibilities. Of particular interest, therefore, is the extent to which the markets/information enrichment of an SP-2 economy may lead to Pareto-inferior outcomes. As one may expect, since SP-2 economies under some conditions have properties equivalent to SP-1 (Proposition 4.9), Pareto-inferior outcomes can occur. (In this context, recall Propositions 5.6 and 5.8.) The original example demonstrating this significant fact for market enrichment is due to Hart (1975). Although Hart's class of economies has fewer restrictions on beliefs/preferences/goods/markets, etc., than the model considered here, his conclusion remains intact.

The ideas supporting the potentially adverse welfare conclusion associated with enriched markets can be outlined as follows. The heart of the

---

[15] The following illustrates an implication of the problem. Let $\bar{\alpha}''$, A'', η'' and $\bar{\alpha}'$, A', η' specify two SP-2 economies (possibly with endowment neutrality). Suppose further that $C(\hat{A}'') \supset C(\hat{A}')$. One can then conclude that α'' is not Pareto-inferior compared to α'. But this conclusion is endowment specific, in sharp contrast to the SP model. (Recall Proposition 3.10.)

matter deals with the *partial* elimination of the set of attainable consumption patterns. The consumption opportunity set derives from a combination of the two trading rounds' opportunities, and both the spaces $C(\underline{\underline{P}})$ and $C(A_{e,\eta})$ serve as inputs when one identifies attainable consumption mixes. (Recall the analysis in section 4.6.2) Thus, consider a comparison of (A',η) and (A'',η) where $C(A'') \supset C(A')$ and $\eta \neq \eta^0$. Market enrichment implies that $C(A''_{e,\eta}) \supseteq C(A'_{e,\eta})$, with the possibility of a strict subset relationship. However, the opportunities in the presignal round must be considered too; the single- and double-primed equilibria may differ, and one cannot rule out that $C(\underline{\underline{P}}') \supset C(\underline{\underline{P}}'')$. What actually happens to the span of the $\underline{\underline{P}}$ matrix as markets change must be traced back to the implicit prices. Unless the implicit prices remain unchanged, thereby satisfying the conditions of Proposition 4.10, more markets do not necessarily enlarge the set of attainable consumption patterns. In the extreme, two different equilibria may imply that rank$[\underline{\underline{P}}''] = 1 <$ rank$[\underline{\underline{P}}'] = Y$: the *single*-primed economy satisfies DCM and is as efficient as an SP-3 economy, while in contrast the *double*-primed economy transforms into the generically inefficient SP-1 economy (this follows from Proposition 4.9). The welfare effects can be negative since, depending on the preferences/beliefs, the sharing of risks *across signals* may be relatively more crucial than the improved second-round risk sharing made possible through second-round market enrichment. In sum, very roughly, the loss in efficiency due to $C(\underline{\underline{P}}'') \subset C(\underline{\underline{P}}')$ dominates the gain due to $C(A''_{e,\eta}) \supset C(A'_{e,\eta})$.

The putting together of an actual example consistent with the above reasoning presents certain problems since $C(\underline{\underline{P}}'')$ and $C(\underline{\underline{P}}')$ are endogenous and depend on A'' and A', respectively. For example, rank$[A'] = S$-1 would not work because it results in a complete A'', further implying that the double-primed economy reaches FPE relative to the underlying information function (Proposition 5.10). Nevertheless, one can construct incomplete markets settings such that rank$[\underline{\underline{P}}''] = 1$. To frame the double-primed economy as a SP-1 economy has the advantage of "maximing the chances" for "truly inefficient" allocations. The preferences/beliefs underpinnings for nonrandom P''_y price vectors follow if one derives the posterior probabilities that sustain a posited equilibrium of (nonrandom) prices, preferences, and allocation α''. (The approach has much in common with Proposition 3.6.) The allocation α'' should ideally differ little from $\bar{\alpha}_i$ since $V_i(\bar{\alpha}_i)$ serves as a lower bound on expected utility. This raises another complication that relates to a trading requirement. One shows without difficulty that $\bar{\alpha} = \alpha''$ implies $\alpha'' = \alpha'$ when $C(A'') \supseteq C(A')$ and a WR2 outcome results. Thus, the double-primed setting should have some, but limited, trading. With respect to the single-primed setting, by letting $Y = 2$ one can be reasonably certain that rank$[\underline{\underline{P}}'] = Y$ given $J' \geq 2$ since linear dependence in $\underline{\underline{P}}$'s columns occurs only in knife-edge cases. Thus the single-primed economy satisfies CPE, a desirable property since the object of the analysis requires all individuals to be better off in this economy. Finally, one exploits the irrelevance of *signal* beliefs in the double-primed economy, that is, Proposition 5.5. Significantly heterogeneous signal beliefs implies a relatively inefficient double-primed equilibrium, since SP-1 admits no risk sharing across signals even though such risk sharing is clearly desirable.

The next few paragraphs describe a numerical example.

Information: let $S = 6$; the information function partitions S into the sets {1,2,3} and {4,5,6}.

Markets: $J'' = 3$ and $J' = 2$ where

$$A'' = [\bar{A}''\bar{A}''],\ A' = [\bar{A}'\bar{A}'],$$

and

$$\bar{A}'' = \begin{bmatrix} 1 & 0 & 1 \\ 1 & 1 & 0 \\ 0 & 1 & 1 \end{bmatrix},\ \bar{A}' = \begin{bmatrix} 1 & 1 & 0 \\ 0 & 1 & 1 \end{bmatrix}.$$

Supplies are, respectively, $Z'' = (0,4,4)$ and $Z' = (4,4)$, so that $W = W' = W'' = (4,8,4,4,8,4)$. Thus, the double-primed economy includes an additional nonredundant zero supply security, namely, security one. It follows that $C(A'') \supset C(A')$ and $G(A'',\eta) \supset G(A',\eta)$.

Individuals: $I = 2$, and both individuals have logarithmic utility. For simplicity, but without substantive loss of generality, the model excludes date-zero consumption. The state probabilities are proportional to

	States					
Individual	1	2	3	4	5	6
1	1	7/3	2	100	2 × 100	100
2	100	9/5 × 100	2/5 × 100	1	2 × 1	1

Endowments are symmetric, that is, $\bar{z}_i = \frac{1}{2}Z'$, $i = 1, 2$.

Equilibrium in the A''-economy: assume, tentatively, that the posterior round prices do not depend on y; then $\text{rank}[\underline{\underline{P}}''] = 1$, $\bar{z}_i = \hat{z}_i''$, and the equilibrium derives from an SP-1 setting. The trades, $\Delta z_i''$, and the conditional equilibrium values for each of the two signals follow:

$$y = 1.\quad \Delta z_1'' = -\Delta z_2'' = (1/2,-1,1/2)$$

$$w_1'' = (2,4,2) + (-1/2,-1/2,1) = (1.5,3.5,3)$$

$$w_2'' = (2,4,2) + (1/2,1/2,-1) = (2.5,4.5,1)$$

$$\lambda_1'' = \lambda_2'' = (1,1,1), \text{ and}$$

$$P'' = (1,1,1).$$

Since $\Delta z_1'' \cdot P'' = 0$, the trades satisfy the budget constraints.

$y = 2$. The *conditional* beliefs *are* homogeneous, and the equilibrium has no trading. Again, $\lambda_1'' = \lambda_2'' = (1,1,1)$ and $P'' = (1,1,1)$.

Hence, $\text{rank}[\underline{\underline{P}}''] = \text{rank}\begin{bmatrix} 1 & 1 \\ 1 & 1 \\ 1 & 1 \end{bmatrix} = 1$ and the hypothesized allocation does indeed constitute an equilibrium. The individuals' expected utilities, after normalizing the probabilities, equal

$$V_1'' = V_1(1.5,3.5,3,2,4,2) = 1.04$$

and

$$V_2'' = V_2(2.5,4.5,1,2,4,2) = 1.13,$$

respectively.

Equilibrium in the A'-economy: first, suppose that $\text{rank}[\underline{\underline{P}}'] = 1$. Then $\hat{z}_i' = \bar{z}_i$ is optimal. For $y = 2$ a no-trading equilibrium ensues with $P_{y=2}'' = (1,1)$. The requirement $\text{rank}[\underline{\underline{P}}'] = 1$ therefore holds only if $P_{y=1}' = (1,1)$. But the latter price vector does not support an equilibrium. (This one demonstrates readily via a direct analysis of the two individuals' optimality conditions and using the fact that $w_{is=2} = 2$, $i = 1, 2$, for all z_i satisfying $z_i \cdot 1 = \bar{z}_i \cdot 1$.)

Hence, $\text{rank}[\underline{\underline{P}}'] = 2$ and the economy satisfies DCM. The equilibrium can therefore be derived in an SP-3 setting with market structure

$$\delta(A',\eta) = \begin{bmatrix} 1 & 1 & 0 & 0 & 0 & 0 \\ 0 & 1 & 1 & 0 & 0 & 0 \\ 0 & 0 & 0 & 1 & 1 & 0 \\ 0 & 0 & 0 & 0 & 1 & 1 \end{bmatrix}.$$

Given the asymmetry of signal probabilities, in this economy individual one consumes heavily in states 4–6, while individual two consumes heavily in states 1–3. An approximate calculation of the equilibrium yields the following.

Consumption by Individual	States					
	1	2	3	4	5	6
1	0.1	0.3	0.2	3.98	7.96	3.98
2	3.9	7.7	3.8	0.02	0.04	0.02

The expected utilities equal, respectively,

$$V_1' = 1.68, \quad V_2' = 1.67.$$

Hence, $V_i' > V_i''$, both i, and the A''-economy results in a Pareto-inferior outcome compared to the A'-economy.

The previous example embodies Hart's result; the next proposition states it as follows.

PROPOSITION 5.11. *There exist incomplete markets sequential (SP-2) economies such that enriched markets make all individuals strictly worse off.**

It should come as no surprise that more information may have the same implications as enriched markets, that is, Pareto-inferior outcomes may result. The theme that the economics of information is equivalent to the economics of markets retains its validity. To demonstrate Pareto inferiority, the example that follows revolves around two economies satisfying rank$[\underline{\underline{P}}''] = 1$, rank$[\underline{\underline{P}}'] = Y'$, although η'' is strictly more informative than η' (and $C(A_{e,\eta''}) \supset C(A_{e,\eta'})$). The trading in the double-primed economy will be insignificant (i.e., $V_i(\alpha_i'') - V(\bar{\alpha}_i)$ is small), thereby in the limit guaranteeing that $V_i(\alpha_i') > V_i(\alpha_i'')$. Similar to the market-enrichment case, part of the difficulty in constructing an example relates to the necessity of having *some* trading in the double-primed economy, because otherwise $\bar{\alpha} = \alpha'' = \alpha'$.

Let $S = 6$; the information functions η'' and η' induce the partitions

$$\{\{1,2\}, \{3,4\}, \{5,6\}\} \quad \text{and} \quad \{\{1,2,3,4\}, \{5,6\}\},$$

respectively. Hence, η'' is strictly more informative than η'.

Let $J = 2$; the markets are specified by

$$A = \begin{bmatrix} 1 & 0 & 1 & 0 & 1 & 0 \\ 0 & 1 & 0 & 1 & 0 & 1 \end{bmatrix}.$$

Let $I = 2$; both individuals have logarithmic utility and the model excludes date-zero consumption. Individuals' state probabilities are proportional to:

	States					
Individual	1	2	3	4	5	6
1	1	1	$k(1+\varepsilon)$	$k(1-\varepsilon)$	K	K
2	1	1	$1-\varepsilon$	$(1+\varepsilon)$	K^{-1}	K^{-1}

where $k > 1$, $\varepsilon > 0$ is small, and K is large. The individuals have identical endowments: $\bar{z}_i = \frac{1}{2} Z$ where $Z = (1,1)$.

Consider first the equilibrium in the η''-economy.

Suppose (tentatively) that $\hat{z}_i'' = \bar{z}_i$, that is, the SP-2 equilibrium reduces to an SP-1 equilibrium. The claim works when rank$[\underline{\underline{P}}''] = 1$, a fact that subsequent analysis substantiates. Specifically, the prices and the trading for the three signals are as follows:

$y = 1$: Trivially, no trading occurs and $P''_{y=1} = (1,1)$.

$y = 2$: The constant k does not affect the equilibrium since the conditional probabilities $\pi_{i=1}(s/y = 2)$ are independent of k. With this independence the setting becomes symmetric for the two securities, and $P''_{y=2} = (1,1)$. Some trading occurs independently of k, provided that $\varepsilon > 0$. However, the trading approaches zero as $\varepsilon \rightarrow 0$.

$y = 3$: Regardless of K, there is no trading, and $P''_{y=3} = (1,1)$.

Since P''_y does not vary with y, it follows that rank$[\underline{\underline{P}}''] = 1$. This confirms the hypothesized first-round equilibrium, $\hat{z}''_i = \bar{z}_i$. Further, given any k and K, $V_i(\alpha''_i(\varepsilon)) \rightarrow V_i(\bar{\alpha}_i)$ as $\varepsilon \rightarrow 0$ for both i. In other words, for small ε, the η'' information function adds almost no welfare compared to the no-trading lower bound benchmark.

Consider next the equilibrium in the η'-economy.

Suppose that the rank of $\underline{\underline{P}}'$ equals one. Then $P'_{y=2} = (1,1)$ since $P'_{y=2} = P''_{y=3}$. But $P'_{y=1} = (1,1)$ does not support an equilibrium for any $k > 1$ and $\varepsilon > 0$. This one can verify through a direct analysis of the individuals' optimality conditions. Individuals' security holdings have explicit solutions, and further analysis shows that aggregate demands do not equal to total supplies. ($P'_{y=2}$ does depend on k and ε, and because $k > 1$, $\varepsilon > 0$ one may show that in equilibrium $P'_{1y=2} > P'_{2y=2}$.) Hence, rank$[\underline{\underline{P}}''] = 2$ and markets satisfy DCM since $Y' = 2$. Consequently, the SP-2 equilibrium is equivalent to an SP-3 equilibrium in which the markets equal

$$\delta(A,\eta') = \begin{bmatrix} 1 & 0 & 1 & 0 & 0 & 0 \\ 0 & 1 & 0 & 1 & 0 & 0 \\ 0 & 0 & 0 & 0 & 1 & 0 \\ 0 & 0 & 0 & 0 & 0 & 1 \end{bmatrix}.$$

The trading in this economy adds materially to individuals' well-being. In states 5 and 6 individual one (two) consumes relatively more (less), and in states 1–4 the converse applies. This outcome occurs because K is large. Such exchange clearly improves welfare regardless of k and ε, and it does not vanish as $\varepsilon \rightarrow 0$ or even if $\varepsilon = 0$. Formal analysis readily shows that $\alpha'_i(\varepsilon)$ does not converge to $\bar{\alpha}_i$ as $\varepsilon \rightarrow 0$ for sufficiently large K (e.g., choose K such that $\pi_{i=1}(s = 5) > .3$ and $\pi_{i=2}(s = 5) < .2$). One concludes that $V_i(\alpha''_i(\varepsilon)) = V_i(\bar{\alpha}_i)$, $V_i(\alpha'_i(\varepsilon)) > V_i(\bar{\alpha}_i)$, and $V_i(\alpha'_i(\varepsilon)) > V_i(\alpha''_i(\varepsilon))$, as $\varepsilon \rightarrow 0$, both i.

PROPOSITION 5.12. *There exist incomplete markets sequential (SP-2) economies such that information enrichment makes all individuals strictly worse off.**

Both of the examples demonstrating Pareto-inferior outcomes were constructed such that $1 = \text{rank}[\underline{\underline{P}}''] < \text{rank}[\underline{\underline{P}}'] = Y'$. These strong relationships facilitate the development of examples, but they are by no means necessary. The essence of the potential Pareto-inferiority derives from the fact that the attainable mixes of consumption after one trading round generally differ, and one cannot expect the double-primed economy to weakly dominate the single-primed economy on this dimension. As a result, after two trading rounds (combined) the set of attainable consumption mixes in the single-primed economy does not necessarily have a subset relationship to the same set in the double-primed economy, even though the double-primed economy permits greater richness in the second trading round. Expressed in terms of the taxonomy introduced in section 3.5, the *joint* effect on attainable consumption patterns is a Type III market comparison, and these comparisons can lead to any one of the four welfare outcomes. From this perspective the conclusion of potential Pareto-inferiority seems less surprising.

5.5. Information and Issues of Valuation

Section 3.7.2 introduces a class of propositions, collectively referred to as the Modigliani-Miller Theorems, which articulate the relationship between security prices in economies with different market structures. The core of the analysis revolves around conditions for, or implications of, common implicit prices. This section reconsiders the issues; otherwise identical economies with different information functions should also under appropriate circumstances maintain the underlying values of consumption patterns. In the usual fashion, relationships about security prices originate from the concurrent focus on the conditions for invariance of implicit prices and attendant welfare requirements. The analysis emphasizes CPE allocations, although some of the results relate to non-CPE economies.

CPE economies permit reasonably straightforward extensions of Propositions 3.17, 3.18, and 3.19. Because of the simplicity of the measurability constraints associated with (the absence of) information, the analysis often leads to sharp and easily interpretable relationships between security prices in two economies, one that is more informative than the other. Perhaps more important, the analysis, again, highlights the similarities between information and markets.

In what follows, the market structure generally remains fixed, and only the information function varies. This leads to considerable simplifications. Recall, however, that $C(A'') = C(A')$ implies $C(\delta(A'',\eta)) = C(\delta(A',\eta))$; certain generalizations would therefore be direct.

The M-M Theorems showed that the security price vectors in two economies connect with each other if the implicit prices remain constant. The same applies here; accordingly, of particular interest is the relationship between $\{P''_{jy}\}_{j,y}$ and $\{P'_{jy}\}_{j,y}$ for two different information functions (η'' and η'), and where one initially presumes that $R'' = R'$. An obvious starting point in addressing this issue lets one information function be noninformative. The following useful result, which incorporates a converse, can then be stated.

LEMMA 5.13. *Consider two SP-3 economies. The market characteristics* $(A,\eta',\underline{P}')$ *and* (A,η^0,P^0) *have a common implicit price system if, and only if,*

$$P_j^0 = \sum_{y\in Y'} P'_{jy}, j = 0, \ldots, J.$$

The equivalence is most readily appreciated in the context of the SP-3 budget constraint. Two plans $\underline{z}'_i$ and $\underline{z}^0_i$ can lead to the same consumption patterns if one disregards the signals in the more informative economy: $z'_{ijy} = z^0_{ij}$ for all $y \in Y'$ implies $\alpha'_i = \alpha^0_i$. Let $R' = R^0$; then the two plans also cost the same, $\sum_j z^0_{ij}P^0_j = \sum_j \sum_y z'_{ijy}P'_{jy}$, and with $z'_{ijy} = z^0_{ij}$ it follows that $\sum_j z^0_{ij} P^0_j = \sum_j z^0_{jy} \sum_y P'_{jy}$. But the last equality cannot hold for all $\underline{z}^0_i$ unless $P^0_j = \sum_y P'_{jy}$. Conversely, if $P^0_j = \sum_y P'_{jy}$ and $z^0_{ij} = z'_{ijy}$ for all $y \in Y$, then $\alpha_i \cdot R^0 = \sum_j z^0_{ij}P^0_j = \sum_j \sum_y z'_{ijy}P'_{jy} = \alpha_i \cdot R'$ for all $\alpha_i \in C(A_{e,\eta^0})$; hence one can always use R' in the η^0 setting.

From the lemma one infers that signal independent (relative) *security* prices, which were critical in the fineness proposition, Proposition 4.1, require but are not implied by an invariant implicit price system. Formally, $P'_{jy}/P'_{oy} = P^0_j/P^0_o$, all j, implies $P^0_j = \sum_y P'_{jy}$ given the normalization $P^0_o = \sum_y P'_{oy} = 1$, but the converse does not follow. (Proof of sufficiency: $\sum_y P'_{jy} = \sum_y P'_{oy}(P^0_j/P^0_o) = (P^0_j/P^0_o) \sum_y P'_{oy} = P^0_j$ since $\sum_y P'_{oy} = P^0_o = 1$. The case $A = I$ shows that the converse does not hold since $P_{jy} > 0$ for only one y.)

Lemma 5.13 obviously generalizes to η'' and η', where η' need not equal η^0.

PROPOSITION 5.13. *Consider two SP-3 economies. Let* η'' *be as informative as* η'. *Then the market characteristics* $(A,\eta'',\underline{P}'')$ *and* $(A,\eta',\underline{P}')$ *have common implicit prices if, and only if,*

$$P'_{jy'} = \sum_{y''\in \bar{Y}''} P''_{jy''}, j = 0, \ldots, J; y' = 1, \ldots, Y';$$

where $\bar{Y}''$ *defines the subset of* Y'' *such that* $\bigcup_{y''\in\bar{Y}''} S_{y''} = S_{y'}$.*

The M-M Proposition 3.16 developed from the observation that $R'' = R'$ follows if (i) $G(A'') = G(A')$ (i.e., $C(A'') = C(A')$), and (ii) endowment neutrality. This scheme does not extend to varying information since $\eta'' \neq \eta'$ implies that $G(A,\eta'') \neq G(A,\eta')$. However, the M-M Proposition 3.17, which substitutes the weaker condition $g(A'',v) = g(A',v)$ for $G(A'') = G(A')$, clearly generalizes to varying information.

PROPOSITION 5.14. *Consider two endowment neutral economies that achieve CPE relative to* (A'',η'') *and* (A',η'), *respectively. Suppose further that* $g(A'',\eta'',v) = g(A',\eta',v)$. *Then the two economies have a common implicit price vector.**

Proposition 5.3 embeds the key conditions for $g(A'',\eta'',v) = g(A',\eta',v)$ when $A'' = A'$: time-additivity, homogeneous signal beliefs relative to η'', and FPE in the less informative economy ensures that the incremental information has no impact on the equilibrium. Accordingly, the implicit prices remain the same, and Proposition 5.13 determines the pricing of securities. (Subsequent analysis reconsiders and exploits the model more fully.)

Before detailing the generalization of the third M-M proposition (Proposition 3.18), consider a lemma that adds structure to the implicit prices when utilities are time-additive and signal beliefs are homogeneous. Because these particular preferences/beliefs subsume the usual LRT utilities setting, the insights derived from the lemma are relevant for the third M-M proposition. Furthermore, the literature frequently exploits the lemma in a variety of contexts, and it is of interest by itself.

LEMMA 5.15. *Suppose that* (*i*) *utilities are time-additive,* (*ii*) *signal beliefs are homogeneous. Then the prices in SP-3 satisfy*

$$P_{oy'}/P_{oy} = \pi(y')/\pi(y).$$

With the standard normalization $\sum_y P_{oy} = 1$ the lemma's conclusion reduces simply to $P_{oy} = \pi(y)$: the cost of one unit of date-zero consumption in event y equals to the probability of the event occurring.[16] These particular prices of date-zero consumption combine nicely with Lemma 5.13 and Proposition 5.14.

PROPOSITION 5.15. *Consider time-additive utilities and homogeneous signal-beliefs. Suppose further that* $g(A,\eta',v) = g(A,\eta^0,v)$. *Then the security prices in two (endowment-neutral) SP-3 settings connect by*[17]

$$P_j^0 = E[\tilde{P}_j'/\tilde{P}_0'],\ j \in J.$$

Moreover, in (endowment-neutral) SP-2 settings the security prices connect by

$$P_j^0 \equiv \hat{P}_j^0 = \hat{P}_j' = E[\tilde{P}_j'/\tilde{P}_0'],\ j \in J.*$$

The conditions on preferences/beliefs are "almost" redundant. Barring highly specialized cases (such as identical individuals), $g(A,\eta',v) =$

[16] Given homogeneous signal beliefs, note that the prices in SP-1 and SP-2 can *always* be scaled such that $P_{oy} = \pi(y)$. (The latter is unrelated to the normalization $\sum_y P_{oy} = 1$.) Hence, Lemma 5.15 has no content beyond SP-3.

[17] For notation, note that $E[\tilde{P}_j/\tilde{P}_o] \equiv E[P_{j\tilde{y}}/P_{o\tilde{y}}]$.

$g(A,\eta^0,v)$ does not hold without homogeneous signal beliefs and time-additive utilities. This naturally suggests that one can use the essentially weaker condition $g(I,\eta^0,v) = g(A,\eta^0,v)$ rather than $g(A,\eta',v) = g(A,\eta^0,v)$; Proposition 5.15 still holds, since Proposition 5.3 implies the last equality.

The first part of Proposition 5.15 states: on condition that the information has no effect on the allocation, the security prices in the no-information economy serve as unbiased estimators of the (relative) signal-conditioned prices in a more-informative SP-3 economy. The proof follows immediately from prior results since $P_j^0 = \sum_y P'_{jy} = \sum_y (P'_{jy}/P'_{oy})P'_{oy} = \sum_y (P'_{jy}/P'_{oy})\pi(y)$. (Use Lemma 5.13 and Proposition 5.14 for the first equality, and Lemma 5.15 for the last.) The effect of the signals on the security prices permits an articulation because the equilibrium does not depend on the information *function*.

The second part of the proposition states: in the dynamic SP-2 setting, (i) the prices in the first trading round equate to those that would prevail in an otherwise equivalent no-information economy, and (ii) the first-round prices serve as unbiased estimators of the uncertain (relative) second-round prices. The proof of (i) derives from the absence of signal-contingent trading and common implicit prices in the η' and η^0 SP-2 economies if $g(A,\eta',v) = g(A,\eta^0,v)$ (Propositions 5.9 and 5.14). The statement (ii) also follows immediately, since SP-2 and SP-3 have equivalent implicit prices. This equivalence obviously implies equivalence in signal-contingent security prices as well. (Note that P_{jy}/P_{oy} in SP-2 cannot be manipulated through scaling of prices.)

However, it is surprising that conclusion (ii), $\hat{P}_j' = E[\tilde{P}_j'/\tilde{P}_0']$, holds without the irrelevance of information condition. It suffices if the SP-2 equilibrium solves $g(A,\eta',v)$; unlike the previous case, signal-contingent trading may occur.

COROLLARY 5.15.1. *Consider a SP-2 economy with time-additive preferences and homogeneous signal beliefs. If the economy achieves CPE relative to* (A,η), $\eta \neq \eta^0$, *then the first- and second-round prices satisfy*

$$\hat{P}_j = E[\tilde{P}_j/\tilde{P}_0], j \in J.$$

One usually refers to the pricing relationship in the corollary as the *Martingale Hypothesis*. This hypothesis is often also stated as $\hat{P}_j = E[\tilde{P}_j]$, $j \in J$, which poses no problems provided that one keeps in mind firmly that the security prices in that case have been normalized by $\hat{P}_0 = P_{oy} = 1$ instead of the usual $\hat{P}_0 = \sum_y P_{oy} = 1$. (With arbitrarily scaled security prices, the Martingale Hypothesis equals $\hat{P}_j/\hat{P}_0 = E[\tilde{P}_j/\tilde{P}_0]$.)

The risk-neutral valuation relationship implied by the conditions may come as a surprise. A rough explanation is as follows. First, the information introduces no extraneous risks, since the risk sharing is efficient. Second, the first trading round resolves no substantive uncertainty: the beliefs about the events observed prior to the second trading round are homogeneous, and certainty prevails about the marginal utility of the date-zero consumption good. The latter follows because every individual has time-additive utility and certain date-zero consumption. Finally, the valuation relationship needs no adjustment for the time value of consumption because no consumption transpires prior to the realization of the signal.

The third M-M proposition, Proposition 3.18, states conditions such that the implicit prices are independent of the endowment distribution. The result uses homogeneous beliefs and LRT utilities combined with $\rho U_i^2 = U_i^1$. The conclusion in Proposition 3.18 extends directly to economies with information.

PROPOSITION 5.16. *Suppose that utilities are LRT with the same slope parameter for all individuals and that* $\rho U_i^2 = U_i^1$. *Suppose further that beliefs are homogeneous and that the markets satisfy* $1 \in C(A)$. *Then, for each of the three equilibrium settings (SP-1, SP-2, SP-3) the implicit prices do not depend on the endowment distribution. Moreover, the implicit prices depend neither on the equilibrium setting nor on the information function (or the markets).**

That the first part of the proposition subsumes SP-3 follows immediately; SP-3 and SP differ merely by notation, and the extension of Proposition 3.18 is direct. The SP-2 case follows from Corollary 5.3.1 and Proposition 5.9, which jointly assure the equivalence of SP-2 and SP-3 equilibria. Less obviously, the proposition subsumes SP-1 economies, although these do not generally reach CPE (and FPE), even under the conditions used in the proposition. Nevertheless, the SP-1 and SP-3 equilibrium prices are equivalent because they derive from the same "composite individual" single-person economy as in the SP-3 economy. That is, invoking Proposition 3.22 for each signal results in the same prices as in its SP-3 application.

Proposition 3.22 also makes it clear that neither the equilibrium setting nor the information function affects the implicit prices (see also Corollary 5.3.1). The implicit prices' extreme independence of all exogenous variables, except for preferences/beliefs and (per capita) supply, reflects the power of what is effectively a single-person economy.

Finally, generalizations of converses to the M-M propositions may be developed. In the simple two-date economy, the essence of Proposition 3.19 is the weak welfare improvement (WR1 or WR2) that follows from an enrichment of markets and common implicit prices. The result derives directly from the partial equilibrium Proposition 2.4. Similar reasoning extends to varying information: Propositions 4.5 and 4.10, which pertain to SP-3 and SP-2 respectively, can be embedded within equilibrium settings.

PROPOSITION 5.17. *Given fixed implicit prices in an SP-3 setting, information or markets enrichments imply either WR1 or WR2. For SP-2 assume in addition that* $\eta' = \eta^0$ *or* $\eta'' = \eta'$.*

Note that the informative SP-2 economies need *not* achieve CPE.

The last proposition subsumes a converse to the first part of Proposition 5.15 as a special case.

COROLLARY 5.17.1 *Suppose that utilities are time-additive and that signal beliefs are homogeneous. Let* (A,η') *and* (A,η^0) *be two markets/information function pairs. If the two economies achieve CPE, and the two security price vectors satisfy*

$$P_j^0 = E[\tilde{P}_j'/\tilde{P}_0'], \text{ all } j \in J^+,$$

*then either WR1 or WR2 applies.**

In comparing Proposition 5.15 with Corollary 5.17.1, observe that the corollary replaces the welfare assumption $g(A,\eta',v) = g(A,\eta^0,v)$ (i.e., WR2) of Proposition 5.15 with the conclusion of Proposition 5.15 (i.e., $P_j^0 = E[\tilde{P}_j'/\tilde{P}_0']$), such that Corollary 5.17.1 yields a welfare conclusion (i.e., WR1 or WR2). This illustrates again the close relationship between welfare and statements about security prices.

The (weak) welfare improvements supposedly take place in equilibrium settings. Some of the comments that followed Proposition 3.19 therefore deserve repetition. In particular, the endogenicity of implicit prices in general equilibrium impairs the "quality" of the M-M converses. Section 3.7.3 points out that the only known nonendowment specific setting in SP leading to fixed implicit prices and a potential strict welfare improvement occurs when one individual has linear preferences. The observation obviously extends to SP-3 since this setting differs little from SP. But SP-2 also results in a common implicit price vector that equals the (α-independent) MRS vector of the individual who has linear utility. Although the conclusion follows directly because SP-2 is sufficiently similar to SP-3 (i.e., a modified SP-3 problem as spelled out in section 4.6.3), one can also verify the invariance through a direct analysis of the Lagrangean optimality conditions associated with SP-2.

The generalized M-M propositions, and related converses, have virtually no relevance in SP-1 settings.[18] One should expect this since the allocations and prices in SP-1 have no particular relationship across signals. However, an interesting exception occurs for LRT utilities because one can exploit Proposition 5.16. A single "composite individual" determines the

[18] In SP-1 economies with fixed implicit prices, more markets, alone, lead to WR1 or WR2, while the effect of more information (possibly combined with more markets) may lead to any one of the four welfare outcomes.

implicit prices, and thus one can fix the implicit price vector independently of (A,η) (assuming that $1 \in C(A)$). One might suspect that such a sharp statement about prices in SP-1 accompanies a sharp welfare conclusion. Thus, what welfare implications derive from an SP-1 equilibrium with LRT utilities? The solution is rather drastic: incremental information generally makes *all* individuals strictly worse off, and at best only specific endowments lead to indifference. This outcome contrasts sharply with the welfare indifference in SP-2 and SP-3 settings.

PROPOSITION 5.18. *Consider an SP-1 economy in which individuals have LRT utilities with identical slope parameters and* $\rho U_i^2 = U_i^1$. *Suppose further that beliefs are homogeneous and that the markets satisfy* $1 \in C(A)$. *Then endowments exist such that WR4 follows in a more informative economy compared to* (A,η^0). *With arbitrary endowments, WR2 and WR4 constitute the only possible outcomes.**

That no individual under the conditions can be strictly better off basically follows from the invariance of implicit prices across settings, the welfare irrelevance of information/markets in SP-3 settings, and the fact that holdings cannot be coordinated across signals in SP-1 settings. More precisely, let $\alpha_i(SP - n,(A,\eta))$ denote the ith individuals' optimal choice in the nth setting ($n = 1$ or 3) when the markets/information are (A,η). The proposition asserts that, in equilibrium, no individual strictly prefers $\alpha_i(SP - 1,(A,\eta'))$ to $\alpha_i(SP - 1,(A,\eta^0))$. To prove this contention, first note that $\alpha_i(SP - 1,(A,\eta^0)) = \alpha_i(SP - 3,(A,\eta^0))$ since an SP-3 with η^0 equals SP-1. Second, using Corollary 5.3.1, $\alpha_i(SP - 3,(A,\eta^0)) = \alpha_i(SP - 3,(A,\eta'))$. Third, Proposition 5.16 (via Proposition 3.22) implies equivalence in the implicit prices of SP-1 and SP-3 for all (A,η), $1 \in C(A)$. Hence, one can invoke Proposition 4.9: the allocation $\alpha_i(SP - 1,(A,\eta'))$ cannot be strictly preferred to $\alpha_i(SP - 3,(A,\eta'))$. Collecting these relationships, it follows that no individual strictly prefers the more informative SP-1 economy, regardless of his (fixed) endowments. Further, note that WR4 generally occurs because c_{iy} typically varies with y, a condition sufficient for an inferior non-FPE outcome. At least one individual is then strictly worse off, and with no one being better off the conditions for a Pareto-inferior outcome are met.

The proposition would be considerably more difficult to prove using "direct" analytical methods that bypass the critical concepts associated with Propositions 3.22, 4.9, 5.3, and 5.16. This final result therefore fittingly highlights the relative advantage of using a few key conceptual insights rather than mathematical manipulations.

5.6. Concluding Remarks

Although the theory of financial markets develops with few mathematical complexities, the central concept of implicit prices involves a certain subtlety. The tempting perspective that obstructs an understanding of the theory emphasizes security prices rather than implicit prices, and securities rather than consumption patterns. Such an emphasis on financial variables is quite natural since, after all, social scientists prefer to analyze variables that have a real-world representation. Yet, with the advantage of hindsight, one can easily see why the "unobservable" real variables assume such great theoretical significance. Implicit prices provide a unifying valuation support structure regardless of (i) the markets and (ii) the information function. Alternative specifications of markets or information functions can now be compared with relative ease. Note specifically that without the concept of implicit prices for incomplete markets, a cohesive theory is virtually impossible because the analysis will then not properly distinguish, and link, complete and incomplete markets economies. Similarly, dynamic and static economies relate through implicit prices. Having internalized these ideas, one need only keep a few additional guiding principles in mind. The most important among these are:

Implicit prices provide the relevant linear operator for the valuation of securities.

The only relevant aspect of a market structure is its span.

An understanding of the structure of implicit prices follows from an understanding of the efficiency characteristics of the economy. The M-M result exploits this fact: equally efficient economies have identical implicit prices. Also, explicit valuation models generally derive from Fully Pareto Efficient settings.

The comparative analysis of an individual's welfare focuses on his consumption opportunity sets, and not on a direct analysis of his expected utility.

Equilibrium models frequently have complex features that are more apparent than real. In these seemingly deceiving cases the embellishments (incomplete markets or dynamic trading) have no substantive impact on the equilibrium allocation, and the analysis reduces equivalently to the artificial and static Arrow-Debreu markets model. (A cynic might say that modern financial markets theory was precipitated by the invention of more or less well-disguised Arrow-Debreu economies.)

A truly central result is Borch's lemma (Lemma 3.8): under regularity conditions on preferences/beliefs one need not distinguish between states that have identical levels of wealth (or identical payoff columns). Finance theory uses the conditions and conclusions of that lemma with incredible frequency.

In pure exchange, welfare derives from individuals' trading. Prices and wealth are irrelevant to welfare analysis except in those models that exploit fixed implicit prices.

Finally, to understand a financial markets model it helps to consider its equivalent in real terms: each individual selects his consumption pattern subject to (i) one budget constraint, and (ii) the linear space that determines attainable mixes of consumption patterns. The existence of a linear space constraint (ii) triggers two central questions. First, is the linear space endogeneous or exogeneous? Second, does the linear space effectively restrict the optimal consumption choice in equilibrium? Answers to these two questions go to the heart of any particular model.

Appendix 5.1. Proofs

Proof of Proposition 5.7: Given some $\{V_i\}_i$ and allocation α one can determine an R that supports the equilibrium via any one individual's MRS vector. Let $\hat{w}_{iy} \equiv \sum_{s \in S_y} c_{is}R_{0s} + w_{is}R_{1s}$; the $\{\hat{w}_{iy}\}_{i,y}$ define the consumption expenditures across signals and individuals required to support the equilibrium. Finally, one easily shows that an $\bar{\alpha} \in G(I,\eta^0)$ exists such that $\bar{\bar{w}}_{iy} = \hat{w}_{iy}$ for all i,y.

Proof of Proposition 5.10: Section 4.6 shows that complete markets imply DCM.

Remark: CCM cannot replace complete markets. This follows since CCM does not assure DCM. (CCM may hold even when $Y > J + 1$.)

Proof of Lemma 5.13: It is easily shown that $A = T\delta(A,\eta')$, where $T \equiv [I \vdots I \vdots \cdots \vdots I]$; T has J rows and the number of adjacent I matrices equals Y'. Thus, given $R' = R^0$ it follows that $P^0 = AR_1^0 = T\delta(A,\eta')R_1' = T\underline{P}_1'$, which equals $P_j^0 = \sum_y P_{jy}'$, $j \in J(j = 0$ is immediate because of the normalization). Conversely, given the hypotheses on security prices, $P^0 = T\underline{P}_1'$, which equals $P_j^0 = \sum P_{jy}'$, $j \in J(j = 0$ is immediate because of the $= T\underline{P}_1' = T\delta(A,\eta')R_1' = AR_1'$.

Proof of Lemma 5.15: Consider the Lagrangean optimality conditions for SP-3. One shows without difficulty that at an optimum

$$\pi(y)u_i^1(c_{iy}) = \omega_i P_{0y}, \; i \in I, \; y \in Y,$$

where ω_i denotes the Lagrangean multiplier associated with the budget constraint, individual i. (A trivial generalization of the analysis in Chapter 2, section 2.4, yields the condition.) Further, c_{iy} does not depend on y because of Lemma 5.3. Let the scalar c_i denote the optimal date-zero consumption. Hence,

$$\frac{\pi(y')u_i^1(c_i)}{\pi(y)u_i^1(c_i)} = \frac{\pi(y')}{\pi(y)} = \frac{P_{0y'}}{P_{0y}}.$$

Proof of Corollary 5.15.1: Using the notation and result of Proposition 4.8,

$$\hat{P}_j = \sum_y P_{jy}\nu_y \equiv \sum_y \hat{P}_{jy} = \sum_y (\hat{P}_{jy}/\hat{P}_{0y})\hat{P}_{0y}, \; j \in J^+ .$$

But, since the SP-2 setting achieves CPE, the $\{\hat{P}_{jy}\}_{j,y}$ prices are the same as in a SP-3 equilibrium. Further, due to Lemma 5.15, $\hat{P}_{0y} = k\pi(y)$, where the scalar k does not depend on y. Hence,

$$\hat{P}_j = k \sum_y (\hat{P}_{jy}/\hat{P}_{0y})\pi(y), \; j \in J^+ .$$

Put $j = 0$ and it follows that $k = 1$ since $\hat{P}_0 = 1$. This proves the result since $P_{jy}/P_{0y} = \hat{P}_{jy}/\hat{P}_{0y}$.

Remark: As an alternative proof, one can use the relationship $P_{0y}\nu_y = \sum_{s \in S_y} R_{0s}$. (See the discussion that follows Proposition 4.8.) But R is the same for SP-2 and SP-3 given the CPE assumption. The result now follows since, given Lemma 5.15, $\sum_{s \in S_y} R_{0s} = \pi(y)$.

Appendix 5.2

BLACKWELL'S THEOREM IN A MULTIPERSON SETTING

An essential concept in Blackwell's Theorem is that of a *payoff adequate partition* of the set S (PAP, for short). Its definition within a multiperson setting follows. A partition $\{\hat{S}_{\hat{s}}\}_{\hat{s}}$ of S is a PAP if for any $s, t \in \hat{S}_{\hat{s}}$:

(i) $U_{is} = U_{it}$ for all $i \in I$ (local state independence), and
(ii) $\sum_j z_j a_{js} = \sum_j z_j a_{jt}$ for all z_j, that is, equivalently, $a_{js} = a_{jt}$ all $j \in J$. (See Proposition 3.14.)

Condition (i) holds automatically if all individuals have state independent utilities. Condition (ii) means that each set $\hat{S}_{\hat{s}}$ cannot contain states with distinguishable columns of payoffs.

As an example of a PAP, consider state independent utilities and the markets

$$A = [\hat{A} \,\vdots\, \hat{A}].$$

One can now define a PAP of S by letting $\hat{S}_{\hat{s}=1} = \{1, S/2 + 1\}$, $\hat{S}_{\hat{s}=2} = \{2, S/2 + 2\}$, . . . , $\hat{S}_{\hat{s}} = \{\hat{s}, S/2 + \hat{s}\}$, . . . , $\hat{S}_{\hat{s}=S/2} = \{S/2, S\}$. The terminology PAP captures the essence of the analytical conditions. Two states, s and t, are elements in $\hat{S}_{\hat{s}}$, some $\hat{s}$, only if they result in the same utility: conditions (i) and (ii) imply that $U_{is}(z_{i0}, \sum_j a_{js}z_{ij}) = U_{it}(z_{io}, \sum_j a_{jt}z_{ij})$ for all z_i (and $i \in I$). An individual who evaluates his *realized* utility therefore needs to know only his portfolio and *event* realization $\hat{s}$. Thus, while the perfect partition always fulfills PAP, the point is that, depending on markets and preferences, coarser PAP may exist.

A PAP of S implies that all states in each $\hat{S}_{\hat{s}}$ can be brought together in the expected utility evaluation. For each $\hat{s}$, define

$$\bar{U}_{i\hat{s}}(z_{io}, \sum_j a_{j\hat{s}} z_{ij}) \equiv U_{is}(z_{io}, \sum_j a_{js} z_{ij}) \quad \text{if } s \in \hat{S}_{\hat{s}}.$$

Given an information function η, one can restate V_i as

$$V_i = \sum_y \sum_{\hat{s}} \pi_i(y,\hat{s}) \bar{U}_{i\hat{s}}\left(z_{ioy}, \sum_j a_{j\hat{s}} z_{ijy}\right),$$

where $\pi_i(y,\hat{s})$ equals $\sum_{s \in \hat{S}_{\hat{s}}} \pi_i(y,s)$ (or $\pi_i(s \in S_y \cap \hat{S}_{\hat{s}})$). Note that $\pi_i(y/\hat{s})$ does not necessarily equal to zero or one. (As an example, let $A = [\hat{A} : \hat{A}]$, $Y = 2$ with $S_{y=1} = \{1, \ldots, S/2\}$, $S_{y=2} = \{S/2 + 1, \ldots, S\}$; one obtains $\pi_i(y = 1/\hat{s} = 1) = \pi_i(s = 1)/[\pi_i(s = 1) + \pi_i(s = S/2 + 1)]$, which equals neither zero nor one since $\pi_s > 0$, all $s \in S$.)

Consider next two different information functions, η'' and η', that satisfy the following relationship: a function (matrix) $\vartheta(y',y'')$ exists such that

$$\pi_i(y',\hat{s}) = \sum_{y''} \vartheta(y',y'')\pi_i(y'',\hat{s}), \quad \text{all } i,\hat{s},\hat{y} \tag{A1}$$

$$\sum_{y'} \vartheta(y',y'') = 1, \quad \text{all } y'' \tag{A2}$$

$$\vartheta(y',y'') \geq 0, \quad \text{all } y',y''. \tag{A3}$$

Equations (A1)–(A3) do not imply a fineness relationship between η'' and η'. To illustrate this point, consider the case when $\pi(y'/y'') = \pi(y'/y'',\hat{s})$. Putting $\vartheta(y',y'') = \pi(y'/y'')$ one can then show without difficulty that the three conditions (A1)–(A3) hold. In the standard terminology, η' *garbles* η'': the signals received from η' equal to those of η'', except that "noise" has been injected. But as long as $0 < \pi(y'/y'') < 1$ for some y',y'' pair, it is clear that η'' does not refine η' (i.e., knowing y'' does not imply knowing the true y' as required by fineness). The model in section 5.2.3 satisfies (A1)–(A3) because $\vartheta(y',y'') = \pi(y'/y'') = \pi(y'/y'',\hat{s})$. At any rate, garbling is not necessary for (A1)–(A3); see Marschak and Radner (1972, p. 66) for a discussion and examples.

In a single-person SP-1 setting with information/signal independent security prices, the conditions of Blackwell's Theorem, $\{\hat{S}_{\hat{s}}\}$ being PAP of S and (A1)–(A3), result in η'' being at least weakly preferable to η'. (Of course, the subscript i as it appears in A1 has no relevance in a single-person setting.) The conclusion follows immediately. Hence, Blackwell's Theorem modifies Proposition 4.1; adding the relatively mild condition on preferences (i), the informativeness conditions (A1)–(A3) replace the fineness condition.

For a proof of Blackwell's Theorem, see Marschak and Radner (1972, pp. 65–66).

In contrast to Blackwell's Theorem, the subscript "i" as it appears in (A1) becomes important when one considers allocations of securities in the planner's problem. The multiperson conditions (A1)–(A3) suffice in that optimization problem even though the setting has I individuals with possibly heterogeneous beliefs.

Proposition A: Consider MISC $\{V_i\}_i$. Let $\{\hat{S}_{\hat{s}}\}_{\hat{s}}$ be a payoff adequate partition, and suppose that (A1)–(A3) relate the two information functions η' and η''. Let $\{z_{ijy'}\}_{i\in I, j\in J^+, y'\in Y'}$ be any allocation satisfying $\sum_i z_{ijy'} = Z_j$ for all $j \in J^+, y' \in Y'$. There then exists an allocation $\{z_{ijy''}\}_{i,j,y''}$ satisfying $\sum_i z_{ijy''} = Z_j$ for all $j \in J^+$, $y'' \in Y''$ which is Pareto-preferable unless the implied consumption patterns are identical. Hence, it follows that $g(A,\eta'',v) \geq g(A,\eta',v)$ for all v.

Proof of Proposition A: Given some allocation $\{z_{ijy'}\}_{i,j,y'}$ and condition A1, the ith individual's expected utility equals

$$V_i' = \sum_{y'} \sum_{\hat{s}} \left[\sum_{y''} \vartheta(y',y'')\pi_i(y'',\hat{s})\right] \bar{U}_{i\hat{s}} \left(z_{ioy'}, \sum_j a_{j\hat{s}} z_{ijy'}\right).$$

Rearranging the summation signs, one obtains

$$V_i' = \sum_{y''} \left\{\sum_{y'} \vartheta(y',y'')\left[\sum_{\hat{s}} \pi_i(y'',\hat{s}) \bar{U}_{i\hat{s}} \left(z_{ioy'}, \sum_j a_{j\hat{s}} z_{ijy'}\right)\right]\right\}.$$

For each (y'',y') pair, the expression inside [ ] is readily shown to be strictly concave in $(z_{ijy'})_{j\in J^+}$. (Sums of strictly concave functions are strictly concave.) Hence, if one defines

$$z_{ijy''} \equiv \sum_{y'} \vartheta(y',y'') z_{ijy'},$$

and applies Jensen's inequality to the expression inside { } for each y'', then the expected utility associated with $\{z_{ijy''}\}_{j,y''}$, V_i'', satisfies

$$V_i' \leq \sum_{y''} \sum_{\hat{s}} \pi_i(y'',\hat{s}) \bar{U}_{i\hat{s}} \left(z_{ioy''}, \sum_j a_{j\hat{s}} z_{ijy''}\right) = V_i''.$$

The security allocation $\{z_{ijy''}\}_{i,j,y''}$ is feasible since (using A2)

$$\begin{aligned}\sum_i z_{ijy''} &= \sum_i \sum_{y'} \vartheta(y',y'') z_{ijy'} = \sum_{y'} \vartheta(y',y'') \sum_i z_{ijy'} \\ &= 1 \cdot Z_j = Z_j, j \in J^+.\end{aligned}$$

Finally, note that the inequality $V_i' \leq V_i''$ is strict if the allocation α_ι' differs from α_ι''; this follows immediately from the strict concavity of V_i.

The proof shows that one constructs the (weakly) preferable allocation solely from the original allocation and the $\vartheta(y', y'')$ function. Given concave utilities and payoff adequacy, the essence of η'' being preferred to η' derives entirely from the relationship between the two information functions probabilities $\{\pi_i(y', \hat{s})\}_{i,y',\hat{s}}$ and $\{\pi_i(y'', \hat{s})\}_{i,y'',\hat{s}}$. Very roughly, conditions (A1)–(A3) make η'' a preferable information function because it can "smooth" every allocation $\{z_{ijy'}\}_{i,j,y'}$ based on η', and this procedure reduces the extraneous risks (i.e., those risks that do not relate to aggregate wealth and the securities' payoff configurations). The case of garbling illustrates the nature of the smoothing most clearly. The preferable allocation now equals the conditional expected value of the single-primed allocation: $z_{ijy''} = \sum_{y'} z_{ijy'}\pi(y'/y'')$.

The careful reader might wonder whether or not the above multiperson version of Blackwell's Theorem can be inferred directly from the standard single-person version. No such inference is possible. From Blackwell's Theorem one infers only that for any nonnegative $\zeta = (\zeta_1, \ldots, \zeta_I)$

$$H(\eta'', \zeta) \geq H(\eta', \zeta)$$

where

$$H(\eta, \zeta) \equiv \max_{\alpha} \sum_i \zeta_i V_i(\alpha_i) \; (\alpha \in G(A, \eta))$$

provided that the beliefs $\pi_i(\hat{s}, y'')$ and $\pi_i(\hat{s}, y')$ are the same for all i. The maximization problem so defined is a regular "single-person problem" with a given set of beliefs and a utility function for $\{z_{ij}\}_{i,j}$ given by $\sum_i \zeta_i \bar{U}_{is}(z_{io}, \sum a_{j\hat{s}} z_{ij})$. Even with this restriction on beliefs, however, the relationship $H(\eta'', \zeta) \geq H(\eta', \zeta)$ does not directly imply that $g(A, \eta'', v) \geq g(A, \eta', v)$ for all v, although the converse is true. The missing ingredient one needs is the g-function's concavity in v, a condition that the planner's problem satisfies given concave $\{V_i\}_i$ (see page 46, footnote 1 in Chapter 3). Although Proposition A uses concavity, this restriction on preferences has no relevance in the standard single-person version of Blackwell's Theorem.

BIBLIOGRAPHY

Arrow, Kenneth (1964). The Role of Securities in the Optimal Allocation of Risk Bearing. Review of Economic Studies 3:257–273.

Black, Fischer (1972). Capital Market Equilibrium with Restricted Borrowing. Journal of Business of the University of Chicago 45 (July): 444–455.

Blackwell, David (1953). Equivalent Comparisons of Experiments. Annals of Mathematical Statistics 24:265–272.

Borch, Karl (1960). The Safety Loading of Reinsurance Premiums. Skandinavisk Aktuaritidskvift 43:163–184.

Breeden, Douglas T., and Litzenberger, Robert H. (1978). Prices of State-Contingent Claims Implicit in Option Prices. Journal of Business 51 (4):621–651.

Brennan, Michael J., and Kraus, Alan (1976). The Geometry of Separation and Myopia. Journal of Financial and Quantitative Analysis 11 (June): 171–193.

——— (1978). Necessary Conditions for Aggregation in Securities Markets. Journal of Financial and Quantitative Analysis 13 (September): 407–418.

Cox, John C., Ross, Stephen A., and Rubinstein, Mark (1979). Option Pricing: A Simplified Approach. Journal of Financial Economics 7 (September): 229–263.

Dybvig, Philip H. (1983). An Explicit Bound on Individual Assets Deviations from APT Pricing in a Finite Economy. Journal of Financial Economics 12 (December): 483–496.

Fama, Eugene F. (1971). Risk Return and Equilibrium. Journal of Political Economy 79 (January/February): 30–55.

Fischer, Stanley (1972). Assets, Contingent Commodities, and the Slutsky Equations. Econometrica 40 (March): 371–385.

Gale, Douglas (1982). Money: In Equilibrium. Cambridge and New York: Cambridge University Press.

Garman, Mark (1978). A Synthesis of the Pure Theory of Arbitrage. Unpublished working paper, University of California at Berkeley.

Green, Jerry (1981). Value of Information with Sequential Futures Markets. Econometrica 49 (March): 335–358.

Grinblatt, Mark, and Titman, Sheridan (1983). Factor Pricing in a Finite Economy. Journal of Financial Economics 12 (December): 497–507.

Grossman, Stanford (1977). A Characterization of the Optimality of Equilibrium in Incomplete Markets. Journal of Economic Theory 15 (June): 1–16.

Hakansson, Nils H. (1969). Risk Disposition and the Separation Property in Portfolio Selection. Journal of Financial and Quantitative Analysis 4 (December): 401–416.

———. (1982). Changes in the Financial Market: Welfare and Price Effects and the Basic Theorems of Value Conservation. Journal of Finance 37 (September): 977–1004.

Hakansson, Nils H., Kunkel, Gregory J., and Ohlson, James A. (1982). Sufficient and Necessary Conditions for Information to Have Social Value in Pure Exchange. Journal of Finance 37 (December): 1169–1181.

Hart, Oliver D. (1975). On the Optimality of Equilibrium When the Market Structure Is Incomplete. Journal of Economic Theory 11 (December): 418–443.

Hirshleifer, Jack (1971). The Private and Social Value of Information and the Reward to Inventive Activity. American Economic Review 61 (September): 561–574.

Kose, John, and Arditti, Fred D. (1980). Spanning the State Space with Options. Journal of Financial Quantitative Analysis 15 (March): 1–10.

Kreps, David (1979). Three Essays on Capital Markets. Mimeographed notes, Stanford University.

Kruizenga, R. J. (1956). Put and Call Options: A Theoretic and Market Analysis. Ph.D. dissertation, Massachusetts Institute of Technology.

Mangasarian, Olvi L. (1969). Nonlinear Programming. New York: McGraw-Hill.

Marschak, Jacob, and Radner, Roy (1972). Economic Theory of Teams. New Haven: Yale University Press.

Merton, Robert C. (1973). An Intertemporal Capital Asset Pricing Model. Econometrica 41 (September) 867–887.

Milne, Frank (1979). Consumer Preferences, Linear Demand Functions and Aggregation in Competitive Asset Market. Review of Economic Studies 46 (July): 407–417.

Modigliani, Franco, and Miller, Merton H. (1958). The Cost of Capital, Corporation Finance, and the Theory of Investment. American Economic Review (June): 261–297.

Mossin, Jan (1973). The Theory of Financial Markets. Englewood Cliffs, N.J.: Prentice-Hall.

Nielsen, Niels Christian (1978). On the Financing and Investment Decisions of the Firm. Journal of Banking and Finance 2 (June): 75–101.

Ohlson, James A. (1977). Equilibrium in Stable Markets. Journal of Political Economy 85 (August): 859–864.

———. (1984). The Structure of Asset Prices and Socially Useless-Useful Information. Journal of Finance 39 (December): 1417–1435.

———. (1985). Ex Post Stockholder Unanimity: A Complete and Simplified Treatment. Journal of Banking and Finance 9 (October): 387–399.

Ohlson, James A., and Buckman, A. Gregory (1981). Toward a Theory of Financial Accounting: Welfare and Public Information. Journal of Accounting Research 19 (Autumn): 399–432.

Radner, Roy (1968). Competitive Equilibrium Under Uncertainty. Econometrica 36 (January): 31–58.

Ross, Stephen (1976a). Options and Efficiency. Quarterly Journal of Economics 90 (February): 75–87.

———. (1976b). Return Risk and Arbitrage. In I. Friend and J. Bicksler, eds., Risk and Return in Finance. Cambridge, Mass.: Ballinger.

———. (1978). Mutual Fund Separation in Financial Theory: The Separating Distributions. Journal of Economic Theory 17:254–286.

Rubinstein, Mark (1973). The Fundamental Theorem of Parameter: Preference Security Valuation. Journal of Financial and Quantitative Analysis 8 (January): 61–70.

Rubinstein, Mark (1974). An Aggregation Theory for Securities Markets. Journal of Financial Economics 1 (September): 225–244.

———. (1975). Security Market Efficiency in an Arrow-Debreu Economy. American Economic Review 65(5):812–824.

———. (1976). The Valuation of Uncertain Income Stream and the Pricing of Options. Bell Journal of Economics 7 (Autumn): 407–425.

Schrems, Edward Linus (1973). The Sufficiency of Existing Financial Instruments for Pareto: Optimal Risk Allocation. Ph.D. dissertation, Stanford University.

Vickson, Ron G. (1975). Separation in Portfolio Analysis. In W. T. Ziemba and R. G. Vickson, eds., Stochastic Optimization Models in Finance. New York: Academic Press.

Werner, Jan (1985). Equilibrium in Economies with Incomplete Financial Markets. Journal of Economic Theory 36:110–119.

Wilson, Robert B. (1968). The Theory of Syndicates. Econometrica 36 (January): 119–132.

INDEX